Céleste Mogador
Memoirs of a Courtesan in Nineteenth-Century Paris

Translated and
with an introduction by
Monique Fleury
Nagem

University of Nebraska Press

Lincoln and London

Publication of this volume was assisted by The Virginia
Faulkner Fund, established in memory of Virginia Faulkner,
editor-in-chief of the University of Nebraska Press.
Previously published as *Mémoires de Céleste Mogador* by
Les Amis de l'Histoire, 1968. Translation and introduction
© 2001 by the University of Nebraska Press. All rights
reserved. Manufactured in the United States of America

Library of Congress Cataloging-in-Publication Data
Chabrillan, Céleste Vénard de, comtesse, 1824–1909.
[Adieux au monde. English] Memoirs of a courtesan
in nineteenth-century Paris / Céleste Mogador ; translated
and with an introduction by Monique Fleury Nagem.
p. cm. – (European women writers series) Includes
bibliographical references. ISBN 0-8032-3208-X
(cl.: alk. paper) – ISBN 0-8032-8273-7 (pbk.: alk. paper)
I. Nagem, Monique F., 1941– II. Title. III. Series.
PN2638.C5 A313 2001 306.74'2'092—dc21
[B] 2001027147

CONTENTS

ACKNOWLEDGMENTS

My thanks to the Collège International
des Traducteurs Littéraires in Arles, France, for
giving me the opportunity to start on this translation
in the company of helpful translators and in select
surroundings; the Department of Languages at
McNeese State University for giving me a sabbatical to
begin the work; to McNeese State University for
awarding me the Shearman Professorship in Liberal
Arts in support of the translation project. A special
thanks goes to Judy A. Savoie for her critical
reading of the project and to my husband,
Robert A. Nagem, for his support
during the project.

Translator's Introduction

The lives of nineteenth-century Parisian courtesans sparkled with glamour, splendor, and excitement. Many of these women were ardently pursued by young and not-so-young admirers, some of whose names are found today in history books and literary annals. With the rise of a wealthy middle class and the presence of a bored, dissolute aristocracy, Paris between 1830 and 1870 was awhirl with dinner parties, masked balls, stage productions, and gambling fever. The young men of this society were vying with one another for the chance to be seen with the most beautiful courtesan of the day, the one whose exploits on the stage or in the dance hall had placed her name on everyone's lips. For if a young man was seen with this woman, it meant she was his, and showering her with extravagant gifts of jewelry and fancy carriages was a way to keep her. Those men were the dandies of the era and they spent their evenings in pursuit of pleasure and intoxication. Some were talented writers or musicians, some were rich aristocrats (prominent among them was Prince Napoleon, nephew of the emperor Napoleon Bonaparte and cousin of Napoleon III), and others were the sons of merchants and high level bureaucrats. Many of them squandered whole fortunes and often were forced to go into debt, join the army, or emigrate as a result.

The courtesans so in demand were for the most part women who had managed to rise above the level of common brothel prostitutes through their beauty, cleverness, and a lot of good luck. For women whose options were limited because of their poverty or their social status, such a step up seemed to be a dream come true; the reality of their situation, however, was less than glittering. Once their youthful good looks were gone (no later than age thirty or so in those days) or they became ill (tuberculosis and cholera were still common), they became a burden to their admirer and protector instead of an asset and were cynically discarded. Among these women competition precluded most friendships, so they were left alone to return to the brothel or the streets, or to commit suicide, or to die lacking medical care.

Their notoriety, their glamorous lives, and the fascination these pampered and envied women held for the public were the source of inspiration for the writers and musicians of the century. One of the most famous literary renditions of the drama of a courtesan's life is Alexandre Dumas's *La Dame aux camelias,* known in English as *Camille.* The play was first performed in Paris in 1852 and scandalized many people because of its daring dramatization of the redemption of a courtesan through her love for her young penniless lover. Greta Garbo made the character of Marguerite memorable to twentieth-century moviegoers in the 1936 film *Camille.* The Italian composer Guiseppe Verdi based his popular opera *La Traviata,* first performed in 1853, on Dumas's drama. Henri Murger, the French writer who took part in the revelries of this *demimonde,* penned a series of idealized scenes based on his experiences, later published under the title *La Vie de bohème* in 1848. In 1851 the scenes were performed on stage with musical accompaniment. This work, which enjoyed great popularity, became a symbol of this free-and-easy social milieu and inspired Giacomo Puccini's famous 1896 opera, *La Bohème.*

Today we are still fascinated by the lives of these merry rakes and their lovely courtesans, but we are also repelled by the double standard that prevailed. Men enjoyed the freedom to navigate between a life of respectability, possibly including marriage, and a nightlife of promiscuity and revelry without incurring the condemnation of society. However, many of the courtesans were forever reminded of their past as prostitutes by having to appear periodically before the prefect to sign the "vile book" in which they were registered and were unable to appear in respectable company without risking public insult. Unlike the romantic or idealized versions created by the writers of the day, the truth of these women's lives was not glamorous. That might be why, when one of these famous courtesans published her boldly frank memoirs in 1854, the book caused a scandal and was seized, a fate also suffered by the second edition in 1858.

The author of these memoirs was born Elisabeth-Céleste Vénard on 27 December 1824, was dubbed Céleste Mogador during her heyday as a dance hall darling, became Comtesse de Chabrillan when she married Comte Lionel de Chabrillan, and once she had become a widow and a published novelist and playwright was known as either Mme Lionel or Mme de Chabrillan. Several elements combine to make the story of this courtesan exceptional: Mogador's personality and intelligence, her fortuitous escape from the tyranny of prostitution and dependency on various men for her livelihood to a proper marriage to an aristocrat, and a long life as a reasonably respected woman of letters. This bare-boned Cinderella plot, however, overlooks the fierce struggle, the tenacity, and the fortitude this woman displayed on her journey to respectability. Her story as told in her memoirs is not the romantic tale of a courtesan saved by a redeeming love, but a female *Bildungsroman,* as Claire Marrone justly claims. She states, "Céleste's journey toward freedom and her quest for a new sense of self constitutes a portrait of the 'exceptional' nineteenth-century heroine, one who is more gifted and intelligent than most.... Céleste confronts a public that has branded her a 'fallen woman,' and hers is a 'success story.' Satisfaction only occurs, however, after surmounting serious personal and societal hurdles."

Mogador wrote her memoirs at the suggestion of her attorney who was defending her in several lawsuits brought against her by the family of her lover and soon-to-be husband, Comte Lionel de Chabrillan. The de Chabrillans were a rich and powerful family descended from the Knights of Dauphiné who in the twentieth century would be pretenders to the crown of Monaco. Lionel's father, born in 1780, had been attendant to Charles X and married Mlle de Choiseul-Gouffier, daughter of the French envoy to Constantinople. Their elder son, Marie-Olivier-Théodore, held a position at the Council of State. One of their daughters married the Marquis Edouard de Colbert-Maulevrier; the other married the Comte de Montholon-Sémouville. The younger son, Gabriel-Paul-Josselin-Lionel, Mogador's lover, was the typical spoiled rich boy who had a penchant for gambling. Before his father's death, which occurred soon after Lionel met Céleste, he had already squandered much of his inheritance. In the family's opinion, the only solution to his penury was marriage to a wealthy aristocrat. The obstacle to this marriage, however, was Lionel's attachment to one of the famous courtesans of the day, Céleste Mogador. Although they tried to pretend breaking up, the two were so passionately in love that separation was out of the question.

Extravagant as she was in her taste for pretty things, Mogador possessed a natural instinct for thriftiness and, ironically, ended up lending money to her profligate aristocrat lover, including a large sum that she borrowed from her grandfather. In addition, the two lovers bought a small house near the de Chabrillan family estate in the Berry region and furnished it with some of Céleste's furniture. The intermingling of their assets and money, as well as Lionel's decision to make Céleste his proxy while he optimistically sailed to Australia to pan for gold in the New South Wales territory, gave his irate family reason to suspect Céleste's motives in her attachment to Lionel. They attacked her in court in Paris and in Châteauroux, the community near the family estate, and in Bourges.

How does an uneducated twenty-five-year-old woman, whose life has consisted of one struggle after another to survive in a world hostile to her kind, defend herself? In a letter to his mistress before boarding his schooner for Australia, Lionel had recommended Céleste hire a shrewd attorney named Desmarest. Desmarest, who became her lover before her marriage to Lionel and again after Lionel's death, ably defended the courtesan against the powerful de Chabrillan family, who in its arrogance made a few mistakes. But Mogador was not leaving anything to chance. Unschooled though she was (as a young girl she demonstrated an allergy to studies and was indulged by her mother), Céleste began to educate herself by reading, studying law books, and attending trials so she could keep track of her legal proceedings. On the advice of her attorney, she wrote her memoirs to explain her life. This autobiography, which Desmarest most certainly helped her write, was shown to Mme de Girardin, a French writer of note who was known as France's muse; to her husband, Emile de Girardin, a prominent politician; to Camille Doucet, also a writer; and to the great Alexandre Dumas *père*, the author of *The Three Musketeers*. Their verdict was unanimous; the readers compared the text to Jean-Jacques Rousseau's *Confessions* and deemed it worthy of publication. An editor was found and the courtesan became a published author.

In a very direct and simple style replete with reported dialogue, the memoirs present a portrait of an extraordinary woman full of intelligence, passion, compassion, and generosity who was fond of glamour and the theater and possessed uncommon courage. In her memoirs Mme de Chabrillan gives her readers a vivid portrait of the life of a courtesan, but also a quite rare first-hand account of the life of a prostitute in a brothel. In these memoirs, the older woman, although not so old yet, only twenty-eight, looks back with a critical eye and candid self-examination on the journey that brought her to her legal troubles. Like her predecessor in confession, Rousseau, she embroiders on some details or omits others; for instance, she states that she lost her father when she was six years old, when in reality he took off to join the army when her mother was pregnant with her. Although her story has the attributes of a melodrama, she does not sentimentalize her existence nor that of the less fortunate women whom she befriends along the way.

The fierceness of her dedication to her friends is probably Céleste's most endearing quality. For example, when she first meets one of the most popular dancers at the Bal Mabille, the fashionable dance hall of the day, she first observes her and studies her. Then, in spite of the rivalry their profession imposes on them, she forms a friendship with her, and over the years stands by her despite the woman's whimsical and erratic nature. This friend was Lise Sergent, known as la Reine Pomaré, an exotic name given to her by her dancing companions, as was the fashion. Lise Sergent died of tuberculosis at the tender age of twenty-one abandoned by the lover who, as Mogador reports, did not wish to make new sacrifices for someone who had only a month to live. In her naïveté Céleste expected a crowd of mourners at Lise's funeral, but she was the only one in attendance. Céleste sold one of her lace dresses to purchase a marker for the grave. In his novel *Nana,* Emile Zola invents a different ending for la Reine Pomaré, portraying her as an old hag living out of the gutter; the degradation of the fallen queen serves as a warning to Nana and her friend Satin. During one of the first performances of the play based on the novel, someone in the audience shouted protests about the courtesan's depiction. The spectators turned around to see a white-haired woman standing, bravely protesting the insult to her old friend. Everyone recognized this woman as Mogador.

When a friend needed her, or needed some money or some service, Céleste never hesitated to involve herself, even to her own detriment. But when she was crossed, she could be vengeful, as with a flighty woman who pretended to be her dear friend but tried to steal her lover. Céleste doggedly set up a plan to expose the woman for what she was: a double-crosser. Such actions were never undertaken out of meanness but out of her sense of justice. When one of her more experienced courtesan friends who had become bitter and cynical resorted to cruelty toward others, Céleste was appalled and in the end rejected this woman who seemed to be such a bad influence on her as well.

On the other hand, the memoirs also reveal a woman who seems candidly shallow and frivolous. As she relates some of the more tragic moments of her life, she does not hesitate to interrupt their retelling to describe at length some opulent setting that she seems to admire and be drawn to. Is this the strategy of a writer who wishes to relieve the narrative tension with a lighter moment, or is this a genuine expression of attraction to glittery display? In view of her inexperience as a writer and her evident fascination with pomp and ostentation, it is more likely that the latter is correct. It is necessary to remember that this woman was still just a young impressionable girl, and the more mature woman recalling her life is keenly aware of her past weaknesses. In her memoirs the soon-to-be Mme de Chabrillan does not hesitate to paint herself accurately. For example, when her lover the Italian duke puts a lovely little surrey at her disposal, Céleste parades up and down the fashionable Champs-Elysées to show off her good fortune. Similarly, when Lionel gives her a carriage driven by a coachman dressed in English style, she is so dazzled by it, she shows it off to her other lover Richard who, needless to say, is not impressed. The memoirist remarks, "Oh, dreadful flightiness! My first reaction was one of vanity. I nodded to him and signaled for him to come closer. But my carriage did not seem to please him as much as it pleased me. He walked away gloomily."

Her impetuous and fiery nature, however, was the catalyst that determined much of Céleste's life. Many of Mogador's decisions were made irrationally, based on whim and desire. She would regret many of her hasty decisions, none more than the one to enter a brothel and have her name entered in the register of prostitutes. She wished to get away from an intolerable home life (which she left at fifteen because her mother's live-in boyfriend was making sexual advances toward her and once even tried to rape her) and avoid a forced marriage to a dull laborer; based on the conversations she had with a young prostitute, the easy escape appeared to be with these well-dressed women and their glamorous lives. She had not been at the house twenty-four hours when she regretted her choice. Unfortunately her fate was sealed.

By the time Céleste turned sixteen, prostitution was a well-organized profession. The women were supervised closely—on the streets by the police, and in bordellos by the madams. The customers could avail themselves of a publication that served as a "guide to the gentleman." The guide instructed as to prices, places, and specialties. In spite of fears of infections, the recruiting of women was flourishing. The only way a woman could have her name removed from the register of prostitutes was to prove that she had gainful and secure employment. A few times Céleste tried to get her name removed from the register, but the positions she held in the theater or at the hippodrome did not, in the eyes of the police, constitute enough security. When she gave up in this endeavor, she refused to return each year to reregister as the law required, but it meant that she lived in fear of the police, a fear great enough to drive her to attempt suicide rather than face the shame of being arrested.

In keeping with her generous nature, Céleste wanted to adopt her maid Marie's baby girl when Marie died soon after childbirth. As a prostitute, however, Céleste was not allowed to adopt the baby. She had to settle for the title of godmother. It was not until a few days before her marriage to Lionel that, with the help of a powerful friend, Prince Napoléon (who was rumored to have been her lover), number 3748 and the name Céleste Vénard were erased from the register of prostitutes.

Mogador's impetuousness also accounts for some of the more melodramatic moments of her life, at least as she describes them. Her affair with Lionel generated many of them. Like a character in a boulevard drama, a fiercely jealous Céleste gets rid of a rival by storming into her lover's apartment during his absence and ordering the stunned servants to pack up the belongings of the interim mistress to have them taken to a hotel. And when confronting Lionel about this mistress, she grabs a knife and stabs her lover, then stabs herself in the chest and decorously swoons.

A notable significance of these memoirs is their disclosure of a specific class of nineteenth-century French society from the point of view of one of its members. The year that Céleste received her number, the chief editor at the *Figaro* coined the term *lorette,* a euphemism for "prostitute" that Balzac quickly found useful. To become a courtesan, the *lorette* must have one main lover; that is, the woman must be talked about as the mistress of ——, even though she might discreetly have other lovers. And the difference between the two types of women was formally recognized in this subculture of *demimondaines.* For example, some salons did not admit *lorettes,* but they did courtesans. Céleste learned that lesson very early. In the days when she was still innocent enough to believe in love, she became enamored of a young doctor named Adolphe, whom she met when she was still at the brothel. She had not revealed her situation to him, having been told he did not frequent such women, nor had he bothered to let her know he had a mistress, Louisa Aumont, until he took Céleste to a ball at which Mlle Aumont was present. Outraged that Céleste's kind of woman would be admitted, Mlle Aumont demanded her eviction. Young Céleste found out not only that it is quite customary for a man to have several mistresses, but also about the hierarchy among kept women. As she explains in her memoirs, this event began a process of hardening of her heart. The mortification she suffered would not soon be forgotten.

Ever since her mother had taken her to the theater when she was a child, Céleste had dreamed of becoming a stage actress. She never gave up on her dream, although it appears, when she finally was given some acting roles, she did not have much talent. Her practical side and her desire for beautiful things led her to pursue more realistic means to make a living. Many young women sought out popular dance halls to meet young men for romance and maybe to obtain monetary support. It was at one of these dance halls that Céleste's path to becoming a courtesan began.

Present-day chic Avenue Montaigne was then called Allée des Veuves, Widow's Alley. Because of the lack of street lighting, it was a likely place for trysts and other clandestine meetings. In spite of this reputation, in 1813 Charles Mabille, a dance teacher, opened an outdoor cafe, then a dance hall that became popular with working young men and women. Thirty years later, Mabille's sons improved the locale and turned the Bal Mabille into one of the favorite meeting places for lovers until it closed in 1875. It had gardens, harbors, swings, merry-go-rounds, games, and of course a dance floor under the trees, where new dances were introduced to the sounds of an orchestra composed of candidates for the conservatory. After closing time the young men would wait outside for their conquests, anticipating a night of pleasure.

It was at Mabille that Céleste acquired her famous name of Mogador. Mogador, a city in Morocco today called Essaouira, was the site of a notable French victory. The event so captured the imagination of the French that numerous mementos were sold with the name Mogador on them. So when Céleste's dancing partner had to fend off other suitors to dance with the beautiful young woman, he remarked that it would be easier to defend Mogador than his partner. And thus, Céleste Vénard was christened Céleste Mogador, queen of the Bal Mabille. There was, however, another queen, just as admired, la Reine Pomaré, so named because the wild air about her reminded the dancers of the new Queen Pomaré of the French possession Tahiti. La Reine Pomaré was the ill-fated Lise Sergent, whose short and gaudy life epitomized the period: at one time she had lived with the poet Baudelaire; she made it a habit to shock the bourgeois establishment, sometimes dressing like a man; and she wore thick, exaggerated makeup. Now Mabille had two reigning monarchs, each with her own supporters organized in clans like political parties; arguments and debates would ensue. Poets vied with each other to compose poems extolling the glories of the queens. Paris was having fun.

The author of the memoirs is silent on her means of support in those days, but we can assume she found young suitors only too delighted to provide her with a livelihood in return for her favors. She is not so silent, although subtly discreet, on the more well-to-do or famous suitors who would enter her life later. Once she acquired notoriety at the Bal Mabille, and later as a fearless equestrienne at the circus, her name was on everyone's lips; she was recognized in public and was therefore the ideal adornment for a young, or not so young, dandy.

There were many men in Céleste's life, and the majority of them were nothing more to her than a means to an end. Men like the rich Italian Duke of Ossuma or the Dutch baron would set her up in an apartment and furnish it for her; they would give her carriages and sometimes money. If on a whim she wanted a piano, she would get one and lessons to go with it. Some men were sincere in their professed love for her. A famous Italian tenor, although he could barely speak French, fell in love with Céleste and finally stopped seeing her only after she forced him to hide in a cubicle by her bed one day when the duke paid her an impromptu visit. The tenor, sickened by the vaudevillian scene he had been forced to play, could not forgive Mogador's callousness. Others were fatuous dolts like Léon, a shy admirer of her triumphant deeds as a circus rider, who fought a duel over her, but who, to her great embarrassment, ignominiously abandoned her in the street the moment he saw his mother and his grandfather walking toward them. In their eyes, to be seen walking with Céleste Mogador was scandalous.

Céleste was easily impressed by the literary and artistic set. She yearned for the company of intelligent and witty people, and through her association with Lionel, she finally met such people. She became friends with Alexandre Dumas *père* and, much later, with his reticent son. She caught the eye and captured the heart of Thomas Couture, the painter, who used her as a model for his important painting *Roman Orgy*, which now hangs in the Musée d'Orsay, and who did a plaster cast of her hand, today on display at the Musée Carnavalet in Paris. She had come a long way from the days at the brothel, when she was the plaything of the poet Alfred de Musset. She met him not long after the breakup of his love affair with the writer George Sand. Musset, about to turn thirty, already famous, had replaced Sand with the famous actress Rachel. That relationship did not prevent him from spending most of his time in pursuit of other pleasures. He was frequently seen at various Parisian cafés drinking his favorite drink, a mixture of absinthe, cognac, English beer, and an egg yolk. He also was a regular at the brothel where Céleste was employed. His acquaintance with the new young prostitute, who, according to her memoirs, was not afraid to contradict and provoke him, revived his indolent disposition. Then one day he took her to a restaurant and for no apparent reason picked up a syphon of seltzer water as if he were going to pour himself something to drink and, aiming the opening toward her, drenched her from head to toe. When sixty years after her last, and humiliating, encounter with the great man of letters, on the occasion of the inauguration of his statue, a newspaper reporter reminded Céleste of the incident with the seltzer bottle, she stated that she never forgave him.

The true loves of her life were few. When she was sixteen she fell in love with Adolphe the doctor, until he broke her heart. She seems to have also truly cared for a young talented Jewish musician named Hermann Cohen. By then, however, she was too jaded to recognize his sincere passion for her. When she finally did, it was too late; he had renounced his religion, become a Roman Catholic, and joined a monastery.

The true passion of her life, however, was Lionel. She fell in love with him the night she met him and remained true to him, in her fashion, until she died. Her love for Lionel, like all passions, was complex. Certainly he was a very handsome man; his portrait at the Musée Carnavalet in Paris reveals a dark-eyed young man with an intelligent face and a majestic bearing. He was charming and kind but prone to arrogance and selfishness. She was of course impressed with his title and pedigree, but she had had other aristocratic lovers. She certainly was not loath to carry on an affair with the rich and gentle Englishman, Richard, all the while professing to love Lionel. The comte seemed to have been primarily attracted to her beauty, and his desire for her became an obsession that seemed to have more to do with lust than love; he could not stay away from her, however much he tried, in spite of his good sense and class responsibilities. Eventually the two lovers matured emotionally, and their physical attraction turned into love. During his absence from Céleste as he panned for gold in Australia, Lionel's heart grew fonder of the woman for whom he had lost everything: family, reputation, and fortune. Left behind in Paris, Céleste also matured and began to gain more self-respect as she struggled to defend herself against the de Chabrillan family, so that upon his return from Australia a few years after their first meeting and the drama of their stormy relationship, they were married and remained devoted to each other.

The de Chabrillans were of course opposed to such a marriage, so the wedding took place on 4 January 1854 in London with French citizens residing in England as witnesses. It was a triple wedding, possibly so there would be no doubt as to the legality of this marriage. There was a ceremony before the registrar, a second at the Church of Saint-Paul, and a third at the French chancellery. Half a century later, the Comtesse de

Chabrillan would recall that Queen Victoria, curious about this celebrity in her city, wanted to see her. She is supposed to have remarked to a friend that she thought the French beauty was lovelier than the Empress Eugénie.

The marriage was fraught with adversity. Lionel, who had been able to obtain a post of French consul in Melbourne, Australia, sailed with his bride and her godchild, Solange, to find upon their arrival that his wife's reputation had preceded them. The publication of her memoirs had made Céleste even more notorious. She had tried to stop their publication before her departure but had been unsuccessful. From Australia, she wrote to all her friends begging them to burn the books. Because the memoirs caused such a scandal, they were eventually seized and banned from further publication, but it was too late to put out the wildfire they had ignited. Yet Céleste's desire to continue writing was not dampened. The two years she spent in Australia were not idle. In spite of, or because of, her social ostracism by the French and English community, she used her time wisely, including trying to learn English and writing another set of memoirs that would eventually be published in 1877 under the title *Un Deuil au bout du monde, suite des mémoires de Céleste Mogador* (translated in 1997 by Patricia Clancy and Jeanne Allen as *The French Consul's Wife: Memoirs of Céleste de Chabrillan in Gold-Rush Australia*). And so it is in Australia that Mogador's career as a writer began in earnest. The second memoirs not only describe her impressions of the wild frontier life in Australia and the few years after her return from the faraway continent, but also depict the love she and Lionel shared.

With her usual indomitable energy and vivid imagination, Céleste also began writing novels; her first one, the 1857 *Les Voleurs d'or* (translated as *The Gold Robbers* by Lucy and Caroline Moorehead in 1970), a novel on the struggles of pioneers in the new world, met with much success back in France. In his review of the novel, Alexandre Dumas *père* stated that the book was not a chef-d'oeuvre but was certainly one of the most moving and interesting novels of the year. This was the beginning of thirty years of writing novels, plays, operettas, poems, and songs.

Becoming ill in the inhospitable climate of Australia, possibly also nostalgic for the city she loved and the social life she lacked, Céleste returned to Paris after two years in Melbourne. Lionel took a leave of absence and joined her a few months later, but regretfully had to go back to his post after a few months. During the long and arduous voyage back, he became ill and died very soon after his arrival. He was forty years old. At a crossroads between Poinçonnet and the forest of Châteauroux, Céleste de Chabrillan had two large iron crosses erected with marble plaques on which is inscribed: "To the memory of Comte Lionel de Chabrillan, born in Paris 3 December 1818, deceased in Melbourne 29 December 1858. Pray for him!"

The widow survived her husband by half a century. During those years Mogador continued to struggle for financial security and social stability. Although her literary publications met with much success and several of her plays were hits, she still had to fight the de Chabrillan family, who wanted her to abandon the Chabrillan name. The family offered to pay her two thousand francs a year, guaranteed, if she renounced the name Chabrillan. They sent her such emissaries as Ferdinand de Lesseps and Sainte-Beuve. She threw them out. Lionel's brother was sent next. He reproached her, not so much for having been Prince Napoleon's lover, but for spending the night before going to London for her wedding at his house. In spite of these strong-arm tactics, she refused their offer and always made it a point to use her husband's name, and to do so proudly.

With the money she had earned from the theatrical performance of a version of her first novel, she bought a lot in the fashionable Le Vésinet suburb of Paris and had an Australian style country villa built, which she called Châlet Lionel. The war of 1870, however, brought many changes, not only in the widow's life, but also for the country; the empire was coming to an end. Never one to remain idle, on 15 September 1870, with patriotic fervor, she organized an egalitarian organization of women to care for soldiers and orphans called *Les Soeurs de France* (Sisters of France). She wrote and sang sentimentally patriotic songs. When the Prussians occupied Paris, she disbanded the group and returned to Le Vésinet only to find that Châlet Lionel had been ransacked by the Prussians. Her godchild, Solange, who had been a difficult child but to whom she remained devoted, ran off with a Prussian soldier and was never heard from again. Four years later Céleste's mother died.

The remainder of Mogador's life was spent scrimping to survive financially. In the end she was admitted to La Providence, a retirement home run by the Sisters of Charity and subsidized by the Ministry of the Interior. She died there on 18 February 1909, at the age of eighty-five, surrounded by souvenirs of her life as Céleste Mogador. Her funeral services were discreet according to her wishes, and she was buried next to her mother at the cemetery of Pré-Saint-Gervais. On the grave stone appears just her name, "Céleste," and above is a marble plaque with the crown of a *comtesse*. (In 1992 her remains were moved to le Poinçonnet, a few miles south of Châteauroux.) Today, no one remembers the name Chabrillan, but when most French people hear the name Mogador, they readily recognize it. Not far from the cross she had erected in memory of her dear Lionel, there is an oak that the villagers call "Mogador's Oak."

Céleste Vénard, both in spite of herself and because of her courage and her spirit, transformed herself into a true nineteenth-century heroine. Were it not for her memoirs, however, she would be just a footnote in other people's recollection and history books.

A WORD ON THE TRANSLATION

The first edition of the memoirs appeared in 1854 in 5 volumes bearing the title *Adieux au monde, mémoires de Céleste Mogador* (Farewell to the world, memoirs of Céleste Mogador); the second edition appeared in 1858 in 4 volumes with the shortened title of *Mémoires de Céleste Mogador* (Memoirs of Céleste Mogador); and the third edition appeared under the same shortened title in 1876 in 2 volumes. These editions are of course all out of print and can be found only in a few libraries around the world. The author herself made a few changes and additions to the editions following the first one, including a preface in which she defends herself, claiming that it was not her intention to make her kind of life attractive to other young women, but to show the perils of such a life. Her main desire in this painful endeavor had been to confess her life to avoid losing the love of the one who had so generously given his life to her. This translation is based on the 1968 republication of the first memoir by Les Amis de l'Histoire. This edition differs from the original in a few respects. First, some passages that could have appeared redundant were omitted; so were her direct addresses to her attorney. Second, subtitles were added to each chapter title as well as to the title of the memoirs, giving the whole a romance novel style. And finally, where Mme de Chabrillan used the name Robert, the 1968 edition substituted the real name Lionel, and his château is identified by name, le Magnet.

FOR FURTHER READING

Readers wishing additional information on Céleste Mogador and her times can consult the following works, which were examined for the above introduction. Françoise Moser, the author of the 1935 French biography of Céleste Mogador, claims in her introduction to have had in her possession several notebooks in Céleste's handwriting of unpublished memoirs covering the latter part of her life. According to the translators of Mogador's second set of memoirs, these notebooks have not been traceable.

WORKS CITED

Clancy, Patricia and Jeanne Allen. Introduction. *The French Consul's Wife: Memoirs of Céleste de Chabrillan in Gold-rush Australia.* Melbourne: Miegunyah Press, 1997.

Haldane, Charlotte. *Daughter of Paris.* London: Hutchinson, 1961.

Leclercq, Pierre-Robert. *Céleste Mogador, Une reine de Paris. Biographie.* Paris: La Table Ronde, 1996.

Marrone, Claire. "Male and Female *Bildung:* The *Mémoires de Céleste Mogador,*" *Nineteenth-Century French Studies* 25, nos. 3 & 4 (spring-summer 1997): 335–47.

Moser, Françoise. *Vie et aventures de Céleste, fille publique, femme de lettres et comtesse (1824–1909).* Paris: Albin Michel, 1935.

Richardson, Joanna. *The Courtesans: The Demi-Monde in Nineteenth Century France.* London: Weidenfeld & Nicholson, 1967.

MEMOIRS OF A COURTESAN
in Nineteenth-Century Paris

1

My Stepfather

A Dreadful Individual—Toward the Unknown—Storm on the Saône—
First Friend—Refuge in a Bawdyhouse—Saved!

EVERYTHING I HAVE NOT DARED say out loud, I am going to put down on paper. I do not plan to transform my life into a novel, and I do not intend to try to clear my name or pretend to be a heroine. As I describe what I have suffered, what ill or good I might have done, I shall tell all without holding back, and you will see that I need great courage to face my past.

I was six years old when I lost my father. He was a kind and honest man who, before dying, would have killed me if he had had any notion that a few years later I would be called Mogador.

We were living in Paris, on Rue du Puits.[1] My mother was busy with her thriving shop. As for me, as long as my hair was in pretty curls and my mother dressed me in a lovely frock, the rest was not important to me. And so by the time I was ten, I still did not know how to read.

There was no way to force me to learn anything, and as soon as there was talk of sending me to school, I would start to cry and scream. I would always eventually get my way.

We were hatters. There were always five or six employees coming and going in the workroom. These employees transferred the affection they had had for my father to me. I was a very fortunate child.

A tall man often came to the shop. I hated him. It would please me to say unpleasant things to him, which was often. But instead of getting angry, he would give me lots of little presents and would marvel at my beauty.

All this fuss over me was futile. There is no denying the fact that children and dogs can sense who really loves them and who pretends to.

G—— was a thirty-five-year-old man from Lorraine. He was at least five feet seven inches tall, had broad-shoulders, dark hair, rather large, slightly recessed eyes, very thick eyebrows that seemed darker than his hair, a round head, a flat face, a pale complexion, a pinched nose, and lips that were so thin their red part could only be seen when he spoke.

His dark sideburns blended with his silk tie. I never saw him wear a shirt collar, and most of the time his frock coat was buttoned up, which made me say that he looked like a spy.

When he wanted to play with me the way one plays with a little girl, or he wanted to give me something, or take my hand or kiss me, I always ran off, and I did not come back to the house until I was certain he was gone.

Almost a year had gone by. I did not like M. G——, but I had become used to him. When I was scolded, he would defend me. When I wanted something, I would ask for it in front of him, and if I was told I could not have it, he would bring it to me the next day.

I later learned that M. G—— had already asked Maman to marry him and that, without saying yes or no, Maman had answered, "I shall see later. If I am going to give my daughter a stepfather, I must be certain that he will make her happy."

That was the reason for all those acts of kindness toward me. My intuition as a child had not been wrong.

A DREADFUL INDIVIDUAL

He was a mechanical engineer and a very talented craftsman. He had a house back home. Everyone thought well of him. The marriage was decided and concluded in a matter of two months.

My mother had not been married more than six days when twenty persons came to demand money. G—— was riddled with debts.

All those good people told my mother, "You married a scoundrel. If it had not been for the fact that he owed us money, we would have warned you, but he threatened us, saying that if we prevented the wedding, he would never pay us back."

My mother cried a lot, and he would beat me for no particular reason. Our lives had become a series of violent scenes.

After one year all the money was gone. My mother requested a separation from her husband, but the authorities always tell unhappy wives, "Be patient. Your husband promises to stop beating you." Friends interfered and reconciled them. There were more scenes. Again, they made up. He did not want a separation.

My mother was very industrious! She was working for two, and besides, my grandfather was rich. G—— had set his sights on the inheritance.

One night at midnight, G—— returned home full of wine, came to my bed, and removed my covers. When my mother said to him, "You are mad, waking up this poor child and uncovering her. It is freezing cold," he went into a wild rage, grabbed my mother by the waist and threw her down the stairs. My poor mother's head hit a sharp corner. She was instantly covered with blood. She had the strength to go back upstairs and pick me up in her arms, telling him, "If you touch a hair of my daughter's head, I shall kill you."

We had barely gone down two stories when she fell taking me down with her.

The cold, the fear, and the pain caused me to faint outright. We would have both died right there if a carpenter who lived in the building had not opened his door.

His first thought was to bring us into his home, but he was a bachelor. Fearing that people might form conjectures, he thought it would be better if we waited for daylight at the military post.

When I came to, I was in an armchair, all wrapped up in a greatcoat. Near me was a soldier who was warming my hands in his. My mother's wounds had been bandaged and she was resting.

Our young protector had taken us to the post. Since I was not dressed when I was taken from my bed, four men had been sent to my stepfather's for some clothes. When they arrived the soldiers found a woman in my mother's bedroom. She and my stepfather were both arrested and put in the lockup at the post where we had taken refuge.

G—— wanted to throw himself on us but we were well protected.

When daylight arrived my mother and I were placed on a stretcher and brought before the police chief who sent G—— to prison and had my mother taken to the Hôtel-Dieu hospital.

My mother's convalescence was long. She came down with erysipelas.[2]

The poor woman feared recovery more than her pain. As for me, with the insouciance of youth, I was comfortable at the clinic. In a month's time I was plump, rested, and healthy. Everyone loved me and thought I was beautiful.

In anticipation of my departure, the nuns covered me with kisses and caresses.

I thought, my goodness, a clinic is a wonderful place! I had transformed it into a world of perpetual enchantment for the inpatients. That is the term used in hospitals to designate the patients who, sick with incurable diseases, bedridden and hopeless, have spent years watching the varying population of persons with acute illnesses parade before them.

TOWARD THE UNKNOWN

The moment of departure had arrived. We received notice from the police station that my dear stepfather was being released from prison. My mother would have rather died than see him again. She was advised to leave Paris.

One of her former employees told her, "I am supposed to leave for Lyon where I have a position working for M. Pomerais, a hatter. Do you want to take my place?"

I thought my mother was going to choke her she hugged her so tight.

"Henriette, you are saving my life and I shall always remember this favor!"

Two days later she obtained a passport in the name of her friend at indigents' cost, three sous per league, and we left the next day. Henriette accompanied us with a cabinetmaker named Honoré who had wanted to marry my mother and later be my godfather.

In those days the roads near Paris were still paved and lined with tall trees. As I listened to the sounds of carriages and the wind howling in the branches and rustling the leaves, I could feel myself getting impatient.

Henriette gave me a little dress, Honoré, a wide-brimmed straw hat. Neither one was rich, yet they both offered us some money. My mother reassured them, "I have what I need for me and Céleste."

Their kind hearts swelled, because they knew very well that we had just left the hospital without a sou, but they did not dare insist.

We walked all day long without eating. At eight o'clock, having completed one leg of the journey, we went to a roadside farm. I was very tired, but I pretended to be gay. I hopped around and bantered with the members of the household. My graciousness pleased everyone, and we were treated as if we were rich.

The next day my mother went to city hall to get road assistance, and our journey to Chalon-sur-Saône progressed without incident. Each time we came upon a church or a roadside cross, we asked God for protection.

When we arrived in Chalon large rain drops began to fall. In spite of our fatigue, we ran all the way to the steamboat pier. It was stiflingly hot, and I had been so burned by the sun that my neck was covered with blisters. The boat was leaving at five o'clock in the morning. To make sure there would be room for us, my mother paid in advance. The girl at the inn woke us up at four o'clock. We went down to a large room for coffee.

STORM ON THE SAÔNE

The weather was atrocious. We could barely see anything. A plank had been set up to get the passengers from land to the boat. The wind blew so furiously that we could have been swept away.

The fear of losing her seat caused my mother to be careless. She picked me up and risked running across, but her weight shook the plank; she missed her step and I fell in the Saône.

I was pulled out dazed from this fall and this unanticipated bath.

Of course, we were in second class, a small square room with benches all around. Once I was changed and dry, I looked at the people around us. There was a kindly and venerable looking priest, two nicely dressed workmen, and a bold looking woman wearing a loud dress and an outlandish bonnet.

Somewhat recovered from my adventure, I went toward the priest and tried to look in the book he was holding. He motioned for me to approach, showed me the holy pictures, and encouraged me to pray to God.

I was lying down and sleeping on the bench when the sound of thunder suddenly woke me up. Everyone was crying out in despair. As it went under a bridge, the boat almost broke in two and its smokestack was partly broken.

FIRST FRIEND

As soon as we arrived in Lyon we asked for directions to Célestins Square where the master to whom my mother was assigned lived. We were able to sublet a very small room in a house nearby.

I have already said that my mother had taken out a passport in the name of her friend Henriette. The passport therefore bore the name of an unmarried woman. When I called her Maman, she received strange looks.

We had been in Lyon two days. Maman had met the master-hatter who greeted her kindly, but she had not dared tell him she had a daughter. Therefore I had to stay cooped up in my room all day.

If our landlady, a short skinny woman of about fifty, had seemed a little friendlier, I would have wormed my way into her favors, but her only love in the world was a big gray cat.

I became more reasonable. I promised to be good and to hem handkerchiefs. I must have really been softened up to make such a promise because I hated sewing.

This was Friday. My mother did not have to start work until Monday. We went for a walk to the Brotteaux.[3] We had taken a lunch with us and sat in the shade of a beautiful chestnut tree. We were about to eat when I felt something cold and damp against my neck. I was so scared I did not dare turn around. I looked at Maman, who started to laugh so loud I decided to look around, and I saw a big brown and white water spaniel. At least that is what we later determined he was, because on that day he was so muddy it was impossible to make out anything about him except his clear gray eyes, his black nose, his white teeth, and his pink muzzle. He was a poor creature. I gave him my bread.

After an hour we got along so well together that he did not want to leave me, and I thought he was magnificent. We went home and he followed me to the door. Maman had her hand on the knocker. I plucked up my courage: "Dear mother, may I please, I would like to keep him until Sunday."

"You are mad, child. You want us to be evicted. Do you not remember that the landlady hesitated before renting to me because I had a child? So now if I bring her a dog!"

I could not promise to hide my friend, since he was the size of a large poodle. The door opened and my spaniel entered with me. Even though I repeated, "Go away, go away!" he wagged his tail and stayed put. Maman took my hand and baptized my dog as a sign of adoption when she said, "Come on, Mouton, you will be company for Céleste."

Because my mother was very good at her job and she had good taste, after she had worked a while her masters were very kind to her. She explained her position and revealed my existence. She was scolded for not bringing me with her. The lady wanted to go get me right away.

"Do not go," said Maman. "She has a dog that she will not part with. She is crazy about it!"

The lady insisted on going to fetch me and my dog.

Several months went by like this. We would receive letters from Henriette who would tell us what was going on in Paris. To find out where we were, my stepfather went begging to all of our friends, but no one was persuaded by his posturing. He ran around, drank, and gambled. After six months he was riddled with debts.

My mother was in charge of sales at the hatter's where she worked. One day a man came in and recognized her.

"I am not mistaken," he said to her, "you are Mme G——. I saw your husband two months ago. He is telling everyone who will listen to him that you ran off with a lover, but my wife gently set him straight."

"Please, take care not to tell him that you saw me," replied my mother.

The man promised most sincerely to be discreet. The first thing he did was to write to his wife: "Guess who I just saw in Lyon. . . ."

Not long after that my stepfather knew where we were. Since he did not have a sou, he got himself hired on as pilot on one of the steamboats that provide service to Lyon. I already said that he was a mechanical engineer.

REFUGE IN A BAWDYHOUSE

One day, or rather one night, since it is already dark at four thirty in the winter, I was walking my dog. I was in the middle of the square when a man grabbed me and lifted me like a feather.

I was going to scream, but suddenly I lost my voice. I had just recognized my stepfather.

I tried to tear myself away from him and to scream, but he was squeezing me so hard that my bones were cracking and my voice died on my lips. I could not breathe.

"Listen," he said, "your mother is a wretch. She is going to pay me back today for all the misery she has caused me. I am well aware that she does not love me, but you are another matter. She will want to find you!"

I was going to close my eyes when I saw my dog following me. I took heart. I was no longer alone.

We went through several streets, then in front of an alleyway where animal carcasses dripping with black and coagulated blood were hanging on doors. At the entrance smoky oil lamps produced a dark and drab light. We entered some sort of cul-de-sac and he stopped about midway. I took a look at the house he was about to enter. It was tall and narrow, and the windows were closed. On the second floor, there was one shop whose windows had been whitewashed. The alley was dark. As we entered I stiffened my body and called my dog. But as G—— turned around, he kicked the dog. Such a sharp pain went through my heart that I collapsed on my tormentor's shoulder. I do not know whether I had fainted or if the will to not see any more, to not hear any more, had numbed me for a few moments. Finally I heard someone speak. It was a woman's voice. I opened my eyes and jumped off the chair where I had been deposited. I ran toward this woman. I saw G——'s eyes dart toward me, so I turned my head and did not dare say a word. We were in a room that seemed strange to me. It looked like a café and yet it was not one. There were chairs, tables, a counter, liquor bottles, several scantily dressed women in low-cut gowns. One of these women was seated next to G——. She is the one I had gone toward for refuge. She had a harsh voice and seemed mean. Two other women were at a table with two men; a blue and red flame burned among them. Two other women were playing cards. I saw yet another one who, behind me, was working on a child's little dress.

The frosted windows did not permit me to see outside and the door to the street was boarded up. I made a startled move: the woman near me was about to drink a glass of clear yellow liqueur and some of it spilled on her dress.

"Idiot!" she yelled. "Now my dress is stained."

And she shoved me so hard, I rolled several feet.

After a few moments I felt someone gently tugging at my sleeve. It was the woman who was sewing. She sat me on her lap. My heart relaxed a little.

The two women who were at the table with the men said to the one who was near G——, "Hey! Louise, do you want some punch?"

"No," the one by that name replied, "that mess of yours is only good for children. I prefer pure brandy."

She finished drinking the glass that had been the cause of my disgrace. Then, addressing G——, she resumed the interrupted conversation. "So you say that this kid is yours? You should have left her at home because the rules are very strict."

G—— slowly emptied his glass, and, most probably having thought of what to say, began thus: "I got married eight years ago and I loved my wife. She deceived me, so we separated, but the laws are unfair; they give the daughters to the mother. My wife is living here in Lyon with her lover. I came from Paris to take my child away from her, and I intend to leave tomorrow. But I was afraid that they would look for me tonight and I figured I would not be found here. Therefore you must keep us here tonight."

I sighed deeply. I did not dare say anything to the woman who held me in her arms, but I looked at her. She squeezed me gently and motioned for me to keep quiet.

SAVED!

"Oh," continued G——, "if she could run away, she would, so I have to keep an eye on her."

"As you wish," replied Louise, "but I do not want her near me."

Then my protector spoke up in a casual tone, "I shall keep her, if you want. It is late now and it is almost certain that I shall be alone. I shall take good care of her. I know something about children."

This proposal seemed to please Louise.

"Is that all right with you?" she asked G——.

"Yes, just so long as she does not let her go out."

"Do not worry. She has a daughter she takes good care of! Come on, little girl," she said, turning toward me, "you are going to stay with Marguerite and your father will come get you in the morning."

Marguerite took me to a room nearby and said to me, "Now, talk, but softly, because your father is next door and there is only a wall separating us."

I told her that I had just been kidnapped. I begged her to go tell my mother. She put me in her bed, turned the key twice to lock the door, and left.

After her departure I fell asleep. I did not hear Marguerite come back. She was sleeping near me when I woke up. Everything came back to me, and I asked her news of my mother.

"I saw her," she said to me. "I told her where you are. She is going to come over pretending that someone on the outside alerted her, because this man could beat me if he knew that I was the one who had gone to inform her."

We heard loud voices coming from the room below. I let out a scream. I had just recognized my mother's voice.

I ran toward the door. Marguerite held me back and, knocking on the wall, said, "Do you hear the commotion downstairs? It is a woman asking about her child. This might concern you. Come get your daughter."

At first there was no answer from the room next door. Marguerite pushed me toward the stairs, waited a few seconds to give me some time, and exclaimed in a loud voice so she could be heard by everyone, "Oh, no! While I was talking, the little girl ran off." The poor woman was trying to reconcile the successful outcome of my escape and her fear of G——'s anger.

I had not reached the bottom of the stairs when I heard a door open and G—— coming after me. But before he could reach me, I was at my mother's side and in her arms.

G—— rushed toward us, but using their bodies, the women formed a wall of defense around us. In a matter of a few words, my mother had explained her position to them. Just the sight of her had dispelled the effects of G——'s lies.

"I am going to kill them both!" he yelled.

"So I was right to send for the guards?" said Marguerite, who had come in last.

Those words had their effect. G—— stopped, fists clenched, mouth foaming. Marguerite took advantage of this moment of hesitation and led us out through the courtyard.

2

The Hunter and the Hunted

At the Mathieus'—Flight Once More—Attempt to Escape from the Enemy

"WELL," SAID M. POMERAIS, "now we need to find you a safe hide-out. You would be too exposed here. I am going to send you to one of my friends, a wholesaler. I shall get word to him, and you will leave tonight. In the meantime, go up to my wife's room and we shall fetch your belongings."

We had barely started up the stairs when G—— showed up. We saw him pacing back and forth in front of the shop.

Tired of not seeing anything, he entered and asked for the address of a woman who, according to what he had been told, worked in this house.

M. Pomerais was on his guard. "What is this person's name?"

"Sir, I am looking for my wife. After ruining me and deceiving me, she stole my daughter. I would abandon this miserable woman if I had my child. I cannot tell you under what name she came to live in Lyon because she conceals the one I gave her to dodge the law and my pursuit."

M. Pomerais answered calmly, "All that does not amount to a name. I have fifty women working for me, and as long as they are punctual, I do not ask for details about their private lives."

G—— was very disappointed, especially since M. Pomerais was about to turn heel. "Oh! Sir, how unfortunate I am! You must have been warned about me. I am sure that she deceived you too."

"You are mistaken. I have not been warned about you. I do not have the honor of knowing you."

"I told you my name is G——, and I want to find my wife. In case she changed her name, this is what she looks like: she is five feet tall, has a nice figure, an oval face, a high forehead, and fine shiny dark hair.

She has nicely arched dark eyebrows, bluish-gray eyes that have a harsh expression, an aquiline but broad nose, a large mouth, thin lips, and wonderful teeth. Her daughter, I mean my daughter, is seven. She is a precocious child. She will be strong-willed like her mother." Then, afraid of letting his hatred for me show, he added, "She is ill-mannered! All that will change!"

M. Pomerais bit his lips to avoid replying with all the disdain this act inspired in him. "It is true, I know the person you just described. She is a hardworking woman who seemed quite honest to us. She told us yesterday that she was leaving Lyon for a few days."

So saying, M. Pomerais took leave of G—— and turned his back on him.

G—— remained stunned for a few moments, and then, realizing that he would get nothing from this man, became furious and left.

AT THE MATHIEUS'

At ten o'clock that night, an apprentice came to tell us that G—— was no longer at the shop entrance near which he had been prowling all day.

At half past midnight we left accompanied by M. Pomerais, two workmen, and the concierge. We were going to the Guillotière.[1]

When we got there it was past one in the morning. We were expected. The person who let us in was a healthy-looking man approximately forty years old, short and fat, with a nice complexion. His frizzy, grayish-brown hair framed his face. He was bundled up in a large frock coat.

"You are quite late, my children, I was about to go to bed."

"Excuse us, dear Mathieu," said M. Pomerais, "but this poor woman did not want to go out earlier for fear that she would be followed. She cannot leave your house for some time."

"Do not worry," replied M. Mathieu. "We shall be vigilant, and my son will keep the little one from becoming bored."

"Well, take heart, dear Jeanne," said M. Pomerais to my mother. "You are with good people."

The door closed behind him. We went across the courtyard. M. Mathieu led us up two flights of stairs.

"Here is your room," he told us.

My mother thanked him profusely.

When I woke up the next morning my mother was up and walking softly so as not to make any noise. She was combing her hair. I have never seen anyone with hair that beautiful. Our room was nice and clean. The sun shone through flowers clinging to a window that looked out on the courtyard. I felt quite cheerful.

"Oh, what a lovely garden, Maman. I am the one who will take care of it."

My mother kissed me.

"Someone is going to come for us. Come here and let me dress you."

At that moment someone knocked softly on the door. We looked at each other without moving.

"Yes," replied my mother.

The door opened, and a woman of about thirty looked in.

"I hope I am not disturbing you," she said, "but I go to the workroom early. Do you want to have breakfast downstairs or in your room?"

Maman told her that of course she was ready to follow her and she did not know how to express her gratitude.

"Oh!" said Mme Mathieu. "If I can be frank with you, I am coming to get you not so much to take you to the workroom but rather to please my son."

We went down to the dining room where I found a boy my age, cute as a button. His brown and naturally curly hair was shoulder length. He seemed to look down on me, which embarrassed me greatly, but during lunch he was sweet.

FLIGHT ONCE MORE

I was so happy that a month felt like a day.

One morning a shaken M. Mathieu came into the workroom. He was holding a letter in his hand.

"I am summoned before the police chief to face M. G——."

My mother looked at the letter and turned pale.

"My God!" she said breaking into tears. "Is there no way I can avoid bringing torment to those who come to my aid? I do not want to be the cause of unpleasantness in this household. We shall leave tonight."

"Oh," said M. Mathieu, "you are getting carried away! Nothing can happen to us because we welcomed you into our home. Your work is enough to pay for what we are giving you. I shall go see the police chief, and if you must leave us, we shall find you another hideout. As for Céleste, she is not his daughter, she is yours. So we shall keep her. My boy likes her so much he could become ill if she went away. And so, I am on my way to find you a little room."

I had heard this whole conversation and my heart was divided between two sorrows, the choice between which seemed inevitable. Either

I would have to leave the house of young Mathieu or be separated from my mother. I went down to the office where my friend was studying, and I told him everything. He began to stamp his feet and scream at the top of his voice, "I do not want you to go. If you leave, I shall stop learning how to read!"

M. Mathieu returned at four o'clock and told us he had found a room in the house of one of his friends, M. Raoul, a *canut*.[2]

The next day my mother got up very early.

"Take me right away to your friend's house," she told M. Mathieu. "I am leaving you my daughter. Bring her to me as soon as possible, because I would not have the strength to go on without her near me."

M. Mathieu took her to his friend's house and I impatiently waited for his return. When I saw him come in, I ran toward him. He took me in his arms and, going toward the window, he lifted a corner of the curtain and asked me, "Céleste, is that man over there not your stepfather?"

I was so agitated that I could not answer right away. I was looking without seeing.

"Where is Maman? Has he seen Maman?"

"No, thank goodness he has not seen her, but her premonition was right. I am glad she asked me to take her away this morning because I had intended to wait until tonight. The doorman told me when I returned that a man had come asking all sorts of questions. He pointed him out to me. Look, he is the one who is still in front of the house."

I looked and I recognized G——. My mother was in a secure place, so for now we did not have to worry about his presence; however, I did not sleep well. I thought I could see G—— emerging from each piece of furniture, from every corner of the room.

M. Mathieu left at ten o'clock to go see the police chief. G—— was already in his office. Walking in front of him without looking at him, M. Mathieu addressed the chief: "Would you please tell me, sir, what is requested of me? I am a merchant and I have sixty persons in my employ, men and women."

"I understand. This is the complaint brought against you: M. G——, here before you, accuses you of hiding his wife and his daughter in your house. Supposedly his wife has a bad reputation, so she is not the one he misses, but he wants his daughter back. What do you have to say?"

M. Mathieu looked G—— up and down, then turning toward the police chief said, "I give you my word as an honest man that this gentleman is a scoundrel who beats this poor woman and this poor child. He is profligate and lazy, and the only reason he wants to find his wife is so he can take from her what she has earned since she left him. Yesterday, when she learned that you had written to me and guessing that it concerned her, she ran away leaving me her daughter's birth certificate. Here it is. You can see that he is deceiving you and that this child is not his. His wife, on the other hand, is respectful and thrifty, and Mme Mathieu says that she does not know of a more gifted worker."

"Well, sir," said the chief looking at G——, "what do you answer to that?"

G—— was not disconcerted. "My answer is that this man is my wife's lover; that is why he speaks so well of her."

The police chief frowned. "Be careful; when such accusations are made, they must be proven." Then turning toward M. Mathieu, he said, "So you say this woman is no longer at your house. What about her child? Did she take her with her?"

M. Mathieu hesitated, but he did not know how to lie.

"The child is at my house."

G—— pinched his lips. The police chief said, "Sir, you heard, your wife has left. As for the child, she is not yours. I advise you to leave them both alone."

M. Mathieu left feeling victorious, but he could detect a sinister smile on G——'s face. So he promised himself to be even more careful about keeping my mother's refuge a secret.

When he went to see her that evening, he took a circuitous route because he had once again seen G—— lurking about.

ATTEMPT TO ESCAPE FROM THE ENEMY

My mother could not get used to the thought of being without me. She wanted to come for me. M. Mathieu had a devil of a time calming her down.

"Now, my dear friend, give me three days and in three days, I promise, you will have your daughter back."

I had a heavy heart that whole next day. My little Mathieu went for a walk with his father. They saw G—— at a spirits shop almost across the street from the house where we lived. As soon as G—— saw them, he paid his bill and followed them the whole way.

The next day, same routine. M. Mathieu and his son went into a house with two exits, stayed a half hour on the stairs, and took off again in front of G——.

The third day, after dinner, M. Mathieu told his wife, "We must get Céleste dressed. I am sure that her mother must be going insane. If we wait too long, she will do something rash."

15

"Oh! In her situation I would feel the same way," said Mme Mathieu. "The little boy is in bed. He must be asleep already. Come, Céleste."

And, taking my hand, she led me to her room, opened the cabinet where her son was asleep,[3] and came back with some of his clothing under her arm.

"Come here, I shall unfasten your dress!"

I undressed so quickly that I was tearing everything. Dear little Mathieu's clothes fit me perfectly. The father came to see if I was ready. I flew into his arms.

"Woman, give her the little mackinaw coat. It is rather cool out. And bring her cap down over her eyes. Does she not look cute dressed like this. Pierre is going to come with us."

Pierre, the servant, entered at that moment. He was coming to tell us that G—— was at his post again.

"Well," said M. Mathieu, "we must go."

He grabbed his cardigan and the three of us left. My legs were shaking and I would have fallen down if M. Mathieu and Pierre had not held on to me.

G—— was following us. One time, he came so near us that I thought he had recognized me. But he backed off and, when he saw that we were taking the same route that M. Mathieu and his son had taken the day before, he left us.

We reached the house where my mother was living.

M. Mathieu picked me up. We saw a light at the top of the stairs and heard my mother's voice.

When she saw us arrive, she let out a yell, "Oh! That is not my daughter. She was taken from you!"

I ran toward her and frantically said, "Maman, you do not want to kiss me?"

She recognized my voice, lifted me in her arms, and almost suffocated me with her caresses.

Kind M. Mathieu was laughing heartily.

"Now, calm down. Our ruse worked. Do not worry, I shall come back as soon as possible and I shall give your address to Pomerais."

3

The Lyon Insurrection

M. Raoul's Naïveté—Shadows over the City of *Canuts*—
A Villainous Plot—To Fire and Sword—Urchin at the Guillotière—
Two Bullets to the Head

THE LODGINGS M. Mathieu found for us included a cabinet and a
bedroom with two large windows looking out on the wharf. The view
was splendid. We could see a great number of boats going up and down
the Rhône. Across from our windows there was a long bridge, and at
each end of the bridge were two towers that served as toll booths.

Two days later M. Mathieu had a cart full of walnut furniture brought
to us: a bed, a dresser, chairs, a table, a mirror. We put our trestle bed
in the cabinet, and that became my room. Dear Mme Mathieu sent us
sheets and towels. We had never been that well-off.

That evening, we spent some time with our neighbor M. Raoul. As
we entered his workplace, the regular sound of four Jacquard looms
made us dizzy. M. and Mme Raoul were wonderful people, but so dull
that as soon as evening had descended upon the room where we would
gather, I went into a deep sleep.

M. RAOUL'S NAÏVETÉ
We had been in our new abode two months without anything happening to disturb us. My mother worked like a dog almost every night.

The *canuts* employed children to tie the threads to their bobbins.
These children, who are approximately ten or twelve years old, earned
ten sous a day. After some observation, I learned how to do it. M. Raoul
noticed and told my mother, "If you wish, I can hire Céleste, and if she
earns some money, that can help you a little. I shall put her at my frame.
She will not get tired."

My mother hesitated, but I pleaded so much with her that she relented. She would settle near me to do her work.

17

After two weeks a new dress was purchased with my money, and we went to see M. Mathieu. You cannot imagine how proud I was. I was earning my keep; that meant I was a grown woman! I was the one who had bought this dress. I spent so much time prancing around in front of my poor little friend that we did not get to play all day.

Early the next day I was at my post. My mother worked near me and M. Raoul. I can still see him raise his eyeglasses over his forehead and say, "My dear friend, do you realize what a sad life you are leading? Living alone at your age, always working, no holidays, no Sundays off. . . . Perhaps you should have tried once more to see your husband."

"If you knew my husband," my mother replied, "you would understand that there is no recourse with him."

My mother did not like saying anything bad about her husband, so it was only when pressed that she talked about her suffering. She did not provide many details; therefore, kind M. Raoul did not perceive motives serious enough for separation in her vague complaints.

"Now," he told my mother, "I do not want to scare you but I must tell you what happened yesterday. You had just gone out, when a nice-looking, well-dressed man asked to speak to me alone. 'Sir,' said this man, 'I hope that my name will not scare you. I was in the wrong, but every sin can be forgiven. My name is G———. My wife lives here, in lodgings you are renting to her. Because you are an honest man, I come to you for help in obtaining forgiveness. I was unfair and violent. I regret it, and I swear I shall not do it again. Tell my wife to try once more to live with me. We shall reside in this house, and you will be able to judge my conduct. Sir, believe me, I am sincere.' And as he spoke, his eyes filled with tears.

"I asked him how he got your address. He replied, 'I sent the wife of a friend of mine to M. Mathieu's and she said that I had left, and she wanted to know Jeanne's address to tell her the good news. Pierre, the domestic, gave out your address. I have earned eight hundred francs in six weeks doing mechanical repairs. I can entrust you with the money. It is for my wife.'

"I told him that I could not take his money but that I would pass on the message."

My mother listened to Raoul without breathing. "Well," she said, "I am doomed. Where will I escape to now?"

M. Raoul was alarmed. "My dear, what are you talking about, escaping? You cannot abandon all your things. What do you have to lose in trying? With the money he is offering you, you will be able to pay off what you still owe on your furniture, and you can keep part of it in case a need or a problem arises."

My mother let out a cry rather than a sigh. "The thought of seeing this man again drives me mad and if he comes into my room, I shall throw myself out of a window!"

"Now, what a fine way to solve everything! And your daughter, madame, do you plan to throw her out of the window also?"

My mother slumped into her chair, twisting her arms. I ran to her and, as I kissed her, I told her, "Since he promises not to harm us any more, try it, Maman. Here, we have nothing to fear."

She sorrowfully shook her head. "What time is he supposed to come?"

"Soon."

The clock struck twelve.

She got up, went out for a few minutes, and came back with a roll of paper in her hand.

"Here," she told M. Raoul, "read this and you will know the man who was deceiving you yesterday and who is going to lie to you again."

It was a copy of the request she had made in Paris to try to get a separation.

After reading it, Raoul lowered his head, returned the paper to my mother, and apologized to her.

Someone came to let him know he was expected in the next room. He motioned for my mother to accompany him. She followed him, leaning on each piece of furniture.

SHADOWS OVER THE CITY OF *CANUTS*

G—— was holding his hat in his hand. His back was to the window. He made a move as if he was going to grab me, but my mother positioned herself between the two of us and asked him, "What do you want?"

"But," he said slightly taken aback, "I want to make peace with you. I shall make you happy. I swear it before this man. Come and give us a little kiss, Céleste!"

Needless to say, I did not move an inch. My mother was thoughtful for a while, then she leaned toward me. "Go, Céleste," she whispered, "go kiss your stepfather."

Pushing me toward him, she said to me, "Go on, he will not harm you. You see, M. Raoul, my daughter cannot overcome her fear; that is because, under the pretext of kissing her, he used to kick her legs and leave marks as black as ink. Or else he would pull her pigtails so hard that when I combed her hair big clumps would fall out."

"You exaggerate, Jeanne," said G—— to my mother, "but I shall make you forget all that."

The next day he was settled in our room. He pretended to be happy. Since he had brought trunks, which were in our way, M. Raoul let us have an attic whose door faced ours on the landing and formed the slant in the roof. The house was only three stories tall, and we were on the third floor.

G—— did not stay home much. He always had plenty money even though he gave some to my mother, who would hide it for future needs.

Many men would come see him. My mother begged him to entertain his friends elsewhere because their visits interfered with her work. Each day he went out more frequently. My mother thought it best to let M. Raoul know.

"G—— is not working. He has money. Sinister looking individuals come to visit him. I am afraid that he is about to do something evil."

It is possible that in very different circumstances M. Raoul would have paid less attention to my mother's premonitions, but we were, unbeknownst to us, on the eve of a terrible tragedy. The rebellion in Lyon was beginning to loom menacingly. For some time now M. Raoul had been noticing early signs. He found out that G—— was keeping company with all the men who were suspected by the police, that he was going to reunions where very violent passions were being stirred up.

Revolutions have a quite horrible side, and I have kept a dreadful impression of all that I saw then. All trade stopped; groups were forming in the streets; workers were in revolt; hideous men, who looked like they had escaped from prison, would participate in those gatherings. Shaking like a leaf, I could hear around the neighborhood where we lived all sorts of death threats and arson plans being uttered.

A VILLAINOUS PLOT

One day G—— came home with a menacing look in his eyes. He told us that he had friends he needed to see and ordered us to vacate the apartment. My mother answered that she did not want to be compromised, that he would have to go somewhere else. G—— angrily tightened his fists.

"I am going to come at noon and you had better be gone from here or I shall squash you both."

Then, noisily opening the windows, he added, "Look, Jeanne, all these people on the wharves. A revolution is starting. Three days from now, I could kill you, and no one would ask me what happened to you.

Your friend Raoul, no doubt your lover, will be hanged from this window and bled dry like a pig. The rich are in for it! Those idiots who give us money to serve them! We shall demolish their houses and find their safes."

I ran to my mother. He pounced on me, furious, took me by the arm, and threw me across the room. I landed dazed against the door of the cabinet where I slept. My poor mother stood up like a wounded lioness.

"Coward! Wretch!" she screamed.

He simply grabbed the poor woman's body, brutally forced her to go down on her knees, and left, repeating, "I want this room at noon."

As soon as the door was closed, my mother crawled over to me. I was softly crying. She looked at my arm. The internal bleeding had left a bluish mark.

"The monster! The monster!" she was yelling. "Who will rid me of this murderer?"

She took me in her arms to lift me off the floor where I had remained. I showed her my hip and my knee. Both those parts had hit the tiles and were bruised.

"I am going to put you to bed."

Once I was in bed, she applied water and salt compresses to the bruises and went down to the druggist to buy some poultice. Muffled sounds were coming from the wharf.

I was feverish. I asked for something to drink. My mother did not have any sugar, so she went back downstairs. She saw G—— talking to a group of men just a few feet from the house.

She came back upstairs, frightened.

"What am I going to do?" she said to herself. "Going to Raoul's would be exposing him to danger. And my daughter, in her condition, I cannot take her with me. Oh, God! what am I going to do? If he finds us. . . . Oh!"

And she ran to the table and picked up a knife.

"If he touches my child, I shall kill him."

She was listening. I saw her run to the door.

"It is too late, they are here!"

She ran into my cabinet, closed the door and removed the key, leaned over my bed and put her hand over my mouth. "Be quiet, be quiet. . . ."

The front door opened and closed. We heard the footsteps of several men in the room.

"This is not all of us," said my stepfather.

"No," a voice answered, "the others are coming. We did not want to all come at once for fear of being noticed downstairs. The miser on the first floor always fears for his coins. He is constantly watching who comes and goes."

There was a knock at the door and the voice was silent. The new-comers were talking in low tones. There must have been eight or ten of them.

Gradually the conversation became animated, the sounds more distinct.

My mother and I were listening with all the lucidity of fear.

"It is impossible," G—— was saying. "If, while we are over there, things do not get going here, we shall all be arrested. We have to start here."

Another voice interrupted him, "Nothing ventured, nothing gained. When things are set in motion here, it will be too late over there. You have to scare off the hen to get to her eggs."

"But are you certain," said G—— softening his tone, "that there is as much money as you have been told?"

"Rather than less," said another voice.

"How long will it take?" asked G——.

"Barely six hours. It is three leagues from here. We shall leave tomorrow at first light."

Some of the men in the room left. Once their footsteps were gone, G—— told the men still in the room, "We have to watch Antoine: he could expose us for no reason."

"That's a good one!" the others answered. "The two of you suspect each other. Just yesterday he was saying that you cannot be trusted!"

A voice near the window said, "This is a good location. We shall have a good view and we shall be able to help."

"You are welcome," said G——.

Since they were all near the window now, or were speaking very low, we could not hear any more. Then the words "farewell," and "see you tomorrow," reached our ears.

My mother sighed, "Gone. They are gone!"

I sensed, because of the fear that I still felt, that she was mistaken, and I motioned for her to wait.

After a few minutes we heard someone walking, opening drawers, closing the window, and going out, carefully turning the key in the lock.

My mother opened the door to our cabinet.

"We are locked in. What are we going to do?"

She thought for a while, then knocked on M. Raoul's wall. He came to our door. We told him that we were locked in, and we entreated him to go get a locksmith.

"It is not necessary," said Mme Raoul, who had followed her husband. "Here is the key. It was given to me downstairs. I met M. G——on his way out. He asked me if his wife was in the building. I said that I did not know. He asked me to give you the key that he took with him by mistake."

M. and Mme Raoul came into our room. My mother told them what she had heard.

"They are going to plunder, maybe even commit a more serious crime. We must try to warn those poor people."

"But do you have their names and address?"

"Unfortunately, no."

TO FIRE AND SWORD

The next day a storm descended on the city. Around four o'clock G——came home, ashen, grim, his clothes in disarray, his tie partially undone. There was perspiration on his brow.

"Hide this," he told my mother. "That is an order."

And he threw a sack full of money on the table and a package on the floor. Turning toward the door, he told two men who had followed him, "Come in with your trunks. There is no one here but my wife, and I can vouch for her."

Motionless, my mother was looking at the scene.

"Let us see," said G——, "let us open the packages."

He pulled out of them silk dresses, lace, some jewelry. Once he had stashed his loot, G—— left without a word.

For a few minutes my mother remained pensive, then, taking me in her arms, she told me, "Let us go to Raoul's. I just had an idea!"

She spent a long time talking to M. Raoul who then stood up and said, "You can count on me."

The next day, very early, a man was knocking on our door. G——jumped out of bed and hid in my cabinet. The new arrival asked in a loud voice, "You are Mme G——?"

"Yes, I am."

"Where is your husband? We need to talk to him."

"He is not here, but if you wish to leave your name, I shall be able to tell him that you came."

"No," the man answered, "we are going to wait downstairs for him to come home. He was one of those who plundered ——'s château. Do you have anything here that comes from this robbery?"

"No," my mother answered in a firm voice.

"Watch yourself; hiding the truth would make you an accomplice. Good-bye, madame."

And he went back downstairs.

G—— came out of the cabinet, his face distorted by fear.

"Oh! Jeanne, my good Jeanne, you saved me!"

"Yes, for an hour maybe, but the police will be back. They are going to search the place. Your only recourse is to flee tonight. Until then, you must hide. There is an attic off the landing."

An hour later five men came and made a lot of noise. G——, hidden in his attic, did not miss one word of the conversation.

"Is your husband back?" asked the man who had come earlier.

"No," my mother answered.

"I regret it, madame, but we cannot rely on your statements. We must see for ourselves."

On that note, two men entered the room, the cabinet, and pretended to search everywhere.

"Nothing," they said on their way out, "but he will not get away; he has been betrayed by one of his accomplices."

They left.

G—— was more dead than alive. My mother had the devil of a time making him leave the attic.

"Now," she told him, "you can see that you are doomed if you do not flee far away."

G—— left at midnight.

Raoul was waiting for us. As soon as he saw us he said, "Well! You are now rid of him. Did my men not play their part well?"

"Splendidly!" my mother said. "You have done me a great favor!"

Indeed, the men who had come were none other than *canuts* engaged to frighten G—— and to force him to leave.

The next day Lyon was put to fire and sword.

Fire had been set at each end of the bridge across from us. The naval toll booths were there and contained much flammable material: oil, alcohol. . . .

We could see the poor employees throwing the furniture out the windows and everything else they could save. We could hear their pitiful cries, soon lost amid a huge uproar intermittently interrupted by savage bursts of laughter.

We saw a poor man jump from a window. He broke his leg when he landed, could not get up, and was trampled by the crowd.

24

Suddenly an urgent rumor erupted through the crowd of men assembled on this one spot. We saw them flee in all directions. Troops were arriving from the other end of the bank, now deserted. But it was a false alarm; we heard the steady steps of the cavalry horses departing, leaving behind a cloud of dust.

Once the cloud had vanished, we saw everything return to the way it had been. The dark mob had re-formed even more terrible than before.

The most excited ones took advantage of the time they had left before new troops arrived. They smashed every door, raided every house.

"Arms, arms!" they would yell.

Our door opened and we were asked the same thing.

"Nothing here, there are only women. . . . What about you, old man, do you have a rifle?"

They were addressing M. Raoul.

"I do not have any more arms. I gave them all away."

The house shook under this avalanche of wooden clogs and steel shoes charging up and down the stairs.

The cavalry returned. This time it was coming in our direction. Swords drawn, the soldiers were charging. Furious cries echoed through the crowd.

"They're murdering citizens; they're slaughtering our brothers! To the houses! To the houses!"

On that signal, they went through stores, through alleys. In less than an hour the roofs along the bank were covered with rebels. The worst were the twelve- to fifteen-year-old children. They would make slingshots with leather straps. Others, using their shirts as bags, would haul the sharp pebbles that paved the streets of Lyon in those days to the rooftops. With their makeshift slingshots, they could send their projectiles a long way. Others aimed at windows. Those who had no weapons would toss whatever was handy through windows.

I can still remember a caged parrot someone had rushed to the third floor of a house; for a half hour it emitted such sharp cries that its voice could be heard above the fighting.

Our house was totally occupied. The firing from the street had smashed every window. They had just destroyed M. Raoul's looms, and they were throwing the parts down on the troops. M. Raoul and his wife were crying. . . . They were ruined! Part of our furniture suffered the same fate.

After several hours of fighting, the riot seemed to subside. My mother took advantage of this lull.

"Come," she told me taking me by the hand, "tomorrow this area will be up in flames. We must try to get to the Mathieus'."

It was almost nighttime. Once I had reached the second floor, my foot slipped and I fell flat on my face. I got up, and we went downstairs to a place with more light. My mother screamed. I was covered in dried blood. They had killed the second story lodger.

A group of armed men was guarding the entrance. My mother approached them resolutely.

"Gentlemen," she said, "I must leave this house. I want to seek refuge at the house of some friends."

"Are you going far?" said a husky voice.

"No, just a few feet from here."

"You will be escorted part of the way. You, men, go!"

And he turned toward two of his comrades who were sitting on some hay.

We walked in silence. Once we had reached a military encampment, the two men stopped.

"I am not going any farther," said one of them. "We do not want to throw ourselves into the lion's jaws."

They turned right around without looking at us. My mother talked to a captain who ordered two soldiers to accompany us.

The Mathieus were having dinner. Everyone shouted in unison when they saw us.

They had not heard anything in this part of town. They only knew that there was fighting going on elsewhere, but the sound of shooting had not been heard in this neighborhood.

The days that followed were bloody, but we were fortunate enough to no longer be witness to the fighting.

TWO BULLETS TO THE HEAD

Peace had been restored for some time when we received a letter from City Hall asking my mother to appear the next day. I wanted to go with her, but she would not let me.

She came back half an hour later, all out of breath.

"Friends, my dear friends, my husband is dead!"

"Your husband is dead! . . . Well, that is good riddance for you!" exclaimed M. Mathieu.

Maman did not give any sign of approval, either for the sake of appearances, or because her heart was less austere than her reason.

G——— had been found at the Croix Rousse with two bullets in the head. The papers found on his person, a card with his name and several letters that were not addressed to him but that were in his wallet with his passport, meant there was no mistake possible. G—— did not exist anymore.

This event changed all of my mother's plans. Nothing was keeping her from returning to Paris now, and she was even more inclined to do so now that her furniture had been smashed during the riot. She announced her intentions to the Mathieus.

A few days later we left Lyon.

4

M. Vincent

A Peculiar Family Reunion—The Stonemason Was
Chasing Skirts—M. Grange and His Daughter—Tragedy at the
Saint-Martin Canal—Horrible Domestic Scenes—The Enterprising
Cohabitant—Alone in Paris

ONCE WE WERE BACK in Paris we had to live with my grandfather.
That was very painful for my mother. After his divorce from his first
wife her father had remarried. Maman had much to complain about
her stepmother, who did not like the children of her husband's first
marriage.

There were three of them: two girls and a boy. They zealously learned
their trade so that as soon as they could support themselves, they could
leave a house that the memory of their mother, replaced by a stranger,
rendered unbearable.

Adèle, the oldest, was placed with a lace merchant. One evening she
was carrying a box of Mechlin lace[1] on Rue de la Lune around ten
o'clock when a man assaulted her, knifing her three times: in the cheek,
piercing her tongue; in the breast; and in her side.

Nearby, a woman saw a man run away shouting, "Oh! What have I
done, I made a mistake."

The victim was taken to Hôtel-Dieu hospital where she died a few
hours later without having a chance to reveal her name. It was thanks
to the box of Mechlin lace that what had happened to her was later
revealed. The identity of the murderer was never discovered.

My mother was placed with a milliner. Her brother wanted to learn
how to paint. My grandfather had a slight preference for this son, and,
except for the disagreements with his wife, he was more hospitable to
him than to his sisters.

On a day that he had been refused some money, he returned with two pistols and told his father and his stepmother, "I want money; I know there is some here. Open this desk or I blow your brains out."

He got it all, down to the silverware. Midway down the stairs, he was laughing his fool head off, shouting, "The pistols were not even loaded!"

He left France and was never heard from again.

My mother learned her trade and settled down without asking anything from her father. She could not forgive him the harm he had inflicted on her mother. In twelve years she had seen him only twice. She would send me there for New Year's.

I could love passionately or hate furiously. I adored my mother, but I cried when I had to go see my grandfather.

A PECULIAR FAMILY REUNION

I was still under this negative impression when we arrived at his house upon our return from Lyon. We reached his house at 8 Rue de Bercy-Saint-Jean at ten P.M. The street was actually a covered alleyway.

His shop was a furniture store. Its sign jutted out at least two feet and read: Rental house run by ———. Old and new furniture bought and sold.

The entryway was an alley door so narrow that one could only go in sideways. A half-door with a bell announced someone's arrival and departure, which was not necessary, since my grandfather was at once owner, doorman, bellboy, and furniture salesman.

His own room was on the second floor. It was a lovely room with two large windows and a balcony bordered by a rusty iron railing. It jutted out over a street so narrow that once out of bed one could shake hands with the neighbor across the way.

That was the room where we made our entrance, hearts heavy and heads bowed.

The room was an annex for the shop. It contained so many pieces of furniture, clocks, and paintings that we could not find a place to sit.

My grandfather was seated in a comfortable chair. The bell had alerted him, and he said indifferently, "So, it is you, girl. What the devil are you doing here at this hour? We were about to go to bed."

He had not seen us in two years!

"Father, I just arrived from Lyon. I have come to ask you to lodge us for a day or two."

The stepmother jumped in her chair. "We do not have room."

"That is true," said my grandfather, "we shall make up a bed for you on the floor."

My mother told everything that had happened to us. The stepmother pretended to sleep, and as Maman was saying to her father, "I have a lot more to tell you, when we are alone," she pretended to wake up and said, "Good night, I am going to bed."

She went into the next room, taking care to leave the door open. My grandfather got up and closed it.

"Well, my child, what do you plan to do?"

"But, Father, what I have always done: work, once I am settled. Tomorrow I shall look for lodgings. If you want to furnish it for me, I shall pay you as soon as possible."

"Certainly, but to avoid problems, she must not suspect anything." And he was looking at the door through which he probably was afraid she was listening because he continued in a low voice, "Do you have any money?"

"No, since I had to pay full price for my daughter, my resources have been depleted."

He pulled several keys from his pocket, very quietly opened a chest, and took out a bag.

"Here, put that in your trunk. It contains one hundred *écus;*[2] that should help you out. But not a word in front of her! . . ."

The next day my mother had found lodgings on the corner of Faubourg du Temple and the canal.[3] We moved in.

A few days later my mother went to see some manufacturers she knew, who gave her enough work that she could hire a few women.

I worked with her. On Sundays we would go for walks in the country, or she would take me to the theater.

I was eight and a half years old. I was tall, thin, pale. I looked twelve. I was jealous of anything my mother seemed the least bit interested in.

THE STONEMASON WAS CHASING SKIRTS

Above us lived a stonemason who sang from morning until night. He looked like he was about thirty-five, had blond short hair, and blue eyes.

I ran errands for my mother and would meet him on the stairs. He would laugh with me. He seemed like a really nice fellow.

One day he told me, "Little girl, why don't you tell your mother to let you come spend an hour in my studio to pose for a head."

I told him that I did not know what that meant but that he should ask my mother himself. He did not hesitate. I had not even climbed the stairs, he was in our apartment. He had already explained what he wanted because I heard my mother answer, "I do not mind."

We became great friends. He was always at our home.

He had one fault: he was a libertine. When a woman he fancied walked by in the street, he would follow her all day long. Maids, workers, wives of his friends, the pretty ones, the ugly ones, the old ones, the young ones—he knocked on every door.

His mother often came to visit him. She would come down to see us. One day she invited us to dinner. Then we became inseparable.

I grew jealous. My active mind saw too clearly. I looked for ways to be mean. In the end, I became unbearable.

When we would go for walks and M. Vincent wanted to hold my mother's arm, I would throw myself between them and cling to her, "Maman, please. . . ."

M. Vincent was nice to me the way G—— had been in the beginning, but like him, he was wasting his time. If he served me at the table, I would not eat.

I was so miserable and became so hateful that I asked my mother to place me in apprenticeship. The next day she announced that the following Monday, I would enter the service of M. Grange, Rue du Temple.

My heart was mortally grieved by the fact that I could be gotten rid of so promptly. I was already proud. I did not shed a tear.

M. GRANGE AND HIS DAUGHTER

That Monday my mother took me to see M. Grange. I cannot imagine anything so ugly as this man! And nothing so pretty as his daughter! Petite, with reddish blond hair, but fair and fetching, coquettish and elegant, barely fifteen. At the time, I was eleven and I was taller than she. I had a forest of very dark hair. I was pale, my skin was dark. We were total opposites.

M. Grange asked my mother if she wanted me to be lodged. Before she could reply, I said, "Yes, let me sleep here. I shall be less in your way."

My mother replied, almost angrily, "Not at all, little mademoiselle, you shall come home every day."

I left in the morning and came home at night. Often, Maman was out and did not come back until late. I would wait in the street. I could have stayed at the shop, but I was not happy there.

My master's daughter had keys to everything. She stole from the sales to buy her frippery. This child, who lost her mother when she was very young, had always been spoiled.

She took great pleasure in humiliating me. She was incompetent. I was more skillful than the main seamstress, and yet, sometimes the daughter would throw my work in my face, telling me, "Undo this, it is poorly done." I would fume and wait five minutes, then I would undo my work without a word.

There were ten workshops in this building. In the evening, during the summer, the men and women would gather at the entrance.

If someone spoke to me, she would come over and say, "Why do you not leave? Your mother is waiting for you."

When my apprenticeship was over, I asked M. Grange if he wanted to keep me on as a day worker.

"Certainly, I shall pay you twenty sous a day, and if at the end of the day there is something pressing, you shall be paid per unit."

He said, looking at his daughter, "You are upset now, Louise, you will not be able to scold her any more. She is a woman. How old are you, Céleste?"

"I am almost fourteen."

"Oh, really, I thought you were older. You are strong."

Out in the courtyard there was a wallpaper factory. The office clerk was always in the shop or at the entrance.

Whenever my master's daughter saw him, she would go outside. She would turn red when he went inside.

One day he was standing in front of my loom, looking. In those days lots of rich gold trimming over velvet was fashionable. I did all the embroidering, and they said I was very talented.

My young mistress came near me, angry as a little rooster. She leaned over my work.

"This is poorly done," she told me. "Do not finish this; nobody will want it."

I looked at my embroidering, and I said, laughing, "You are talking about something that you cannot judge, since I have never been able to teach you how to do this kind of embroidering."

And I handed my work to the main seamstress.

She had been with the house for ten years and thought of Louise as a mere child.

"Céleste's work is good," she said. "Incompetent as you are, you have no right to advise others!"

Louise ran off to the back of the shop, and, when her father came back, she began to cry her eyes out saying that I had mistreated her.

That evening, at home, I found my mother very agitated because M. Vincent had not been seen since the night before. When he came home—entering without knocking—my mother did not greet him well.

As the source of tenderness that I felt for my mother was drying up, I could feel emerging inside me unfamiliar emotions. Instead of sleeping, I would spend whole hours staring at the stars. I could picture myself rich, happy, and loved.

The plays I had been taken to when I was very young had spoiled my mind and inflamed my nature.

M. Vincent would eat at our house. He went up to his studio only to work. When he addressed me I would answer, "Mind your own business. Do I know you? You are not my father."

My mother would warn me to be quiet.

"Well," I would tell her, "I know that you do not love me. If I were old enough, I would leave, I would rent a little room where I would stay by myself."

I was making myself hated.

TRAGEDY AT THE SAINT-MARTIN CANAL

We often went to M. Vincent's mother's house. One evening as I was returning from the shop I was told by the concierge that my mother was at Rue Popincourt. I went to meet her there. Mme Vincent told me to wait, that they would be back.

We both fell asleep, I in a straight chair, she in an armchair. When I woke up the lamp was fading.

"It must be very late," I said rubbing my eyes. "They are not coming back. I am leaving."

It was almost midnight. It was cold. There were very few houses along the canal—just a few laundry stalls, a few streetlights very distant from each other, and squares of driftwood piled up to dry near the water.

I was almost at the Ménilmontant bridge when I heard voices.[4] I stopped, and, not knowing why, I huddled up against a door. The voices started up again. They were coming from the edge of the canal, behind the piles of wood.

"Do not hurt me, I told you this is all I have."

"That is a lie. You got paid. Today is Saturday."

"No, I am being paid every two weeks again."

"That is not true."

And I heard footfalls, then two or three moans, and later something falling.

"Hurry, search," the man who had already spoken, said.

"I cannot find anything," replied the other one, "you should not have killed him."

"Oh, yeah! So he could finger us. You are a smart one!"

33

And then I heard something fall in the water. I let myself drop to my knees in the corner of the door. I wrapped my head in my black apron so my white bonnet would not attract attention and . . . I fainted.

When I came to, I was in a large room lighted by at least five or six candles fastened to the wall. There were large vats with smoke rising from them, a fire under each, steam filling the room like a cloud, and through the mist, moving shadows.

A large woman came toward me and asked, "Well, are we feeling better?"

"Yes, madame."

"What in the world were you doing there, at that time of day?"

"Where, there?"

"Why, there, on our laundry's doorstep. On our way to rinse our wash, we found you lying on the ground."

"Oh, I remember! . . . Close your door, quick, quick! . . . They are still there!"

I told them what I heard.

"My poor girl," they told me, "a drowned man is not rare around here."

They picked up a candle and went to inspect the shore of the canal. There was no trace of the struggle.

I was taken back home and to my mother, who, knowing that I had gone to Mme Vincent's, thought I had stayed there. I was ice cold and my teeth were chattering. The doctor said he feared typhoid fever. He was not wrong.

I was sick for two months. Grief played a big part in my illness because now I had no doubt my mother was in love with M. Vincent.

I went back to work, but to get home, I had to cross the canal. I would be seized by fears I could not control, and my mother decided to move.

At first I thought that it was just for my account, and I thought that by leaving this house we would be separated from *all* the lodgers who lived there. I was wrong. M. Vincent followed us, and if my mother was leaving the neighborhood, it was mainly to separate him from all his female acquaintances.

My hatred grew. I told myself, "If only he had been the one thrown into the canal! . . ."

HORRIBLE DOMESTIC SCENES

I spied on his actions. I think he really loved my mother, but it was impossible for him to be faithful. My mother was excessively jealous.

I knew that I wanted her to know, and at dinner I told Vincent, "Say, your new girlfriend is not very pretty!" or, "You are wrong to chase after that one, she does not want you."

They would argue for a few days, but when they made up, I had lost just a little bit more of my mother's affection.

One day a little country outing had been organized at work.

Everyone was going, men, women, children. M. Grange was paying. I went without asking for permission. My mother lost her temper and beat me harder than usual.

I often got slapped. Vincent would take my side, but I did not want to owe him anything, and I would position myself to receive the beatings.

"What right do you have to preach to me. If I wanted to do wrong, it is not your supervision that would prevent me. There is already talk at the shop that you set a poor example for me."

I was a few feet from her. She looked at me with frightening eyes. Vincent looked astounded.

On a table next to my mother was a little mother-of-pearl-handled knife. Vincent had given it to me. She threw it in my face. Her aim was good. Thank goodness the hilt was heavier than the blade. Instead of coming at me like an arrow and going into my eye, the knife cut my left eyebrow.

Blood flooded my face. My mother fainted, and cried a lot when she came to; I got off with just a scratch.

Vincent scolded her. She tried to make me forget with tender attention and caresses. But it was too late, my heart was closed to this tenderness, which up until then had filled it exclusively. Instead of instilling in me trust and affection, she had allowed my bad instincts to grow without fighting them.

If at that moment I had had the means at hand to get an education, I believe I would have profited from one. The void that had filled my heart made me live through my mind. Unfortunately, my desire to know overtook the resources I had to learn, and I could barely read.

I was going on fifteen. Supposedly I was pretty. Louise was becoming ugly and had lovers, and that did not enhance her looks.

We moved to 23 Rue Neuve Culture-Sainte-Catherine. The house was on the corner. The windows looked out on Rue Culture, but from our house we could see the Eglise Saint-Paul and the Rue Saint-Antoine.[5]

The house was clean; however, the alley was strangely laid out. The stairs ended on the street. The only shop, which extended all around the house, was occupied by the owner, a wine merchant.

Our lodgings were on the third floor and were composed of three rooms: a kitchen, a large room with an alcove, and another room, without a fireplace, whose light source came through a door that could be locked. A muslin curtain covered the glass half of the door, but that did not prevent being able to see everything going on in my mother's room.

M. Vincent had given up being a stonemason. He found work in an office. He lived at our house. They were a couple.

In spite of all that I did to him, he seemed to like me more each day. He would give me presents, was loving, and seemed to care more for me than my mother.

One night when I had just gone to bed I heard him tell my mother, "I tell you that you must take her back in to work with you. She is almost fifteen and those crickets over there are after her."

My mother answered, "You know very well that it is not up to me. She would not want to leave her shop."

"Pooh! There is always a way to make a girl stay with her mother, and I shall assume the responsibility of watching over her."

My mother told Vincent that he was crazy, and that if I suspected in the least he was watching over me, I would try to run away from home.

My grandfather came down with scurvy. He had gone to stay with one of his brothers in Fontainebleau.

Feeling very ill, he wrote my mother entreating her to spend a few days with him. My mother left, advising me to do the housework.

THE ENTERPRISING COHABITANT

I would go home every evening as usual. M. Vincent would come home very late.

Two or three times I woke up suddenly. He was standing near my bed, a light in his hand.

"What do you want?" I would say to him.

"Nothing. I have to watch over you during your mother's absence. You have suitors. Do you know that you are almost of marriageable age? The one who will get you will be mighty happy."

Then he would leave staring at me with fiery eyes.

He received a letter from my mother. He told me that my grandfather was very sick, and that my mother would stay with him another week or so.

That day I came home in tears. I had quarreled with Louise. Her father took her side. I asked for my wages, which they gave me. I was now unemployed.

"Why do you torment yourself so," said Vincent. "I love you, even though you hate me. All that I shall have will be for you."

And taking me in his arms, he kissed me several times. Then he held me tighter and tighter, so close to him that I began to tremble.

I did not reply, but I ran to my room.

"What is the matter?" he asked.

"Nothing," I answered, because I did not know why I had run away.

I came back, contrite, and I sat down near the window. He sat next to me.

"You must have quite a grudge against me that you run away when I come near you! You are jealous of me because of your mother. You are wrong because, had it not been for you, I would have been long gone."

I looked at him surprised. He took my hand and continued, "I am a skirt-chaser, I like women, but until now, I have not been capable of loving the same one for very long. You, however, I have not been able to leave."

He looked me straight in the eyes and held my hand.

"You are wrong," I replied. "I have never been jealous of you. I hate you because my mother loves you more than she loves me. If you stayed because of me, you made a mistake."

He seemed taken aback. I took this opportunity to say that it was late, and I retreated to my little cabinet. Since he was not keeping the light on, I turned mine out and undressed in the dark.

I spent the next day at home. Two men came to invite Vincent to dinner. They left their names.

He came home around three o'clock. I handed him the note they had written and he left to meet them.

I spent the day mending some of my things. At ten that evening I was still working. I had taken my dress off to redo the hem. I was in my slip and chemise when I heard a knock at the door. I put my shawl around my shoulders and opened the door. Vincent came in tipsy.

"You made a conquest this afternoon," he said. "The short one told me that he liked you. I replied that the stove was not burning for him, that I was keeping you."

"What do you mean, you are keeping me! Are you under the impression that I shall never marry?"

"Unless you want to marry me."

I backed up a little.

"You!" I said, "I certainly hope you would not dare ask me!"

"I told you yesterday that I love you."

I looked at the door. I saw that he had locked it and removed the key. "What do you want from me?"

He hesitated a moment, stretched his arms out to embrace me, and replied in a low voice, "I want you to love me! I want you! I shall have you! . . ."

He grabbed me by the waist and hugged me tight.

I tried so hard to slip to the floor that I was successful, and, hanging on to the bed post with all my strength, I screamed for help. He snatched my shawl and tore my fichu. I crossed my arms to hide my almost bare breasts. He lifted me and squeezing tight said, "Hush up! Give yourself willingly, or I shall have you by force."

His head was leaning against my shoulder, and I felt his damp mouth. On a sudden impulse, I bit his arm so hard he yelled and let go of me.

I ran to the window, opened it, and, climbing out on the ledge, told him, "If you come near me, I shall jump."

He asked for forgiveness, told me that he had had a moment of temporary insanity, but that I could come down and he gave his word he would not try anything again. It is not because I trusted his word that I decided to leave my position, but because of the terrifying void I could see below me.

Tugging on my skirt and my arm, trying to get me down from the window, he told me, "You think that I am going to leave so you can accuse me. I want to be able to tell your mother that you are the one who provoked me!"

I began to scream. He pulled me so hard I broke one of the window panes with my elbow.

At that moment, there was some noise in the street and Vincent got scared. He ran out and the door stayed open.

My arm was cut in three places. I put on my dress, my shawl, a bonnet, and left, not quite knowing where I was going.

ALONE IN PARIS

Once downstairs, I pushed the door open and ran toward Place Royale.

I came back by way of Rue Saint-Antoine. The bells of Eglise Saint-Paul were striking two in the morning. I turned onto Rue Culture. I sidled along the houses.

I saw the light in the window. What was he doing? . . . Why had he come back? . . . He had not seen me go out. He must have thought I had fainted or was dead.

I saw him look out the window, and I hid behind a scaffolding.

This neighborhood is still quite dreary, but in those days, everything was closed after ten at night.

I crossed the street and stood outside the porte cochere of the grain merchant next door.

I had been walking for two hours.

The herb and grain merchant's shop was at the back of the courtyard. The granary where he stored his straw and hay was on the second floor.

I was leaning against his door. Probably someone had forgotten to lock it.

I went inside and corrected that oversight.

It is horrible to be fifteen and alone in the streets of Paris, without a friend.

I walked around the courtyard a little, found the stairs to the hayloft. I went in. I lay down on bales of straw and slept until first light.

5

Thérèse

Corruption of a Minor out of Pity—Vice Squad—At the
House of Detention—Wretched Childhood in the Slums—M. Régnier,
Magistrate for the Prostitutes—The Iron Cage

"WHAT AM I GOING TO DO?" I was saying to myself as I woke up shivering from the cold. "I cannot go back home. My mother wrote five days ago that she would be back in a week. She will be arriving tomorrow or later. But what am I to do for two days?"

I spent that day on the wharf watching people fish. I had ten sous. I spent two on bread.

Five days later, my mother still had not come back.

I was crying . . . , I was hungry, and I could not walk anymore.

I sat on the steps of Eglise Saint-Paul and put my head in my hands. Several people walked by without looking at me. I felt someone tap me on the shoulder.

"What are you doing here, little girl? You have been here more than two hours. Are you crying?"

The person addressing me was a rather pretty twenty-five- to thirty-year-old woman.

She was wearing a black silk dress, a bonnet with ribbons, a jumper with colorful flowers in the style of the day. She hiked up her dress on one side and revealed a well-turned foot in a black high-top shoe. Her very white, perfectly straight stockings denoted habits of elegant cleanliness.

I told her why I was there. She stepped into a corner that separated the shops from the church. It was dark and she seemed to want to avoid being seen.

"Poor girl," she said, "do you think your mother will be back soon?"

She asked me if I had written to her. I answered that I did not know how to write, and that, in any case, I did not know her address in Fontainebleau.

"You cannot sleep in the street. . . . I cannot take you. . . . Oh, well, never mind, you have to eat. You see, I cannot walk by your side. Follow me a few steps behind and enter where you will see me enter."

CORRUPTION OF A MINOR OUT OF PITY

I was so afraid of losing her that I was walking on her heels. I saw her laugh with women who were walking back and forth.

She stopped in front of a wine merchant's door and glanced inside the shop, which was crowded.

She took an alley that abutted the shop, opened a door that probably led to one of the wine merchant's rooms, and picked up a candle and a key with a brass number. Once on the second floor, she opened a glass door draped with poppy-red calico curtains.

The ceiling was low. There was a bed, a sort of sofa, two chairs, a table.

"Come in," she said. "Tomorrow, I shall go see if your mother is back. You will be better here than in the street."

She came back with bread, wine, and cold cuts. I had been so hungry that my stomach had shrunk.

"Well," she asked, "are you feeling better?"

"Yes, madame. I want to thank you! . . ."

And I kissed her enthusiastically.

I asked her what she did. She replied, "What I do! . . . I am doing something bad bringing you to my rooms. I was like you. A man ruined me the way one wanted to ruin you six days ago. I did not defend myself, and this is where it led me. I have to hide the fact that I am keeping you here for a day or two. If it was known that you are here, we would be suspected of things you or I could not even imagine, and I would be in a lot of trouble. How old are you?"

"I am going on fifteen."

"Fifteen!" she repeated. "My God, that would cost me six months!"

"Six months!" I said without understanding.

"Yes, girl. Corruption of a minor!"

"I do not understand."

"It is not easy to explain. I am not Thérèse anymore, I am a number. I do not follow my will anymore but the regulations on a card. If I want to go out bareheaded, the regulations state that I must wear a bonnet. If I want to go out during the day, the regulations forbid it. I am not allowed to walk down certain esplanades. I must never appear at a win-

41

dow, and I especially must never go out with an honest woman. Judge for yourself what would happen with a fifteen year old girl! They would say I want to sell you."

I looked at her. This confession did not distance me from her.

"Be very careful, little one, and never fall prey to this vice! Because you see, I would regret not letting you die of hunger. Now go to bed. Here are some clean clothes; you can return them to me later."

I had spent six nights without taking my clothes off. I cannot describe what sheer joy it was to put on a white gown and to lie down.

In the morning, around ten, she went to our house and came back to tell me that my mother was not back.

Thérèse promised she would keep me another day or two if it was necessary.

She would go out in the evening and come back late.

VICE SQUAD

On the third day, realizing that she could no longer keep me, she offered to take me to the house of my mother's stepmother, who probably stayed in Paris to take care of the furnished house. We were not far from it when two men stopped us.

"What is your name?" one of them said.

She told him her name, but she had turned so pale I thought she was going to faint.

"And that one," he said, pointing to me, "is she registered?"

"No, she is an unfortunate girl who does not know where her mother is and I have been hiding her for three days."

"How old is she?"

"Fifteen."

"Well, she will follow us. She will be just as well taken care of at the house of detention."

She told them I was a good girl and they started to laugh.

"I am done for," she whispered to me. "They are going to sentence me to six months."

I was devastated when I saw that I was being taken to the police prefecture. I ran toward the bridge and I wanted to jump in the Seine. These men took pity on me and told me that I would be out the next day.

We walked along the quays. We arrived in front of an archway and we were led into a large courtyard.

Our guide walked toward a little door with iron bars and frosted glass behind them. The man went up two steps, grabbed the metal hammer, and knocked. We were let into a square room.

On the right, at the entrance, was a counter with bars. That was where you were asked your name. On the left was a trestle bed where the turnkey slept, and farther back, numbered hallways.

"This way," we were told by a man wearing some sort of uniform.

He led us to the end of the hallway, on the right. All this was lighted by an oil lamp.

I saw a door with bolts behind a counter. The man opened it.

"You will have company," he told us as he closed the door on us.

I was in an enormous room with cots along the walls.

The bolts creaked. The door opened and my name was called.

"I made a mistake. There is one here for the small room."

I came out and was led up three flights of stairs.

I was made to enter what is called the room for little girls. It was dark. The floor was covered with mattresses.

I heard a small voice say to me, "Hey, there is room for you, lie down here."

I spent the most horrible night imaginable. I vainly tried to peer through the darkness. I had such strong hallucinations that I lost self-awareness. I cried and uttered incoherent words.

Someone took my head in her arms and said, "Do not cry like this. Tomorrow someone will come claim you."

AT THE HOUSE OF DETENTION

Finally I saw dark rays form against a dark blue background. It was a window with iron bars.

The room was large, four meters square. The walls, oil-painted in a light color, were covered with inscriptions made with the point of a knife. Extending all across the room was a metal pipe for the heating. A wooden bench was all the furniture there was. In a corner there was a water pitcher, and in another, a tub. . . .

The mattresses were made of sackcloth, the blankets, of brown wool.

I had three prison-mates. I could not see the two who were at the other end of the room. Their blankets covered them entirely. Stitched in white letters on my blanket were the words "House of Detention Prison."

I looked next to me. As soon as I did, I had to lean against a wall, horrified.

At the lower end were two bare feet, black as ink, with long nails. What passed for a petticoat must have been made of dark wool, but it was muddy and so full of holes that its edge was lacy. A camisole of light flowered cotton, faded and torn at the back, revealed a dirty rag that must have been a shirt. All that was spotted with lice.

I have always been headstrong, but I believe I have a good heart. I remembered that this poor creature had had good words for me.

I came nearer to look at her face. Her head was bent against her shoulder. Her brownish hair was thick and tumbled untidily around her neck and over her cheek, preventing me from seeing her face.

I decided to wait, and I sat on the bench.

My three roommates woke up at the same time.

"Oh, it is daylight," one of them said. "It is so stupid to be awakened like this. I was sound asleep!"

"It is the new one," said the other girl. "She never stopped bawling all night and I did not sleep a wink."

"Sure," said the one who had comforted me, "you snored like a bumblebee."

I looked at the one who had just spoken, and I was quite astonished. I had thought she was a repulsive, ugly monster, but instead I saw a pretty child's face, pale, but the kind of pallor that poverty and squalor inscribe on the purest of faces.

"Oh!" she said. "I thought you were lying down next to me!"

I was reluctant to tell her why I had gotten up. She shook her head.

"I disgusted you, I am so wretched! That is all right, better sleep next to me than Rose, she has the mange."

I looked at Rose, dressed like a market vendor, with a scarf on her head. She was short and could possibly be fourteen.

She walked toward the little ragamuffin and told her menacingly, "You lied; I do not have the mange. *It is* blood pimples and if you ever say that again, I shall smack you."

"If you hit me, I shall try to hit back, but I am not going to like it because I would have to touch you."

"That is true," said Rose. "I do not want to get dirty hitting a beggar."

And she turned her back on her, picked up a mattress, placed it in a corner, and sat on it.

The beggar picked hers up and went to put it on top of the other. Rose got up without a word. Peace was restored.

On the way back, the beggar said to the one lying down in the middle, "Why do you not get up, the guard is going to be here. If the beds are not put away, you will be punished."

The one being addressed uncovered herself and stretched her arms. She was probably eight or nine. Her skin was tanned, her hair braided in the back. Two velvet ribbons circled her head. On her ears were brass rings.

She was wearing a short black velvet jacket and a checked skirt. Her little boots, too big for her feet, were tied with strings.

"Oh," she said, "I was dreaming that I had just sung at the Champs-Elysées, I was passing the hat, and got forty sous."

WRETCHED CHILDHOOD IN THE SLUMS

The door-hatch opened, and a needlessly harsh voice sounded. "Are your beds up so I can sweep? . . ."

"Yes," my neighbor answered.

The door opened. A man entered, took the tub and left.

The guard stopped at the door and asked, "Who whimpered all night?"

"So, can we not cry in jail anymore, these days?" replied the beggar. Besides, you are so friendly. . . ."

"That does not prevent you from coming back, vagrant!"

"It is not my fault if I keep coming back."

Once the room was swept, they left. The beggar yelled out to them, "Send us the soup."

This carefree attitude seemed unnatural to me. So, it was possible to leave this prison since she had come back. But how, once outside, could one get in a situation to come back?

I asked my neighbor, "Why are you here?"

"Because I was begging."

"Why did you beg?"

"Well, to eat, of course!"

"Do you not have a father or a mother?"

"Oh! I have Maman. . . . My father was a roofer but he was killed at work five years ago. There are five of us children, and I am the oldest. My brother and I, one day that there was no bread in the house, we left without a word and we went our separate ways and begged! . . . That evening I had fifteen sous, my brother, nine, and I am certain that he did what I did, that he ate some cookies. Maman was feeding my youngest sister. I went to buy bread, milk, and sugar. I did it again the next day. I thought it was fun. I always had more than my brother. One day I asked for money from a man who brought me here. I stayed a week. Maman came to get me. It was obvious that she was destitute, so they promised her some help and I was allowed to go. We were given one loaf of bread a week. That is not much for six. I went begging again. I ran into the man who had brought me here and he pretended not to see me. Another one saw me and arrested me two days ago. They said I would be sent to the reformatory. Good! I shall learn to read and work."

The singer said, "I tweak a guitar in front of cafés. Several of us had gotten together: a hurdy-gurdy player, a woman who played the harp, and a violinist. The latter kept all the money, and I worked for nothing so I left them. Three days ago on the Champs-Elysées two men brought me up to their rooms to sing and had me arrested for that."

This girl was nine years old, and she had been lost for two years. She left the house of detention to go to a hospital.

They were bringing the bread, a dark round loaf covered with bran. Its core was like putty.

Someone opened the hatch and yelled, "Vendor! Who wants to buy something?"

Rose asked for white bread and some sausage. The singer also took some bread and some writing paper. The beggar started prancing around the supplies, and the singer gave her half her bread.

"Come on," Rose said to her, "cut a piece of my sausage, you nasty shrew, and I dare you to say that I have the mange!"

The beggar took half and said, "Give me a little bit of your bread."

She returned to my bench and handed me half of what she had, and said, "It is for the two of us."

My first inclination was to push her hand away, but she seemed so sad, I took half of her bread. I was trying to think of something to give her. . . . I had an idea! I got up and took off my colored petticoat; since my dress was lined, I could do without it. I gave it to her. She was elated.

"She is always the one," said the singer.

Rose untied a little package and threw her a checked cotton scarf.

M. RÉGNIER, MAGISTRATE FOR THE PROSTITUTES

I had arrived at night. Someone came to get me for questioning.

"Farewell," said the beggar. "You might not come back if your mother is there."

I was led down some stairs, and at the bottom I recognized the door through which I came in and the lobby where I had waited.

There were two municipal guards and three women. I was placed next to them.

"You are going to be in charge of six," said the guard.

I approached a guard and asked him, "Where are you taking me?"

He laughed and did not answer.

I asked one of the three women.

"To see the doctor," she bluntly answered.

I looked at this woman and her two companions. One had tousled gray hair sticking out from under a kerchief; she was taking tobacco and smelled of brandy. The other, who was saying she would rather be at the school gate than here, wore a red and green dress and a bonnet covered with flowers. The one who answered me must have been about thirty years old. Her attire was decent and elegant.

Just then the guard entered and two other women were following him. I recognized Thérèse. I was about to go toward her when I saw her look the other way. I understood that I should not speak to her. I waited.

We lined up, one guard in front, another behind, and we were led outside.

The entrance was full of people, men and women. They were probably waiting for those they knew to come out.

The thought of walking through this courtyard with municipal guards, like criminals, of hearing these women insulted, hearing myself insulted, made me want to die of shame, so I hid my face in my hands, a gesture that drew gibes.

"Oh, that one is ugly. She is hiding her face."

We had walked across the courtyard and were at Rue Jérusalem. A group of women accompanied by municipal guards were coming out of an alley and we waited for them to come out before we entered. We were led up two flights of stairs and were brought into a room where there were again more women. It had four walls with benches all around and a window that looked out on a dark courtyard. Thérèse came over and sat next to me. She advised me, "Tell M. Régnier what I told you and he will send you to your mother's."

I watched this blend of pain and joy, tears and cheer. Some came in laughing.

"I am acquitted."

"I am leaving tonight."

They took messages from the others who came back crying.

"I shall be transferred tomorrow. I got two months."

I saw another one, pale, beaten down, who was telling one of her friends, "I am sick. I am going to the hospital."

Some poor wretches would gaze at all of this without emotion, remorse, or pity.

Bursts of laughter would respond to complaints, curses, and such

47

cynical words that the guard threatened those who uttered them with solitary confinement if they continued.

Two of these women were drunk and did not seem to want to stop. Thérèse was called. Then the door opened again without my noticing it. My name was called. Thérèse was brought back in and someone said, "The little one first."

I ran toward the door.

"Whoa! My pretty, not so fast," said one of the guards.

We were in an office that served as an anteroom.

Someone rang from the next door, and I was led into a room where there were a lot of cardboard boxes and a large desk. A man was seated behind it. Without looking up, he told me, "Well, come nearer!"

Twice he asked my name without my being able to answer. He decided to look at me and, probably noticing that I was in no state to speak, he said more gently, "Calm down. . . . You were arrested yesterday with a bad woman who was giving you shelter so she could corrupt you. What did she advise you to do? What did you see at her house?"

Thinking about this poor girl who had compromised herself out of the goodness of her heart, I had recovered and answered firmly.

He looked at me with suspicion.

"Were you in a state of vagrancy when she found you? Why did you not go home to your mother's?"

He looked at me as if he wanted to read deep into my soul. Apparently this examination went in my favor because he then said, "I shall have to keep you until she comes. I shall send an aide."

He rang and someone came to get me. Thérèse was waiting for me impatiently.

"So," she said, "what happened?"

"I have to wait for my mother here."

Thérèse was called. I shook her hand.

She came back all cheerful: she was going to leave! This thought woke me up. I looked at her with envy: she was free, and I had to stay.

After roll call we went into the house of detention.

When we walked through this cursed door and I heard it shut behind me, it seemed like its hinges had just crushed my heart.

THE IRON CAGE

The door opened and someone called out, "Céleste!" I thought they were coming to get me and I ran to the door. I was handed a package and a piece of paper. I read:

48

Thérèse

My dear Céleste, do not worry, I am going to see your mother. I am send-
ing you a comb, some soap, a towel, a scarf. I am leaving but I shall not
forget you. I am sorry I am what I am. You will soon hear from me.
  Thérèse

Night was falling and we arranged the mattresses on the floor like
cots. The singer was gone, and there were two new ones—two children—who began to quarrel. They were sisters.

"It is your fault. I told you to be careful."

"No, it is not my fault. The lady had wrapped her purse strap twice
around the chair rung and I thought it was loose. The chair moved and
the old woman woke up. I brought you the purse. She let me do it and
then she had us arrested."

"Be sure to say you found it on the floor, or you will see!"

And, saying this, she walked toward her. The little one backed up,
and I let her hide behind me.

"Why not leave this little girl alone. Are you planning to beat her
now?"

She started to hurl insults at me and wanted to get through anyway.

I have never had much endurance, but I have always been strong:
with one shove, I sent her rolling to the other end of the room.

Luckily for her, the mattresses were spread out, but she returned to
the attack, furious, saying that she would stab me with a knife.

"Try it," said my beggar. "I am going to call, and I shall say why you
want to beat us."

I stayed there six days and six nights, without news, without a word.
Finally the four of us were sent for. We were told to take all our things,
that we were leaving the house of detention.

I saw a large car, like a bus, but with wire mesh all around it.

Someone tugged at my skirt: it was Thérèse, who, huddled on the
stairs, watched me leave.

"Oh," I said, "have you not seen my mother?"

"No, she has not returned and I could not write you: there are no
letters in correction. Be patient, I shall not forget you. This man knows
where you are.[1] I told him. He did not want to give me your mother's
address, but I am watching for her return."

The women were coming out so she ran off.

"Well!" The warden told the municipal guard, "Why do you let the
prisoners talk?"

"Really now! Do they look like state prisoners?"

"You must be joking! I would rather have traitors than these women. Some are quite devilish! Come on, aboard. . . ."

And he pushed me up.

I was horrified to find myself in this sort of iron cage. I wanted to throw myself out of it.

"I do not want to stay in here!" I shouted. . . .

And I was struggling among five or six women.

"If you do not sit still, I shall have you sent to solitary confinement," said the guard.

He pushed the door saying, "She does not belong in prison, she belongs in Charenton."[2]

The car departed. I rolled under the others' feet. I felt someone pick me up and try to make me sit down. I did not fight back, but I started to cry.

"Cry," said my little beggar, "cry, it will make you feel better."

I had not noticed her yet in the car. Her presence was a comfort and I hugged her tight.

The car stopped and we heard a voice shout, "The door, please!"

We were entering Saint-Lazare![3]

6

Denise

Saint-Lazare—Special Friendships—Fair Marie—
Galley Slaves at Prayer—Corrupting Prison—A Not-Very-Helpful
M. Vincent—To the *Pistole*

I HEARD A VOICE SHOUT, "Here comes the paddy wagon, come see
the new ones. Are there many?"

Another voice, probably that of our driver, answered, "In fact, I am
full up."

We got out. One man came toward us. He was handed a sheet of
paper.

"Oh," he said, "there are some candidates for the house of correction.
Where are the thieves?"

The thought that I could be confused with them made me look toward
the two sisters.

We went through gates, courtyards, halls, and then up to a large
room.

There was a double wire fence in the center. It was a visiting room
where we could talk only from a distance.

The condemned women did not yet know the length of their sentence.

"I hope I have only one month!" one said. "I had a fight with my man
at the wine merchant shop."

"Oh," an old one whispered, "I have only one fear, that my sentence
will be too short. I have been out just one week and I have no shelter.
I am happy only at Saint-Lazare."

I had a chill at the thought that it was possible to like a prison. I asked
one woman, "Madame, do you know, when you are sent to the house
of correction, how long you have to stay there?"

"It depends on your age. They can keep you until you are twenty-one."

"Six years here!" I exclaimed. . . . "Oh! You must be saying that to scare me."

I had been addressing a girl of the Cité, one of those dreadful women, heartless, soulless, who glory in their vices, who tell each other, "I drank a whole bottle of brandy! I stabbed or was stabbed this many times! My lover is a famous thief." These women wear a scarf over the ear and other rallying signs. Often there are very dangerous fights between them and the guards.

I had addressed one of these creatures, so she took pleasure in torturing me.

"All those little tramps," she said out loud, "are not good for us. You are done for! It will be a long while before you get to laugh again!"

SAINT-LAZARE

It was nighttime. The man who came in turned up the light so he could see us, and recognizing several faces, he said, "Oh! A few regulars!"

We were led into an office, and each name was called out one after the other.

"La Huche!"

The woman of the Cité moved forward, head held high, one fist on her hip.

"La Huche, for fighting on a public street, three months."

She ran at the guard, fists clenched. The attendants took her away. She was fuming.

"One week in solitary confinement," said the guard, still pale, as he was writing at the bottom of the sheet.

And so each one's sheet was read. Then it was the two sisters' turn.

"Thion girls! For stealing a lady's purse on the Champs-Elysées, three years in reformatory."

"Take them where the little ones are."

That left only me and the beggar.

"Which of you is called Céleste?"

"I am, monsieur," I said approaching the light.

"You have never been arrested?"

"No, monsieur."

"Take these two to the insubordinates' section," he told the boy. "You will recommend this Céleste."

Then he added, as if he were speaking to himself, "Although what is the use. If she is only partially lost now, amid that lot she will be totally lost."

We went around lots of corners before reaching a huge hallway. All along it were small numbered doors. Each one of us was made to enter a cell.

I felt my way in and found an iron bed. I sat on it and finally fell asleep with my clothes on.

It was almost dawn when I was awakened by someone speaking in hushed tones.

In each cell there was a large square window without a glass pane, just wire mesh. That window was on the hallway side and it was there that the voices were coming from.

"I say, go away," said a voice. "You know very well that it is forbidden to speak to the insubordinates. But if you want to add a month to your sentence, go ahead."

Complete silence! I did not go back to sleep. A bell rang. My door opened and a woman entered carrying things.

She told me to undress and made me put on the house shift. On the chest were the words "Saint-Lazare Prison."

"Stretch your arms out so you can try on this dress."

And then she slipped some sort of gray homespun sack on me, a blue apron with thousands of stripes, a three-piece black wool bonnet, without lace, and a cotton print fichu. She took the liberty of keeping my shoes.

We went up to what is called the refectory. There were three very long tables with wooden benches on each side.

We said a prayer together, then we were served some soup. We moved to a classroom designed so we could take writing, voice, and math lessons. Those lasted two hours. Then we went to a workshop where we embroidered crepe de chine.

Between the two windows was an elevated desk where the mistress, Mlle Bénard, was seated. She was approximately thirty years old and too gentle, too nice for the devils she had to instruct.

At noon we had another meal, after which we went downstairs for recess in some sort of treeless and flowerless enclosure with fifty-foot-high walls around it.

We would play all sorts of games. The oldest girls would pair off and rarely spoke to the younger ones. Their love for each other was so strong they would become jealous.

Among us was a Denise who from the first day had become attached to me. She would give me little presents: sometimes it was a needle, sometimes feathers.

One day her friend became so jealous she made a scene. Mlle Bénard asked me not to speak to Denise anymore.

She would write to me. One day one of her letters was found and she was put in the isolation room.[1] When she came out a week later, she came to my loom, kissed me, and said, "They can put me in the isolation room my whole life, but that will not prevent me from loving you always."

Mlle Bénard scolded me for letting myself be kissed like that.

That Denise had a boy's disposition. Her look was bold and daring. Nothing scared her. When she was being punished, she would sing. Since she was forbidden to speak to me, she would make dates on the sly. She was so affectionate with me that I had become attached to her, and instead of avoiding ways of seeing her, I looked for them.

It was now my turn to feel dejected when she would speak to others. I would pout.

She would send me charming drawings she made with the multicolored flat silks that we used to embroider shawls. Or else she would draw flowers or birds on white paper, and we would exchange them. The mistress did not see a thing.

When in the evening, after work, the others played, I would go sit by a window to listen to the carriages going by and the merchants shouting. The Normands selling lettuce in baskets seemed so happy to be free!

Denise would come near me and say, "Ingrate! You would like to leave! To abandon me. What do you care that I have to stay here?"

Then she would cry.

"It is true that I would like to leave. I shall try to help you go also."

"Oh! Me, not a chance. I still have six months. I want to be registered. You have to be sixteen. If no one comes for you, you can do the same. I know some nice houses where we could make lots of money."

She gave me the address of the one where she wanted to go.

I did not pay attention to it—not then.

"You will come see me, of course?"

She was so insistent that I promised I would.

Still, I told her to give up this idea. I was thinking of Thérèse.

"You are wrong," she said. "You have seen only the lower class of these women, the ugly and the dumb. But I have known some who had lovely apartments, jewelry, carriages, who associated only with people from high society. What will it get you to marry a laborer who will beat you or make you work for two. And besides, you have been here. No matter what you do, that will be held against you."

All she had told me danced through my head all night. I saw myself rich, covered with jewels and lace. I looked in my little shard of mirror. I was truly pretty, and yet my attire was not flattering.

FAIR MARIE

It was a Sunday. As usual we went to mass. Every Saint-Lazare group was there, but separated.

The chapel was built somewhat like the auditorium of the Théâtre Chantereine. On each side of the altar there was a staircase leading up to a balcony enclosed with wire mesh. On one side were the young thieves who were called *les petites jugées*.[2] On the other side, where I was, were the insubordinates. The *jugées* and the insubordinates deeply reviled each other. We were closely supervised. Communication was severely punished.

The space below was also set up like a theater. There were sections, the loges, the orchestra pit, and the orchestra seats.

Behind me, Denise was giving me explanations.

"Look, those who are entering now and who are being placed in front are the adulteresses and the *batteries*.[3] The ones being placed on the other side are the *prévention*.[4] Some have been here for six months. Perhaps they will be acquitted!"

A third row of girls entered and was lined up behind the first.

"Those, look at them well so you will know to avoid them later. They are thieves. . . . When their sentences are short, they are kept here."

All this had occurred very quietly, but soon we began hear some noise. A mass of women rushed in the part I compared to the orchestra seats. They were jostling each other, trying to grab the first benches with such unseemliness that the attendants had to intervene.

Each condemned woman had to go down to the workshops. In those days they were required to make matchboxes. There were some very good workers and when they left, they had a small amount of money.

Later I would recognize many of these women, elegant and proud, whom I had seen in this sad and shameful uniform! There were some old ones, disfigured by scars and illness, and there were some very young, very pretty ones. Among the latter, almost all had a certain stylishness. Some wore a lace bonnet under their uniform bonnet;

others wore white camisoles and silk fichus. The more elegant ones belonged to houses.

The madams at those houses sent them clothing, money, and food. It was said about them, "So and so! She is getting a basket." Some had money. The men they attended to when they were free sent them a lot of things. As a rule they paid for everyone. They were called the *Panuches*.

During services all these women would look up in the air, chat, pass little pieces of paper to the infirmary women, the thieves, the defendants. While the attendants listened to the mass, they played their little games. Time left to serve was announced with fingers. Sunday was a play day.

Denise had been at the house of correction for three years. She had been quick to introduce me to her friend Fair Marie, as she called her.

"Look, do you see on that back seat, next to the one-eyed woman, a girl with a large-checked handkerchief, her head down, with blond hair, a blue and white scarf around her neck? She is writing on her lap. See, now she is raising her head. What do you think of her?"

I watched for a long while before answering. She must have been eighteen or twenty. Her hair was so beautiful that I looked above her head to see if there were not a ray of sunshine that could be giving it such a shiny and golden luster. Her eyes were large and pale blue. Her mouth was big, her teeth crooked but white.

"She has a strange appearance: the bottom part is hideous and common but the upper part is stunning."

"Her personality is like her appearance, which means that she has two. She is whimsical and carefree. You can tell her or do unpleasant things to her and she will not get angry. Then, another day, when no one is saying anything to her, she will lose her temper for no reason. She ran away from home because she had a stepmother."

GALLEY SLAVES AT PRAYER

I turned my head and saw, at the other end of the wire mesh fence, a little girl, twelve or thirteen years old, who was making extraordinary efforts to be noticed from below.

"Look at how this little girl is moving about."

"That is so her mother, who is among the defendants, can see her. Do you see this large woman who is looking our way? That is her mother. She sold her daughter and she is going to be sentenced to at least three years. Her other daughter, whom she sold two years ago, turned her in."

At the other end of the defendants' bench was a small dark-haired woman with delicate features who looked ill. I pointed her out to Denise.

"Oh! That is the woman who just gave birth! She was married to a nice man who adored her. Her husband went on a long trip and was away for a year. When he came home, a neighbor told him that he had been a father for a week. He had his wife arrested along with his assistant who had gone upstairs to take care of her."

"Poor woman!" I said looking at her.

"You think she deserves pity?" said Denise, surprised. "I do not pity her. If she did not like this man, she should not have married him. Look, you see the second woman on the sixth bench, now that is a woman to pity! She is from Bordeaux. A man propositioned her and she married him thinking he loved her. Nothing of the kind. He put her in a shop where her beauty drew people in. He finally said what he expected of her. He would sell her to the highest bidder and he would beat the living daylights out of her if she refused. The police arrested the two of them. He gave his consent for her to be registered."

Once mass was over, everyone left in the order they came in. We went downstairs. On the last step Denise bent down and picked up something she put in her fichu.

Once in the garden, she led me to a corner and pulled out a tiny folded paper. She read:

My sweet darling, The time for your departure is approaching. As for me, I am not lucky; this is my third sentence. I spent the night in a hotel of the Latin Quarter. I was caught in the round-up and now I am in for a month. I am sad. I am afraid I misunderstood your sign. I think of you often. I even miss reformatory.

Fair Marie

"Marie is weak," said Denise. "She has a crush on a student who is leading her on. She must have been caught at his place."

In those days, there were some forty of us in the reformatory. It was a real republic. We were constantly arguing and fighting.

There were some who were incredibly perverse and astonishingly bold. For example, a twelve-year-old girl fled over the walls, which are at least seventy to eighty feet high. Another one fled taking the place of a laundress.

CORRUPTING PRISON

In the days that I am talking about, the most damaging part of this establishment was the associations formed between twelve- to fifteen-year-old girls and thirty- to forty-year-old women.

Each letter coming in and going out is read and marked. In spite of these precautions the recruiters managed to practice their despicable profession.

The recruiters are women who find a pretty girl and give her the address of the wicked houses they represent.

They put ideas into the heads of poor children, lead them toward schools or the Cité, into squalid dives where they die young if they are weak.

It is not rare to hear ten-year-old children say what they want to be, and where they want to go when they are old enough.

The parlor is on the first floor, reformatory on the fourth. In the wall there is a tube that comes from below. When someone rings, it is a signal to put an ear against the funnel. Someone is wanted in the parlor and everyone looks up, everyone hopes.

Those who are called run like crazy, the others are sad. Then, when one of them comes back up with food, all the others surround her. She has seen someone from the outside and it seems that she is bringing back news from another world.

I had been there a month without anyone contacting me. For that reason I had moments of rage when, overtaken by the violence of my nature, I would swear I would avenge myself, I would be worse than everyone else. These moments of pique were ruining my heart.

There was among us a girl named Augustine who was about my age. She told us that her father had decided to take her out of reformatory.

"I convinced him that I would become worse here than I already am, and he believed that it was possible," she added, bursting out laughing. "Poor father, I am going to take off before we reach the end of the street!"

I told her that was bad.

"Thank you," she replied. "He promised that if I did not behave correctly, he would use his leather strap in a not so pleasant way."

That night she came to me in the courtyard and told me in a serious tone, "I am coming out tomorrow and I do not have any clothes. You are my size, could you lend me yours? I shall send them back to you in two days."

I pointed out to her that was all I had, and that if I lent them to her, she had to return them right away. She made such heartfelt promises that I believed in her sincerity and I relented.

She left. A few days later, since she had not returned anything, I confided my worries to Denise.

"Silly girl! Why did you not tell me about this? It is going to be funny when it is your turn to leave!"

Denise

In our enclosure there was a door that was a subject of everyone's curiosity. This door, arched at the top, was raised off the floor and you had to go up two steps to reach it. That is where the infirmary amphitheater was. Interns worked there, but they were forbidden to open on that side. I too was in the dark about this mysterious door.

Probably that day the key had been lost, so someone had entered through the little door and had pushed it back but not completely shut it.

I was going downstairs with Denise who left me to go talk to someone else. I walked by the door, went up the two steps, and slowly pushed on it. It opened and I saw lying on a marble table a young girl whose stomach and chest were open with large incisions. She was not disfigured and her eyes were halfway open. The light the door let in as it opened shined on her face.

"What are you doing here!" said Denise as she approached me.

She made me go back down the two steps saying, "Are you crazy? If that is your idea of amusement, you have some gloomy thoughts."

I had a terrible night.

One of us had just died. I became so sad. I was changing day by day.

A NOT-VERY-HELPFUL M. VINCENT

"Céleste, in the parlor!"

Instead of running like the others, I stayed in my chair, shaking so much that I could not get up.

"Take her down," said Mlle Bénard. "She has never been there."

Denise volunteered to take me there and, without waiting for a reply, led me toward the stairs. I stopped on the third floor. My legs were giving way.

"What are you going to say to your mother?"

"Well, I am going to tell her everything that happened."

"Oh but, if as you say, she loves this man, do not do so until you know whether she is still seeing him. He will have given her his version of things."

My mother was seated on a chair, at the back of a large room with oak benches all around. The floor tiles were white. There was a crucifix on the wall.

She did not take a step in my direction and I was afraid to go near her.

"You poor wretch!" she finally said to me. "Are you not ashamed to make me come here!"

I looked up. I was so certain that I was the one who had the right to criticize that her tone surprised me!

"I hope, dear mother, that you know what led me here. You spent so much time thinking about coming here, you must be used to the thought of my being here."

"Oh!" she said. "I learned three days ago that you were here. It took me that long to get permission to come."

"Five times, you were sent messages."

"That is not true."

"How long have you been back in Paris?"

"A month."

"What were you told when you arrived?"

"That you had let yourself be led astray by a woman."

"And who told you that?"

She did not answer.

"How did you find out that I was here?"

"Three days ago a woman stopped me in the street, the one who got you taken into custody. She told me where you were and recounted some tale about having come twenty times and being told that I had not returned."

"Did you ask the wine merchant if that was true?"

"No. Under what pretext would my door have been denied her?"

I hesitated a little and I asked her, "How is M. Vincent?"

"Well," she replied. "He is waiting for me outside."

"Did you send a petition to the prefect so I can get out of here?"

"I have not had time yet. Vincent is going to write it tomorrow."

"No," I said, "have it written by someone else, and be sure to take it over yourself."

"But why?"

"I shall tell you later."

I had been in the parlor with my mother for an hour, the amount the time we are allowed to stay there.

"Do not forget to write. When will you come?"

"In a few days. I shall write tomorrow."

She kissed me so coldly that, as I was going back upstairs, I began to cry and I told Denise, "You were right, I am done for. I shall never get out of here. Poor Thérèse! I accused her of forgetting. *He* was preventing her from seeing my mother and he was keeping the letters."

TO THE *PISTOLE*

A week went by. My mother returned. She told me that she had made the request but that they had not answered.

I became worried again. Another week went by. My mother finally told me that she had a reply and that I would be free in three days.

And exactly on the third day someone came to my cell to tell me to get dressed, that I was leaving in two hours.

"But I have nothing to wear," I exclaimed. "I did not get my clothes back. I forgot to mention that fact to my mother. Shall I have time to send for some clothes from here?"

"No," the guard answered, "not from here, but from the prison where you will stay until tomorrow. You can keep your reformatory outfit, which will be returned to us in the basket."

I went to Denise's cell. She began to cry so hard that all joy left me.

"I swear that I shall go see you wherever you are."

I left as I had arrived, in the same car, only my attire had changed.

Once at the prison, I was led to the room where I had been before. There was a crowd: seven persons in this little room. I spent three days there without sleep or food.

The fourth day, M. Régnier sent for me.

"Well now, child, I wrote your mother to come get you. Why does she not come? And why are you still in the reformatory uniform?"

"Sir, it is because I lent my clothes."

"Have you been sick? You are very pale."

"Oh, sir, if you only knew! We are very crowded. I am in there with a gang of beggars from Alsace. I have not eaten since my arrival."

"Come on, I am going to send you to the *pistole.*"⁵

Then, pulling out his purse, he gave me two francs.

M. Régnier's kindness and compassion did not protect him from grudges.

Many times I heard death threats leveled against him.

In those days, the women who were arrested were taken to his office. In their presence he announced the administrative punishment imposed on them.

One of these women threw a huge marble paperweight at his face, which luckily did not hit him.

It is in fact since then that this practice has been modified, and that the condemned learn the duration of their time only when they get to Saint-Lazare.

I heard it said, not by one woman, but by hundreds, "Oh! If there is a revolution, we shall take Régnier."

On his orders, I was sent to the *pistole.* It was a four-foot-square room with a barred window, a trestle bed, and a little table.

If they pay one franc a day, all prisoners have the right to go to the *pistole*. Many prefer the common rooms; they are not as somber as this cell.

At eleven o'clock I was called. I went into M. Régnier's office, and my mother was there.

"You are leaving now, my child. Your mother promises to take good care of you. Now, be careful. Do not let yourself be led astray by any of these women that you have met here, because if you come back here, you will find in me a very stern judge. I would have to send you to the Saint-Michel convent until you are twenty-one."

7

The Fall

"I shall leave him, but . . ." — A Trap — Her Sixteenth
Birthday — Neither Depravity nor Pleasure — Vile Book —
A Lunatic — Premature Despair and Belated Remorse —
Smallpox — "Coachman, to Saint-Louis!"

THE AIR SEEMED fragrant to me. I breathed it in as if it were an in-
toxicating flower.

I was yanked from my rapture by my mother pulling on my arm, who
said, "Where are you going? This is not the way."

"Oh! Forgive me, dear mother," I said kissing her several times, "forgive me! I must look like a mad woman, but it feels so good to be free!"

"I am very glad that you prize your freedom so, then maybe you will
be good from now on."

I was not paying attention to what she was saying.

"We are going to go home. You will work with me."

"Yes, Maman."

"Do not be ugly with poor Vincent."

That drew me out of my reverie.

"And," she said, "try to live in peace with him, for the love of me."

"Oh yes, you know only what you have been told. I am going to tell
you the truth."

During my narration, she turned red, pale, cried. I had just made her
suffer terribly.

"I SHALL LEAVE HIM, BUT . . ."

We had arrived. Vincent was at that window where I had gotten hurt.
It all came back to me at the sight of that house and the air was stifling.
But finally I went up the stairs with determination.

I went in looking Vincent straight in the eyes. I thought he would
flinch, but not a muscle in his face moved.

63

My mother turned toward me and said, "All right now, repeat in front of him what you told me on the way here."

It was my turn to turn pale and lose my composure. I saw my mother's face brighten. She doubted me. I was appalled.

I walked on, head held high, eyes forward. Vincent showed no emotion.

"Have you become mute? Why do you not say why I left here? Why do you not say what happened?"

And I repeated everything I had told my mother.

Vincent became even more impassive. "I do not have much to say. You know that your daughter hates me. I, on the other hand, have known her since she was a child and I love her very much. She came home looking very sad, and I tried to comfort her. I do not know what she might have interpreted, but she ran away."

My mother must have been afraid of the state she saw me in, because she asked him to leave us alone.

He picked up his hat and walked by me. On his lips was a smile that infuriated me.

"You believe him instead of me, right? Well, he can have my place. I do not want to live here anymore. You are set on keeping him. I am leaving."

My mother positioned herself in front of the door.

"Now, Céleste, listen to me."

"No, not if you do not throw this man out."

"Well, yes, I shall leave him, but listen to me. He just inherited a few thousand francs and he promised them to me so I can get settled. Be patient for a little while."

I was at the end of my strength. The sleepless nights, the events of the past few weeks had exhausted me. These notions of self-interest and calculations my mother was telling me about so she could delay making a decision dulled my heart. In those days I did not understand what power this emotion called love can have over the soul of women of her age. My mother was forty-seven then. I stopped fighting. That was all my mother wanted. She kissed me with more warmth than she had in a long time.

I went to bed before Vincent returned, and when I got up, he had already left. I avoided all possibilities of seeing him, because when we met there were unending quarrels.

One day he came back during the day, and finding me alone he had the gall to say to me, "Come on, now, let me kiss you, and stop pouting. I told you your mother would not believe you. If you wish, there is still time."

"Listen," I said, "someone is coming up, I think it is my mother. . . . Dear mother, come here and give me some advice. This is what this man was proposing just a minute ago. What do you think I should do?"

"No doubt about it, your daughter is crazy," he said. "She will invent anything to put us on bad terms."

My mother did not reply.

"Now, really," I said, "you promised me you would leave him. Do you think I would have stayed here without that promise?"

My mother became angry at me, saying that she was tired of all this, and that those who wanted to leave were free to do so.

I walked toward the door. Vincent positioned himself in front of me and prevented me from going out.

A TRAP

Where could I have gone? I did not know anyone. I had no family in Paris.

I went back to my cabinet. Through the window I saw him kissing my mother.

"Oh! If only I could run away, if only I were sixteen!"

An awful idea had just crossed my mind, and I went to sleep calculating my age to the day.

After each quarrel, I would say, "Fine, fine! Just two more months, just two more weeks, and I shall leave you and never see you again. I shall come back rich and I shall not need you anymore."

Having witnessed only the narrowest and most miserable side of life, I yearned to move on toward a wider horizon that I filled with ghosts evoked from all that I had seen on the stages of the boulevard theaters!

Then a dreadful idea came to me. Before leaving everything, I wanted to try one last test.

"You see," I told my mother, "I want to convince you. Pretend to spend the day out and hide in my room. Listen and you will know whether I lied to you."

She hesitated for a long time, then finally she consented. We agreed on everything for the next day.

Vincent came in at nine.

"Where is your mother?" he asked.

"She is not back."

He walked around the room without saying a word, then picked up a book.

I looked toward my cabinet with anxiety, thinking that my mother must be rejoicing to see the test turn against me.

"You were right," I said, "when you said she would not believe me. You must have put a spell on her. If I had loved you as much as she loves you, what would have happened to you?"

He looked at me without responding. I thought I saw my curtain move. I moved closer to him.

"You do not tell me anything anymore. You see that I was right not to give in. If I had left with you, you would already be tired of me."

"Try it," he said.

"Try what?"

"To follow me, to be my mistress."

"Well, what about Maman?"

"Pooh! She will get over it."

We heard a noise in my room. He looked at me and I started to laugh without answering him.

He rushed to open the door. My mother had fallen sideways. He carried her to her bed. She had lost consciousness.

And he was truly sad. He kissed her, asked for her forgiveness. "Oh," he shouted, "I am a scoundrel! Poor woman! I killed her. Please, God, forgive me!"

My mother opened her eyes and looked around. "Leave," she told us. "Leave, both of you. I want to be alone."

Only Vincent heeded her request.

"Where do you want me to go," I said.

And I sat down.

She hid her face.

My heart was jumping for joy in my chest. It seemed to me that I had regained my rightful place in the house. Alas! I did not know Vincent yet. Not only did he not leave, but I am certain he did not even entertain that likelihood.

There are some people one cannot ever get rid of, and he was one of them.

My mother kept to her bed for a week. He took care of her the whole time with passionate tenderness. To draw him away from her bed, I would have had to cause a scandal. I would have been bold enough, because I was not scared of him. But in the state she was in, such a scene would have killed my mother.

She would tell him to go away, would reproach him bitterly. All of that would just slide off him. He would beg my mother to forgive him.

He would get on his knees before her and make solemn promises for a beautiful future. He even asked me to intercede for him!

My mother was gently relenting . . . in his favor.

He had asked for some time to put his affairs in order, but he was dragging things out and my mother was not pressing him anymore. All hope was lost. He was the winner.

HER SIXTEENTH BIRTHDAY

I was sixteen less one month! . . .

There was talk of marrying me to a laborer, to be rid of me. I refused. I disliked the man in question. Laborers scared me. The insurrection scenes in Lyon were still fresh in my mind. For me, one who says "laborer," says "insurgent," an absurd notion that I would not rid myself of until many years later.

One more month went by. I was sixteen . . . and my mind was made up.

I am dealing with an atrocious event and a dreadful day in my life. There has been in my life one really horrid day. In the morning I was pure. In the evening I was ruined.

The next day I would have given half my life to take back the step I had taken, but there are ladders we can never go back up. . . .

It is impossible to be more humble than I have been, and than I still am, before the sacred quality of the virtues I did not have the strength to exercise.

Although I never got what is called an elementary education, I have always liked to be aware of my thoughts.

But having reached this point, I realize that if there are some horrible memories, by the same token there are some things that are very difficult to confess.

I do not know how public these pages will be, but even if they have only one reader, I do not want that person to be able to accuse me of having concealed a single shameful act of my life.

The emotion that will guide me through this narration is much superior to the various motives that inspired my conduct. I am going to try to recount, as chastely as possible, the most unchaste life in the world.

I left the house promising myself not to come back if I found Denise where I went looking for her.

Going down the stairs I felt my pocket to make sure my fortune—five francs—was still there.

Outside there was a fine mist. I had put on my best attire, and to protect my bonnet, I hailed a small carriage. I gave the coachman the address. When he heard the name and number of the street, he was dumbfounded.

"Do you not know where that is?"

"Oh, yes!" he replied, laughing.

The route seemed long. We arrived in front of a lovely house, and the coachman helped me down.

"Is that really where you are going?"

"I think so," I replied, embarrassed. "Would you wait five minutes for me? . . ."

He nodded and sat on his running board, which was still down. Past a carriage entrance I found an iron gate, which I opened. A bell tinkled.

At the far end of the courtyard were huge kitchens. I was about to go back out because Denise could not possibly live in such a beautiful house, but the moment I pushed the door, a voice said to me, "Who are you looking for?"

"Excuse me, madame, I am looking for Mlle Denise. Do you know if she lives here?"

"I do not know. I do not know the women. I never go upstairs, I am the cook. Fanny! . . . Wait a minute, the chambermaid is coming down."

Mlle Fanny appeared. She seemed very unpleasant. However, after looking me over, she addressed me in a very gentle tone.

"Who are you looking for?"

"I am looking for Mlle Denise."

"I do not know that name. Wait here a minute," she told me, pointing to the peristyle at the bottom of the stairs. "I shall have you speak to Madame."

I entered. A little later, I heard voices on the mezzanine discussing me.

"Is she pleasant?"

"Better than that."

"Have her come up."

Mlle Fanny came to get me and led me into a pretty little room.

A tall, fat woman entered at the same time, but through another door. Her hair was gray, coiled around her head and tied with a little chain adorned with diamonds and rubies. Her hands, sparkling with rings, leaned on each piece of furniture because her size made walking difficult. She was covered in silk and lace.

She asked me for the surname of the person I called Denise. . . . I told her.

"Yes, she is here, but what do you want with her?"

"I would like to see her, to kiss her."

"Thank goodness. I was afraid you had come to try to take her away. Because I do not want anyone to take my residents away."

She rang and Mlle Fanny appeared.

"It is indeed the one we thought that this young lady wants to see. Tell her to come down as she is, it is one of her friends."

Then she examined me closely. Apparently she was satisfied with what she saw because she asked me if I wanted a position. She told me she was shorthanded. She asked me my age and wanted to know where I had been until now.

I replied that I was barely sixteen and that I had always lived with my mother, but that I was set on leaving her.

"You are not registered?'

"No, madame."

"Oh, well, then you cannot stay here. Leave at once."

And she left.

I was so determined in my disastrous purpose that I felt quite disappointed.

Denise had just entered. She threw herself in my arms.

She was wearing a pink satin robe trimmed with swan feathers, an embroidered petticoat, a shirt so transparent that I could see her breasts through it. Her hair had been curled the night before and was falling in disarray on her neck. Her foot looked adorable in its gold-embroidered slipper.

"You are surprised by my luxurious appearance. Stay here with me and you will have as much."

"That is not what is disturbing me," I told Denise, whose naïve vanity seemed a little ridiculous to me. "But, I would like to stay with you. I even came for that reason, but apparently I must leave right away."

"Silly girl! Do you not see that it is a put on! Madame just told me as she was leaving that you are charming and I should get you to stay. I am going to tell her that you are willing. We shall hide you in my room until it is time to go there."

NEITHER DEPRAVITY NOR PLEASURE

It is as difficult for a young girl in my position to earn an honorable living through work as it is easy for her to slide down the slope toward evil.

Superior minds and generous hearts that have protested in the name of humanity against the black slave trade should also do something about the white slave trade.

Denise led me up four flights of stairs and into a room with two beds.

In this room there were two women playing cards. Another was reading in a chair.

"Ladies, here is my friend from reformatory I told you about many times. She is joining us."

I was coldly greeted and looked over from head to toe.

My new companions began to whisper. I had no difficulty figuring out that they were busy criticizing me.

Denise left me so she could once more confer with the mistress of the house. In her stark enthusiasm for the odious lifestyle she had adopted and that she was endeavoring to introduce me to, she gave herself no rest until she had removed all obstacles that were still in the way of my admission into the house.

When, twelve years later, I ask myself why I took the steps that ruined me, which I would pay for so dearly later, I can attest that the thought of depravity had nothing to do with my decision. The honest woman, now delighting in the joys of motherhood and a contented life, remembers only with loathing sacrificing the innocence of the young woman she used to be.

The two days I spent hidden in this house were for me the most awful torture. The fevered enthusiasm that had sustained me had waned and in my heart was left only remorse, discouragement, and a great loathing for myself and the life I had embraced.

I was alerted that I had to go to the police prefecture to regularize my situation.

I would need to come face to face with my mother, and I trembled at the thought of that encounter. However, I trembled even more at the thought of appearing before M. Régnier.

"Come on," said Denise, "you are not going to start trembling now? If you appear to be weakening, he will send you back to the reformatory."

VILE BOOK

Mlle Fanny had a carriage brought around. I had sent notice to my mother that she meet me at Rue de Jérusalem at noon. She was the first person I saw.

I told her that my mind was made up and that any objections were futile.

"I know quite well that you prefer Vincent to me; that is not your fault. You are weak and you have been so miserable that no one will blame you. Let me follow my destiny. My heart is full of ambitions and I shall be rich. In addition, you see, I have become sickened with my class. I could never have been the wife of a laborer. The misery and privations that you have endured frighten me."

"You are mad!" said my mother. "Who in the world has put those ideas in your head? Give up on your plans and come with me. I swear I shall break it off."

"No," I said, "it is too late."

I was led into the office where I had already been.

"What? Is that you?" said M. Régnier, surprised. "What could you possibly want?"

"I want to be registered."

"Be registered!" he said standing up. "I am going to send you to the reformatory!"

"As you wish, sir. And when I leave, I shall be back so you can register me."

"And your mother consents?"

"Yes, monsieur."

He rang, and, without looking back, he told the boy, "Take this girl to be measured."

My description and height were noted.

My name was inscribed in this vile book and nothing can erase it, not even death!

A complete wardrobe was ordered for me. The next evening I came down wearing a stunning outfit. I had been given a white pinwale corduroy dress, silk stockings, satin shoes, and a coral necklace.

The fat lady seemed very pleased with her new tenant and introduced me to her sister, who, in the house, was called Aunt. She was a tall, skinny woman with white hair and dark eyes. She put on her glasses to better examine me.

Denise was on cloud nine. She would triumphantly look at our companions whose benevolence was far from increasing in proportion to the progress of my improvised elegance.

It is difficult to believe that human beings could become accustomed to these dreadful prisons. I had not been there a week that I had only one thought: getting out.

The visitors were so distinguished and so rich that, deluded by Denise's stories, I imagined that right away I would find someone who would help me get out of there. But time passed, and this unknown protector was not coming. On the contrary, each day my chains became heavier.

The best method the women who run these types of establishments use to govern is the heavy debts they burden these unfortunate victims with. There was an accounting each week: I already owed eleven hundred francs.

I was so sad that Madame allowed me to go out with Denise.

We went to the Chaumière.[1]

Several young men came over to talk to my companion. One of them seemed to pay particular attention to me. Each time I turned toward him, I would see his large, dark, soft eyes fixed on mine.

"But who is this young man?" I asked Denise.

"Adolphe?" she asked, turning around.

"I do not know whether his name is Adolphe, but he is the one who spoke to you last."

"That is right. He is charming. He is studying medicine. His father was a famous surgeon during the Empire and made a great fortune. He had invested this fortune in some companies when he suddenly died. The businessmen went bankrupt. His widow and his son were left practically penniless. Adolphe began his studies, but he was hurt during an autopsy. His arm was in a sling for nine months."

"How do you know all this?"

"He is on intimate terms with a young man I know. Do not say anything if they come to speak to us again. Aldophe, especially, cannot abide women in our position."

The young men came back toward us. M. Adolphe asked if they could come visit us.

Denise pressed my arm laughing and told him that would be impossible, that I was even busier than she, but that the next time she would go see his friend, she would bring me.

When we came home, it seemed to me I hated my bondage even more than before going out because we were allowed to go only once a month.

A LUNATIC

I continued being very difficult and ferociously proud. During my stay in the house where I was, I had the opportunity to exercise this garrulous disposition toward a man whose fame, although glorious, barely eclipsed his behavior. The story of our love affair is not an exchange of venal passion, but a rapid series of acts of violence and quarrels.[2]

The first time I saw him it was, I believe, the day after we had gone to the Chaumière, and I was in a rather bad mood.

I was summoned. I followed Fanny into the little parlor. A man seated near the fireplace with his back to me. His hair was fair, he was thin and of medium size. His hands were white and bony. His fingers were beating time on his knee.

I was observing this premature wreck, because in spite of the wrinkles that furrowed his face, he seemed to be no more than thirty years old.

"Where do you come from?" he said, as if coming out of a dream. "I do not know you."

I turned red and replied, "Do I ask you who you are and where you come from? Do I need a service record to appear before you?"

I was walking toward the door.

"Stay here," he said. "That is an order."

I heard no more and left.

I rushed to tell the fat woman what had just occurred. She shrugged her shoulders and told me I was wrong, that this gentleman sometimes came to stay a whole week at a time and that he was one of this century's greatest men of letters.

Denise was there. She whispered in my ear, "She dotes on him because he has a lot of money but he is brutish."

A violent ring of the bell shook the house. It was my enemy getting angry.

"Do not go back," said Denise.

"On the contrary," I replied, giving the big woman an ironic look. "I would not mind seeing a great genius up close."

I went back into the little parlor.

"So, you are back," he said. "In this house, everyone obeys me. You will do like the others, and, for a start, I want you to drink with me."

He rang and Fanny arrived.

"Something to drink!" he said.

She returned with three bottles and two glasses.

"Now, what do you want? Do you want rum, brandy, or absinthe?"

"I thank you, but I am not thirsty."

He swore like a Templar, and, after filling his glass with absinthe, he gulped his drink.

"Your turn. Drink or I shall beat you."

I calmly took the glass he handed me and I threw its contents in the fireplace.

"Oh!" he said taking hold of my hand and swinging me around. "You are disobedient; that is even better. . . ."

He put a few gold coins in one of his hands, a full glass in the other.

"Drink," he repeated, "and I shall give them to you."

"I shall not drink."

"Well, you certainly are not like the others. You seem different and I like you. Take this gold! You have not earned it, I give it to you. Leave me, go away!"

On the way out, I saw that he was pouring a glass of brandy. Denise was waiting for me at the door.

"I was afraid for you," she said. "It is said that when he does not get his way, he hits!"

Because I had defied him as I did, he could not do without me now. He came to see me two or three times a day. Sometimes he had moments of madness when he would say loathsome things for no reason. That annoyed me.

"Now what do you want from me? You are nothing but a drunkard. Just because some woman has made you angry does not mean you have to hate the others!"

I was a little worried about the effects of my harangue, but I soon could feel reassured, because, after I finished, I noticed that he had fallen asleep in his chair. . . . I tiptoed out of the room.

The next day, he came back to ask if he could take me out to dinner. Madame quickly agreed without consulting me. He came for me at six and took me to Rocher de Cancale.[3]

In the beginning I did not have too much to complain about him, except for a few tasteless jokes.

The waiter who was serving us brought us a bottle of seltzer water.

Who is to know what mad notion went through the head of the peculiar man who had chosen me as the victim of his whims? He picked up the siphon of seltzer water as if he were going to pour himself something to drink and, aiming the opening toward me, he drenched me from head to toe.

PREMATURE DESPAIR AND BELATED REMORSE

I went to Denise to tell her about my trials. She was far from having an insightful personality, but she was loving. She had a manly spirit, and our life was beginning to weigh on her as much as on me.

"Be patient," she told me, "and moreover forgive me. I was deceived even as I deceived you. I too am unhappy. I love a man who would send me away if he knew my situation."

She was crying. It was my turn to console her.

Love cruelly retaliates against women who have profaned its image!

What honest woman, or mother, would want to hire as worker or servant a wanton girl? The fall was intentional, so how is it possible to believe in the sincerity of repentance? The world is not inhuman, just incredulous.

For the woman who has fallen so low, there is no family. Your parents disown you and try to forget you. . . . Marriage is out of the question. The man who would want to unite his fate to yours hesitates before the prospect of asking the police prefect for your hand. Motherhood? Your child's first kiss is torture, its first word a reproach because you cannot identify the father. . . . If it is a boy, when he becomes a man he will scorn you. If it is a girl, you are afraid to keep her near you.

It is not like me to feel in moderation. Joy, sadness, affection, resentment, laziness, activity, I have magnified them all. My life has been one long excess. Knowing these tendencies, you can judge how I must have been suffering when, to please and thereby to earn my daily bread, I had to put up with the presence of odious individuals.

Sometimes, tired of self-reproach, I would blame society. I would tell myself that it is barbaric to allow a sixteen-year-old child to enter into such a despicable contract. . . . The law, which does not allow her to manage her property until she is twenty-one, lets a sixteen-year-old girl sell her body.

My mental torment had finally taken a toll on my health. My head felt heavy, I had fever chills, and I took to my bed. I was told that I had to go down to the parlor after dinner because the fat woman was giving a little party for the house regulars. I got up.

At nine o'clock there were already a lot of people present. I sat in a corner. . . . Champagne was bubbling in glasses and veins. I felt a chill, then a cold sweat. I slumped down on the sofa where I was seated.

SMALLPOX

Someone lifted and led me out.

I gradually came to. The person who had accompanied me or rather carried me was a young man, about twenty-eight or thirty years old. He was of medium height; his attire was meticulous but austere. He seemed worn-out from work or from debauchery.

"You are sick, my child!" he told me. "You must look after yourself."

"Look after myself! Where do you suggest I go?"

And, driven by fever, regret, self-disgust, I told him everything in one breath.

"How much do you owe?" he asked.

I told him. He shrugged his shoulders.

"Listen," he said, "I live alone, but I have a huge apartment because after giving birth, one of my sisters will be coming to Paris in two months. Would you like to use her lodgings?"

Without waiting for my reply, he rang, asked for my things, asked for my account, paid, had his carriage brought around, and told me to follow him.

I asked if I could say good-bye to my friend. He refused. Fanny took care of my good-byes.

We rode a long way. My companion was not saying a word. The car slowed down. We were climbing. I saw a cab stop, and near a gaslight I read Place Breda.[4]

The apartment was on the second floor. A sleepy man opened the door for us.

"Take Mademoiselle to the back bedroom. See that she does not lack anything. If I do not come back, call my doctor."

I followed the butler who took me to a pretty, freshly painted room. During the night I had an overwhelming thirst, but I did not dare call.

In the morning someone knocked softly at my door. It was the doctor and the butler. I slipped on a dress. They chatted as they waited, "He should be looking after himself instead. This wasting disease will catch up with him one day."

Barely dressed, I opened the door. I answered the doctor in half-words, and he left saying, "She has nothing."

M. L—— came home at ten o'clock.

"Well," he told me, "you have nothing. . . . Good! Regardless, take care of yourself!"

He had a lunch brought to me, asked me what I needed for my toilette, and left until the next day.

That went on for a week, seeing him barely more than an hour each day. I was well one day, ill the next. Finally, I stayed in bed two days with a headache. When M. L—— came into my room he told the servant, "Quick, the doctor!"

It was two hours before the doctor showed up. He arrived out of breath from a lunch in town, which he described in detail before taking a look at me.

"Good God!" he exclaimed. "Why was I called so late? She is about to develop smallpox!"

76

He left. M. L—— and the butler followed him. I was alone. I tumbled out of the bed and listened at the door. The doctor was saying, "A lot of good that has done you. What are people going to say when she dies here, in your home? In addition it is a contagious illness."

"Oh!" said the servant. "Monsieur can have her served by whom he pleases, but I am not going into her room again."

M. L—— seemed very affected.

"Doctor, could we not take her to a sanitarium?"

"No, to move her now is impossible. I am going to try to send you a home nurse."

He prescribed a few remedies, and I heard him walk away and leave.

Then I took my hat, which had stayed on a table, my dress, my coat. I opened a door, walked through a room, then two, without seeing anyone, then finally through the anteroom and down the stairs.

Downstairs I climbed into a cab that was stationed across the street and told the coachman as I dropped onto the seat, "Saint-Louis Hospital!"

8

Effects of a Hospital Stay

M. Adolphe and His Friend—How to Get a Start in
the theater?—The Versailles Incident—Plans for Revenge

NOTICING THAT I had passed out in his cab, the coachman asked the
concierge at the hospice to help him get me out of the carriage. The
doctor on call had been summoned and he had me brought to a room
where he gave me the necessary care.

When I came to, he asked me what I wanted. I looked at myself and
understood why; this dress and this silk coat, this flowered hat surprised him.

I told him I had smallpox and I was at the hospice to receive treatment.

He had me turn toward the light, then ran his thumb across my forehead and said dolefully, "Yes, you are right, but what you have just done
was very foolhardy."

He had me brought to a room. An hour later I was delirious. For ten
days I was out of my mind. I was blind for seventeen days. The nuns
were caring for me with great kindness. My face was covered with a
mask of blemishes that kept my eyes and nostrils shut.

I would hear the doctor asking in the morning, "How is number
15 doing?"

The good sister would reply, "Better, doctor. I hope she will open her
eyes tomorrow or the next day."

"Are you keeping her face coated with ointment? . . ."

"Yes, doctor, I do it myself every half hour."

"Good," he said, touching my cheeks. "If she does not scratch, she
will have very few marks. The spots are numerous, but small."

Three days later my eyes began to open like those of a kitten. I was forbidden to try to open them too fast, but I could not help myself. I felt a slight tear.

"Why did you open your eyes? You do not have an eyelash left," said the nun.

I wanted to look at myself, but I did not dare ask for a mirror. She must have read my thoughts because she instructed my neighbors not to lend me one. Futile recommendation! Taking advantage of a moment when the good sister was out, I managed to get a young girl in the bed across from me to pass me her case, and it had a mirror on the bottom.

I dropped the case and fell back on my pillow! Tears surged and my heart fell.

In number 17 there was a woman who had hit her knee. The injury was so serious that her leg had to be amputated. For such cases, the surgeon is accompanied by his students. Two of these young men stopped at my bed and read, "Céleste Vénard, smallpox."

"Oh," said one of the two, "I have to take a look at the one who survived this terrible condition."

He opened the curtain at the foot of my bed.

"Oh!" I said, surprised.

I had just recognized in the one speaking, M. Adolphe's friend, and in the other, M. Adolphe himself. The first one came to the side of my bed and touched my face. He said, "She will not be too marred."

And he started to move away.

I grabbed his coat and said to him, "You do not recognize me! I was with Denise at the Chaumière three months ago."

He was so taken aback, he was at a loss for words; then he made an effort to regain his composure and said to me, "Denise told us you had gone to the country."

"I had asked her to tell you that. She does not even know that I am here. I have kept it from her until now. But I really would like to see her. Would you tell her?"

He promised he would send Denise to me and left.

I heard heels echoing on the wood floor. M. Adolphe, his head bare, his hair pulled back, looking sad, held his hand out to me.

"Poor girl," he said, "if I had known, I would have come to you long ago. I was in the next room and I came to look at you. But I was far from imagining that the one I was thinking of was near me! Because I have certainly been thinking about you."

Visiting hours were starting. He left, saying to me, "I shall be back."

I wanted to fix my hair, but it was falling out by the fistful. The next day I received a few cookies, jam, and some sugar.

That Thursday Denise came to see me. She walked by me twice without recognizing me. Finally I called out to her. . . . She threw her arms around me and began to cry.

Once she had regained some of her composure, she asked me what I was going to do when I got out.

"I ran away from M. L——'s house because I was sick," I said. "I left my things there. I shall give you a note for him. If he wants to return them to me, sell them so I can have a little money, and I shall rent a furnished place."

"Oh, but," said Denise, "you cannot, it is prohibited; you will be arrested."

"That is right. Well, I shall ask M. Adolphe to do it for me."

My handwriting was illegible, yet I had to write to M. L——, so I tried again:

Dear Sir,
You have been so kind to me that I am embarrassed to have to bother you. I just recovered from a long illness. . . . I left with you the few things that I possess. If you would be kind enough to give them to the bearer, I would be twice beholden to you. I am very sincerely grateful.
Céleste

Denise came back that Sunday. She had all my things, plus one hundred francs to help me out when I got out.

"You see," I told her, "I am going to rent a hole. I have been told that I have a pretty voice. I am going to work, and I shall try out for the stage, and once I have an engagement, I shall be able to be taken off the register. M. Adolphe will help me."

Three days later, he told me that he had rented one room and a cabinet on Rue de Buffault. My departure was set for a week from then.

Denise came to get me. M. Adolphe was waiting for me downstairs and took me to my new dwelling and promised to come visit me.

The room that had been rented for me was on the first floor in the back. The window looked out over a boarding school for little boys.

HOW TO GET A START IN THE THEATER?

I had enough money for a month, but after that? Inadvertently I looked at my face, and I started to cry. It was all red, and the doctors had warned me that if I exposed myself to the outside air, the marks would last a long time.

M. Adolphe came to see me twice. He told me that he had just been named surgeon at the military hospital in Versailles. He gave me his address and made me promise I would write to him.

As soon as I could go out without any risk, I put on a black veil and went to the Théâtre Beaumarchais. I asked for the manager. He refused to see me. I insisted. . . . He saw me after making me wait two hours.

He was a big, gray-haired man, a little slovenly in dress.

"What do you want from me?" he said looking me up and down.

"Sir, I would like to be in the theater."

"You have never acted?"

"No, sir, but if you wish I could give it a try."

We were at the door toward which he had pushed me rather than escorted me.

"They are all the same. They think that all there is to it is to go see a manager!"

He was sneering at me as he was speaking to me thus.

I held the door open, then, just before closing it, I told him, "One is not born acting, but I am at the right age to learn. I thought I should go to a small theater. I was wrong, I shall try a more important one."

"The Opera is on Rue Le Peletier."

"Thank you, sir, I am going to the little Lazary!"

"Insolent girl!" he yelled and closed the door.

Once on Boulevard du Temple, I went in the Délassements. A man who looked like he was disguised as an old woman made me enter a little office. On the door was written "Production Department."

He patted his big belly, his gray hair, took a large pinch of snuff and said to me, "One of our dance extras is not here; can you dance in her place tonight?"

I told him that if someone wanted to show me how, I could learn very quickly.

"The devil take you!" he said shaking the tobacco out of his jabot. "I was promised an old coryphaeus from the Opera. I have been listening to you for an hour thinking you were she."

I was sixteen and a half years old! . . .

I went to the Funambules. There, I said to myself, they put on mime shows. I should know enough. Oh! Was I wrong! . . . They would not even hear me. I was too skinny, and my wrists were not strong enough; women have to fight with sabers!

I went home feeling dejected, legs worn out.

The next day Denise came to see me.

"I have come to get you. I am taking you to dine at the house of one of our former acquaintances."

"Who is that?"

"Fair Marie! You know, the one who wrote to me that Sunday at mass. She just bought some furniture. We are going to have a house warming at her house, on Rue de Provence."

THE VERSAILLES INCIDENT

Mlle Marie had a little apartment on the first floor with blue wool hangings and curtains of white muslin. She was reclining on her sofa.

"How charming it is here!" said Denise.

"Yes," replied Marie, "but this is my sixth home. They all get sold."

"Of course, you amass notes and you do not pay them!"

"Oh! This time I shall keep it! Where do you live?" she asked me.

"I live on Rue de Buffault."

"Furnished?"

"Yes, and I am certainly lonely all alone."

"Do you want to come live with me?"

I looked at Denise, who said to me, "Now, that is not a bad idea! You would not have to pay anything."

"I accept, but on one condition, and that is that I pay half the rent as soon as I am able."

I lived with her for several months. . . . She was a good person, but she was extremely disorderly, and we would move every three months. Each day she was surprised that her furniture had not been sold yet.

Occasionally I would spend a few days in Versailles. My relationship with M. Adolphe was, by far, what I cared for the most. By dint of telling myself that I adored him, I had begun to reserve a large space for him in my life.

I had opened a savings account. I would deposit ten francs, twenty francs on Sundays without fail.

When I had three hundred francs I sent for Marie's furniture merchant, and I asked her very humbly if she would furnish one room for me. She replied that she was willing but that she would put the lease in her name and that I would pay notes of fifty francs a month. Since the terms were of too long a duration to go through the store account, I would pay higher ones to her and she would pay them, so that, for a thousand francs' worth of furniture, I would be giving her two thousand francs.

I did not have a choice. I accepted.

Marie was very sad when she learned of my decision.

"You are going to leave me?" she said. "Good-bye savings! A month from now I shall have nothing left!"

A few days after getting settled in my new room, M. Adolphe asked me to go with him to a little soirée being given by one of his Versailles friends.

I accepted. I was quite unassuming but happy to be with him, because I had been suspecting for some time that he had another attachment.

I was asked to sing. I did the best I could. . . . Everyone complimented me. That seemed to make M. Adolphe very proud, when suddenly the scene changed. A woman had just entered the living room. She was wearing a splendid outfit and nodded to everyone in a patronizing way.

"Oh! Here is Louisa Aumont," exclaimed several young men as they walked toward her.

Our eyes met and exchanged darting looks of hatred and jealousy.

Louisa Aumont went straight up to the host, steered him toward the window, and told him, loud enough for everyone to hear, "I had asked you never to invite women, especially that one! . . . I told you how it was. . . . I do not want to find myself in the company of such girls! . . ."

M. Adolphe was biting his lips, but he let the insult ride. I went up to him and told him in a voice restrained by anger, "If you are afraid to defend me, will you have the courage to follow me?"

"Why do you want to leave?" he replied in a sheepish tone. "You are here, stay."

My doubt was being confirmed, and I took off like an arrow.

I waited in the street for two hours, hoping that, worried about me, he would follow me, but no! I became afraid of my despair. I ran toward the road to Paris, and I walked all night, listening to my footsteps. . . .

I arrived home, beaten with fatigue, but more beaten still by my feelings. . . . I was hoping for a letter the next day, some word of explanation! . . . Nothing, nothing. Not one regret, not one apology!

PLANS FOR REVENGE

This first disappointment had a most unfortunate effect on my life.

I became ambitious and unbending.

Marie noticed the change.

"What is the matter with you?" she would repeatedly ask me. "You seem so sad, so preoccupied."

She insisted with so much perseverance that I let my secret out.

"I am in love with a man who does not love me. I love him submissively, sweetly. He does not treat me well and toys with my heart. I can tell you, I have suffered and my soul has become hardened as a result. I shall become like Louisa Aumont."

"What is this Louisa Aumont?"

"Louisa Aumont is my rival."

And I told her about the scene at the soirée in Versailles. Marie seemed frightened by my plans for revenge.

"Now! You might be better off going to see your friend and making up with him."

"He loves this woman, but he will come back. . . . I shall do so much that he will hear about me! It is her riches he likes. I shall have more than she!"

"Come to the ball tonight, at the Chaumière," said Marie.

"No, let us go to Mabille!"

"I have never been there. I would prefer to go to the Chaumière."

"Then I am not going out, because I do not want to run into him. . . . He is coming to Paris and he will be going there."

9

The Bal Mabille

Brididi and His Dancer—The 26 September 1844 Polka—
Louisa Aumont Scorned—The Pomaré Carnival

IT WAS NINE O'CLOCK when we arrived on the Allée des Veuves. . . .
Mabille had been a small village dance hall, lighted by oil lamps. . . .
Admission cost ten sous. . . . It was a favorite meeting place of butlers
and maids in the days when they were less elegant than their masters.

At the time I am speaking of, Mabille had greatly improved. It was
not yet the magnificent gardens that we see today, with flower baskets,
strings of lights, water fountains, a large room with walls lined with
gold, velvet, and mirrors. In those days it was a modest garden! A few
gaslights had replaced the oil lamps, but they were scarce, either out of
economy or discretion. . . . Fabric clerks, grisettes, and milliners could
tell us more about that, since the usual customers had changed. Admission was now one franc.

It was into this milieu that we made our entrance. . . . The orchestra
was in the middle of the garden and sounded good. I loved music. I had
never danced. I wanted to try but the fear of looking ridiculous held
me back.

And yet, Adolphe had told me that Louisa Aumont could waltz well.
I wanted to try. I was invited for a quadrille . . . and I was about to refuse
when a young man from Versailles came to greet me. I accepted. I asked
Marie to be my vis-a-vis. In the same night I learned how to waltz and
how to dance.

BRIDIDI AND HIS DANCER

I walked around the dance hall, stopping briefly by each circle surrounding the good dancers. One of these circles was more crowded than
the others.

I heard laughter, cries of bravo! The circle opened and everyone rushed on the heels of a woman, laughing, talking. This woman must have been five feet tall; her waist was short, her chest round, and her shoulders somewhat high. . . . She held her head proudly. Her hair was a beautiful shade of black, neatly parted. She wore her hair in flat bands; she had a coiled braid at her nape and from underneath this braid hung curly hair that hid her neck. Her forehead was low; her well-arched eyebrows met in the center, giving her a hard look. In addition to that she had large dark eyes, a nose reminiscent of Roxelane's,[1] and a scornful mouth.

She went toward the café, and I followed her so I could be in the first row when she danced. She appeared short of breath. She coughed, placed her hand on her chest, then swallowed two glasses of ice water.

A short man had just signaled to her. He took her by the waist, and the first figure began.

He was as light as a bird. All those leaps, which seemed ridiculous when executed by the others, were graceful when he performed them. I was right to have followed them because there was an even bigger crowd than the first time.

For the second figure, his partner looked at the band leader and as soon as the baton moved, she took off, arms extended behind her, then upon completing the circle, she stood straight up, arched her back, her elbows almost touching, lifted her head, and came back forward.

"Bravo! Bravo!" the spectators were saying.

She was wearing a black wool dress, which signaled poverty. It is possible that she had not eaten all day because she was quite pale.

I heard two young men next to me say, "Let us take her to dinner! . . ."

"No," said the other, "she would cost us an arm and a leg. I bet she has not eaten for a week."

Someone called, "Brididi!" And the short young man who danced so well replied, "Coming! Coming!" and went toward the café.

The next Thursday I went back to Mabille with Marie. We looked for Brididi and his dancer. She was one of the first women I saw. She was wearing a lilac barege dress.[2] Her hair was more elegantly combed.

A man of a certain age, wearing a gray hat, white trousers, a small baggy cardigan, stopped in front of her.

"So, now," he said, "we are in shape again! She looks like la Reine Pomaré."[3]

Everyone around her said all together, "Chicard is right, we have *got* to call her Pomaré."

"Bravo! Pomaré!"

The evening turned into an event. The next day several newspapers wrote about it.

That night Brididi did not seem pleased. He was dancing with pretty girls, but everyone was interested in Pomaré. He decided to give her a rival, and came up to me to ask me to dance. I told him that I barely knew how to dance.

"Well, I shall teach you."

And indeed, he taught me. I took off my little shawl, and I was just in my light short-sleeved barege dress. A lot of people watched me and that encouraged me. At the end of the evening, Brididi asked me unaffectedly, "Do you want to come have dinner with us?"

I accepted in the same way, and we left, a cheerful group, to have dinner at Vachette's.

"Oh," I said, looking around to make sure I was noticed, "if this could be known in Versailles!"

We left the restaurant at six in the morning.

"Nothing for me?" I asked the concierge.

"No!"

THE 26 SEPTEMBER 1844 POLKA

At four o'clock Brididi came to see us.

"Oh! Guess what," he said without saying hello. "There is a new dance: the polka! Come to my house for the evening, we shall learn it and we shall dance it together to make Pomaré fume."

We practiced for five hours. Finally I knew it perfectly. We were performing lots of movements that made us look like trained dogs: arms, legs, body, head, everything was moving at once. We looked like a bunch of telegraph signals and marionettes.

Brididi invited me to stay at his house. It was quite late. I thanked him and declined. He brought us home. Since I did not want him to take me for a prude, I told him about the state of my heart . . . but with each sentence I executed a polka jump and I sang its tune. At home I asked, "No one came? . . ."

"No!"

I stifled a sigh deep in my heart.

Back in my room, I started to polka.

"I am glad," said Marie, "that you are taking your situation lightly."

The furniture merchant came to tell me the next day that my apartment was ready. I took my bags and moved in at 19 Rue de Buffault, in a little two room entresol.

It was lavishly furnished, and looking around at my luxurious dwelling I was worried about the sum I would have to pay. In my bedroom I had a mahogany bed, a dressing table, a Voltaire-style chair covered in red wool, two chairs, a little table. In the first room, which served as parlor or dining room, there was a round table and four fluted chairs.

The next day I put velvet bows in my hair, mended my dress and my boots, and went back to the ball.

Brididi came toward me. . . . I was not unhappy about this partiality. . . . The band announced, "Polka!"

"I could never dance this here! I might do something awkward, and everyone will make fun of us."

"No, no," he said, "let us go in a corner."

I was going to resist, when I heard behind me, "Well! Does not anyone know this dance? . . ."

I recognized Louisa Aumont's voice.

Now I was the one taking Brididi in my arms and forcing him to dance.

Several times I danced by Louisa Aumont, and I leaned so much on my dancer that she could have thought I was kissing him.

I was applauded excessively, I was followed, I was pointed out! . . .

"Pooh! How awful!" Louisa Aumont was saying in the arms of an old man. "Flaunting oneself this way! . . ."

I could tell she was annoyed! I waited for her to come by me. I took hold of her arm to stop her.

"Hello, dear Louisa. How long has it been since you have gone to Versailles to see your lover?"

She turned purple and wanted to go on her way, but I stopped her again.

"Oh! Excuse me, I thought this gentleman was your father. If I had known he was the old bird to whom you say, to get rid of him, that you are going to visit your aunt in Versailles, I would not have talked about your Henri."

I bowed and left laughing. I had just done something mean, and I was beaming. I heard someone say, "She is a lot better than Pomaré!"

All the men came to invite me to dance.

"Oh," said Brididi, "it would be easier for me to defend Mogador than my dancer! . . . Hey!" he shouted really loudly. "I name you Mogador!"[4]

A hundred voices shouted, "Viva Mogador!" Twenty bouquets were thrown in my direction.

There were two camps. . . . On one side were shouts of "Viva Pomaré!" and on the other, "Viva Mogador!" Those who understood nothing and could only catch the sounds shouted, "Viva Pomador!" The guards had to intervene! . . . Pomaré was placed in a carriage, the horses were un-hitched, and the young men themselves pulled her to the Maison-d'or.

Either Mabille had bought some advertisement or the dance masters wanted to make the polka fashionable, but the next day all the news-papers were talking about Pomaré and me. *Le Charivari* pictured us in all positions.

There were two other women who were also making news at the Chaumière; they were Maria the Polka Dancer and Clara Fontaine.

Through the press our meager fame extended into the provinces.

LOUISA AUMONT SCORNED

I had not seen Adolphe for three weeks. He came to Mabille out of curi-osity.

When someone pointed me out to him, he stepped back and said, "You are mistaken! That is not her, that is Céleste."

"Yes," said his friend, "Céleste Mogador!"

Adolphe walked up to me.

"Come, I have to talk to you."

I signaled to my partner that I was coming back.

"You will not be coming back," said Adolphe squeezing my arm.

"And why not?" I asked.

"Do not go," he said, pale, "or I shall have to settle matters with this little gentleman!"

"Might you be doing me the honor of being jealous? Some time back, I admit that I would have been pleased, but today it makes me laugh."

The flower merchant brought me two bouquets of roses that I was being offered. I took them, but Adolphe grabbed them and tore them to pieces.

"Now, really, my friend, what do you want from me? You left me; you did not love me. I did not mess up your love affair. . . ."

"This woman has never been mine! If she were here, I would say so in front of her."

At that very moment, I saw her coming out from behind a grove.

"Look," I said, "here she is! If you do it, I shall believe you."

"You will leave with me? . . ."

"Yes!"

He went straight toward Louisa who was giving him her best smile.

"Come, now, mademoiselle, please tell Céleste that I am not your lover, and that you regret having been so harsh with her."

She made a horrible face, turned red and said, "Yes! . . ."

"That is enough," I told Adolphe, who, I could see, was squeezing her wrist. "Come."

We left in a carriage. He was all sweet and kind to me but I remained cold as a stone!

"You take pleasure in tormenting me," he said with tears in his eyes.

"And do you think I was not tormented when I had to walk home from Versailles the night you abandoned me?"

He was afraid to say any more. I made dates with him . . . and arrived two hours late! He would forbid me from going to public places . . . and I went deliberately! The papers were still talking about Pomaré and me. . . . Whole groups would come see us at night as if we were strange animals. All these gapers fought over a flower from our bouquets.

Pomaré would take on a look of arrogance, practice all sorts of eccentricities, and scare off the curious onlookers who would turn red with embarrassment. That is probably why many of them would come around me and pay me compliments.

I had my following and Pomaré had hers.

"She is delightful!" one of them said, ogling me.

"You will see what a great dancer she is!" the other one said.

"She is so graceful!"

Such were the remarks all these people who disdained me were making. Whatever her position, there is not a single creature who is not susceptible to fame. . . . You can imagine, uneducated as I was, how I could not help but be blinded and misled.

THE POMARÉ CARNIVAL

There is no theater, however small, that does not have its rivalries. My success at Mabille created many jealousies toward me. The men covered me with love and flowers.

I hated Pomaré, and she hated me.

For no particular reason, it was decided that it would be delightful to partner us, and our partisans negotiated the arrangements with all the seriousness reserved for peace treaties.

We walked toward each other and did not take another step. I felt like fleeing, but I came to the conclusion that it would be ridiculous, and so I held my hand out to her. Her face brightened, and she said to me in a most charming way, "I am delighted to make your acquaintance. If you would permit me to visit you, I shall continue my friendship toward you."

She had a patronizing air about her that I did not like, but I took her arm and we went around the ballroom together.

After exchanging a few words with her, I noticed that she took her role seriously and that she thought she was a queen. In fact she was always addressed thus: "Dear queen, are you going to dance? Where will you be so your courtiers can surround you?"

She would indicate a place in a low voice. They would leave proud of themselves and take on a look of protection with their friends whom they led to their places.

One of the usual customers, a high school supervisor, I think, who wore glasses, was called. He was surrounded and applauded with shouts of "Bravo, Pritchard!" The poor man lost his head and pranced about. . . . He was carried triumphantly. . . . He held his head high, imagining himself an important character, but the poor fellow was sent back to his place. He revealed his disappointments to Pomaré who told him, "Come see me, I shall protect you."

She was convinced of her power! . . .

I wanted to get to know this strange person. Since our separation, Marie did not come over anymore; I rarely saw her. I asked Pomaré to come spend the next day with me.

She told me that she did not call for her carriage until four o'clock and that in the morning she received her court.

"Come have lunch at my house," she invited me. "We shall chat and smoke a cigarette."

She left me, then came back.

"Would you like to have dinner with me and some of my friends? . . ."

I replied yes before she had finished her sentence.

We left. At the door she made a frown with her dark eyebrows. . . .

"Jean! Jean!" she said impatiently.

A young boy of about twelve came running up. He was wearing a ridiculous outfit: gray linen pants tucked into his top boots, a frock coat whose waist would have been big enough to make him a cardigan, a very large hat with a flashy braid. In his arms he was carrying a faded cotton tapestry shawl with one end dragging on the ground. Pomaré, furious, grabbed it out of his hands.

"Idiot! Can you not pay attention! . . . You are wiping the pavement with my scarf. . . . If you do not do your work better, I shall dismiss you."

Everyone was laughing around her. The little boy left shrugging his shoulders and brought the carriage around, a two-horse barouche that she rented by the month. . . . It was an almost grotesque conveyance from the shed of an inferior renter.

"The queen's carriage!" shouted ten young boys in unison.

Pritchard walked up to her to kiss her hand. She threw a few coins up in the air. They all jostled each other to pick them up shouting, "Long live la Reine Pomaré!"

The short man was on the seat next to the driver, who wore a hat adorned with the same flashy braid and brown frock coat. Add to that a white horse and a bay one. The interior of the barouche was adorned in some old faded red fabric.

We arrived at the Café Anglais.

"Which room do you want?"

"The large parlor."

It was beginning to be cold, so she requested a fire. Kindling was lit. . . .

"The first cold days are painful," she told me, pale as a ghost.

"Keep your shawl on," I told her.

But she did nothing of the sort. She was wearing a light blue taffeta dress that clashed with her shawl.

She coughed once or twice. She picked up a glass of chilled champagne and gulped it down. Her eyes were shining and color was returning to her cheeks.

Then she was asked to sing a song, of her own composition she said, that passed in review all the gods of mythology.

Her voice was weak. She was accompanying herself on the piano.

She received untold compliments. I was paid very little attention. She talked, smoked; she stood up to everyone. She had an inexhaustible mind and a peerless originality.

The night continued thus. When we left, it was daylight.

At that time of day there are only sweepers and ragmen in the streets. The former, leaning on their brooms, look at you, and each is probably saying to himself, "What these lunatics have just spent in one night would allow me to live for a year."

Sometimes they are handed some money, but more often they are not even noticed.

We were crossing the boulevard when a woman swept some dirt over Pomaré's legs. The queen called her stupid.

The woman with the broom joined in.

"So, look at that, her pesky ladyship! I have been your better, my little one, but I was not proud with the poor people!"

We were already far off.

"See you this afternoon!" said Pomaré. "Rue Gaillon, 19. If you forget the number, ask in the street for la Reine Pomaré."

I thought this boast was marvelous.

10

A "Queen's" Destiny

She Wanted to Be a Nun . . . — Those Roguish Journalists! —
The Kind Young Man from Toulouse — Hired at the Hippodrome —
No More Kind Young Man (from Toulouse) — Camille

AT ELEVEN O'CLOCK I was at my new friend's house. I expected to
see a luxuriously furnished boudoir, but I was surprised to find myself
in a kennel. Anyway that was my reaction to Pomaré's apartment, it was
so messy and dirty.

She lived in a large, sparsely furnished room; her chest of drawers
was covered with a multitude of little objects, souvenirs of her triumphs
at the Mabille dance hall.

Each object was covered with an inch of dust. On a table papers lay
in disarray next to a pile of issues of *Charivari*. Her blue dress was lying
on the floor.

I noticed, hanging on the wall, a plaster Virgin adorned with a little
necklace and a crown. On the mantle the queen had put her hat in
a plate.

She was still in bed, head bare, and hair tousled.

"Forgive me," she said, "my housework is not done yet. The person
I rent from is supposed to do everything and does nothing."

She jumped out of bed and went into a sort of anteroom whose window looked out on a courtyard. She called her porter, who was also her
landlord. He came up.

"Fix us some lunch."

"Certainly, but give me some money."

"I do not have any."

"Now, really," said the old man, "you must have at least twenty sous."

"No," she said, "not a farthing left."

"Well, then, go have lunch wherever you wish, but I am not extending
you any more credit."

"Now, do not be mean! I invited a friend; I cannot send her away."

"Is that right?" said the old man. "Not only you want me to feed you, but I have to feed others as well."

And he went downstairs fussing.

I had heard everything and I was quite embarrassed. She did not lose her composure and told me, as she came back into the room, that we were going to eat out because, as the concierge just let her know, her domestic was not back.

That was really something. I bit my lip to keep from bursting out laughing. I had seen her the night before throwing at least ten francs in change. Obviously she was mad.

SHE WANTED TO BE A NUN . . .

I asked Pomaré to wait for me. I went downstairs, and a few minutes later I returned with everything we needed for lunch.

"I shall reimburse you soon for everything you spent," she said with incredible audacity.

I asked her a couple of questions about her past, but she changed the subject without answering.

And yet I really wanted to know.

"All right," she said after lunch, "you are a sweet girl; promise me you will not tell anyone, and I shall confess all to you."

I promised, and she began.

"I came into the world in Paris in 1825. My father was rich and I was his first child. He had approximately 150,000 francs of capital invested in a theater and it paid fifteen, sometimes twenty percent in interest. I was placed in one of the first boarding schools of Paris. My mother had given me two brothers and two sisters, yet they did not curtail what my parents spent on me. I was seventeen when I heard at the boarding school that there had been a terribly destructive fire on Boulevard du Temple. Two days later my father came to see me. He had been crying.

" 'I am broke,' he told me. 'The fire ate everything up. My poor Lise, I had no insurance!'

" 'Do not worry about me, dear father. You know very well that my deepest desire is to be a nun,' I told him.

" 'No,' he said hugging me tight, 'your mother is almost mad with grief. You must comfort her, help her. I am here to bring you home.'

"Back home, I found everyone in deep despair.

"My mother was slightly out of her head, so I had to take care of the children.

"Soon we were so poor that we let the maid go and I was left to do everything by myself.

"A young man that my father had in his employ often came to the house. He told me so often that he loved me that I gave myself to him without much resistance.

"One day my father came home. I was talking to my lover at the door. My father asked him to visit me in the presence of my mother or himself from now on.

"After a while I began to feel ill and weak. There was a doctor in our building, so I went up to tell him about my symptoms. He looked at me and said, 'You are big with child. That is not a dangerous condition.'

"I ran to see the one who had ruined me. He could think of only one way to save me: destroy my child.

"I took to my room to write. I saw my Virgin Mary and I promised her to live for my punishment and for the poor little creature I was carrying in my body.

"I packed a bag, kissed my brothers and sisters, and left in desperation. I turned into a deserted street and read Furnished House. I spoke to the mistress of the house and explained my situation to the woman, and I pleaded with her so that she eventually relented. I was lodged in an attic.

"I asked where women about to give birth were taken in. I was directed to the maternity ward. I went, but I was told that they took women just two weeks before their delivery date. I was only three months pregnant. . . .

"Little by little, I sold all my possessions. When I had nothing left, I asked for work in the house. I was given clothes to mend and housework to do. The woman at whose house I was residing wanted me to work fifteen hours a day for a piece of bread.

"After much pain I gave birth to a boy. He was so frail that I always listened for his breathing. I was told not to breast-feed him, but I did not listen. I was given a little money, some baby clothes, and I left with my precious bundle in my arms.

"I returned to my hole. I worked a little. My poor child was quite pale. When he was ten months old he would hold his arms out to me. I was happy. However, since I did not deserve this happiness, it was of short duration.

"Although I held him against my heart, his little limbs were contorted, his face was turning bluish. I covered him with kisses.

"This awful struggle went on for a week, then he had an attack, and his body went limp. . . . I thought he was resting.

"For a long time I waited for him to wake up. I picked him up. He was stiff and cold.

"So I ran down the stairs shouting that I wanted a doctor, that my child could not be dead without me.

"I followed my son to the Montparnasse cemetery. I had a sign put on his casket so he could be taken out of the common grave when I would have the means to buy him a cross and a marker.

"For two weeks I was wildly distraught. People took turns taking me in. Some nice young men, to cheer me, took me out for dinner, drinks, and then to Mabille. That is the first time you saw me, wearing the black wool dress. I am proud of myself. Very soon, I shall be rich. I am already fashionable."

She had told me this all at once, and in the most natural manner. From then on, my opinion of her was very different from the one I had first formed.

Even her sweet name, Lise, always retained a certain mysterious warmth.

I took leave of her convinced that she had moments of madness, but feeling that I had become very fond of her.

THOSE ROGUISH JOURNALISTS!

My relationship with Adolphe was gradually getting colder.

Adolphe was certainly not a vulgar character. He was funny, but he was fickle in love and did not have in his heart the kind of feverish passion or the sensitive charm that could long fascinate a woman caught in life's whirlwind as I was.

My visits to Versailles were becoming rarer. When he saw that there was no recourse left, he decided to sign up as surgeon with a regiment leaving Paris.

I preferred the company of Lise, whose whimsical imagination was infectious. However, in my opinion she had one big drawback, that of being closely attached to Rose Pompon.

This short woman had an adorable face and horrible manners. She said any old thing, would spit in your face when she spoke, and dressed like a pile of twigs. She was miserly, oh, how she was miserly! Pompon was pregnant, so Pomaré sent a doctor to her, had the child baptized, and bought baby clothes since Pompon said she had no income. During her absence, Pomaré went to look for something in one of Pompon's chests of drawers. And what did she find, hidden in some stockings? Ten gold louis coins and some jewelry!

The summer balls were closed so I no longer saw Lise, who was getting ready to dance the polka at the Palais-Royal.

My friends encouraged me to take advantage of my success at Mabille. They told me that the time had come for me to try the stage again.

I was accompanied to the Théâtre Beaumarchais, where I was received most kindly once I said that my name was Mogador.

I was hired. The next day I was rehearsing in a revue where I played myself and at the end danced the mazurka. My costume was adorable. My debut was the same night as Pomaré's.

The next day I learned that Pomaré had been outrageously booed. I read a few newspapers where she was covered with derogatory compliments and snide remarks. Journalists treat women like governments.

There used to be only one or two public dance halls. Why are there ten today? Because of the celebrities that the journalists amused themselves in creating during their spare time. Flashy fame caused much jealousy. Thousands of young girls were drawn to those public dance halls by the phony glamour!

Pomaré had a carriage, so they all wanted one, and many did have one. Every day ten new, elegant, and bold young women would be strolling on the Champs-Elysées.

The vaudeville and theater directors, always on the lookout for passions to exploit successfully, had put prostitution on the stage.

During two hundred performances, all of Paris swooned over the tender generosity and the distress of a courtesan; then one day some other vaudeville and theater directors, catching the new trend, had placed us in the pillory of opinion.

Journalists have done those things forgetting that during another era they had beaten brass drums at the door of the Ranelagh, the Bal Mabille, the Asnières ball.

As long as I lived amid this excitement I certainly did not have time to think about my pain nor that of others. Today when I remember how the women who were the most brilliant, the most adored have ended up, I believe that, as in the little drama *Victorine,* if they could be shown their future in a dream, they would all recoil.

THE KIND YOUNG MAN FROM TOULOUSE

Pomaré must have been downhearted about the reviews, so I went to see her. In those days, she lived at 25 Rue de la Michodière, on the mezzanine floor. The house, a furnished residence, was neat and comfortable. Lise was very elegant.

"Oh well!" she said laughing. "My beginning looks a lot like an ending. At the Palais-Royal I have had the kind of success that Lola Montès had. Several in the audience had had perforated keys forged, and they vigorously blew through them; the sound drowned out the orchestra. My dancing was off the cadence!"

"Other than that," I said, "you are happy?"

"Yes," she replied, "look."

She opened a wardrobe and showed me a lot of clothes, which I admired not without a certain amount of envy.

"I am not worried," she said. "I am living with a young man from Toulouse whom I love and is all I could wish for. He works at the post office to please his parents, who want him to have an occupation, but which he does not need since he is quite rich."

"Good! I am pleased."

"Oh! I do not have long to live, so I want to have a good time and not have any regrets."

I left. I saw her that evening in a orchestra loge with a small man with curly dirty-blond hair and glasses. He seemed very attentive to her.

She sent word asking me to join them for dinner the next day. Before he arrived she told me that she could not stand him, but that he loved her so much that she felt sorry for him.

"You see, mademoiselle," he told me that night as he was taking me back home, "right now I cannot do everything I want to do for her, but I am going to come into a lot of money from some property I am selling. I shall give her everything."

A few days later I heard someone in the foyer of the theater say that Pomaré had been arrested as an accomplice in a theft.

An old matron was saying, "Of course! Tarts like that, they will do anything."

"Oh," replied an ugly, dried-up thirty-year-old ingénue, "if I were the judge, I would sentence her to life in prison."

"It would be necessary," I said, "to put all the even merely pretty women in prison. Then there would be a shortage and maybe you would find a position."

As soon as the performance was over, I rushed over to Rue de la Michodière. The mistress of the house told me, "Yesterday a nicely dressed man came to my door and asked me which one was Mlle Lise's room and how she lived. I thought he was her father, whom she fears so much, and I replied that I had no idea how she lived. After that he signaled to two other men who also came in, and the three of them went up to her door, motioning for me to follow them. I could see that they were policemen. Lise opened the door in her chemise.

" 'Get dressed,' one of these men said, while the others inspected the furniture and took some papers. 'You are going to follow us.'

" 'Follow you!' said Lise. 'But where to?'

" 'To the prefecture, of course!'

" 'But, monsieur, I have not done anything wrong.'

" 'That is for the magistrate to decide.'

"She ran into the next room where she probably wanted to pick up a knife, but she was caught before she could open a drawer. Almost naked, she threw herself on the floor. I thought she was crazy! Faced with her despair, they began to treat her more gently.

" 'Come on child, do not fret this way. It is possible that nothing will be done to you.'

"And the three men picked her up off the floor and put her in a chair.

"Her eyes were vacant and she did not seem to hear anything. She got up, then, dry-eyed, got dressed in silence. We did not take our eyes off her. She asked me if Monsieur had come.

" 'No,' I told her, 'I have not seen him.'

"A carriage had been brought around. These gentlemen grabbed each of her arms and sat near her in the carriage. I saw her head jerk back. The carriage was off."

I could not get over what I had just learned. I was certain Lise was incapable of any act of dishonesty.

I made a few inquiries to get some news about her. Twenty times I went to her apartment, but I had to be careful because I, myself, was under surveillance.

HIRED AT THE HIPPODROME

During my saddest time I learned some more bad news.

On occasion I had seen at Adolphe's a young man who had a delightful mistress. Her name was Angéline. She had been registered when she was very young. She had understood what terrible position she had put herself in. So, without becoming a total prude, she lived very modestly with her lover, who knew nothing of her circumstances.

One day that I was returning from Lise's, I met this young man.

He told me, "Oh, you see before you a miserable man. Three days ago we organized a masked ball. There were about a dozen of us. We had a nice dinner before going to the Opera. Angéline was a little too expansive, and a policeman told her he was going to throw her out. My friend, with whom she was dancing, reacted, and there was an argument. They were taken to the station. When she had regained her composure, she was told that she would be taken to the police prefecture. She did not complain, she only asked if she could go home, saying that she could not appear before the magistrate dressed like a docker. She was taken home in a carriage. She asked the policemen to wait five minutes. These gentlemen became impatient and knocked. 'Come in,' she said. When they opened the door, they saw her disappear out the window, then they heard a body fall on the pavement. They found two letters. I was given this one."

He read it through his tears:

My poor friend, I am going to make a very painful jump at my age; I am not yet twenty. I shall not miss life but I shall miss you. See that I am buried. If I am not disfigured, give me a kiss. I am a registered girl. I have been hiding this fact from you for the two years we have been together. I was so afraid of displeasing you! I prefer to give my body back to the earth than to go to Saint-Lazare. Adieu!

"And she killed herself!" I said, moved to tears.

"No. She broke both her legs and she will be crippled the rest of her life. But I shall never leave her."

I decided Angéline was happier than I. After such a terrible accident, it was almost certain that she would be scratched from the register, whereas I . . . my blasted fame was increasing the obstacles.

I had not been able to bring myself to return to the prefecture with these women who must reregister every two weeks. Anywhere I was, I could be arrested.

Each time a man looked at me I thought I saw an inspector. I did not dare go out on foot at night.

One night my watch was stolen. I liked it very much. Well, out of fear that I would have to give my name, I did not dare report the theft.

When I began at Beaumarchais, I thought I was saved. Another illusion. They let me play and dance every night but . . . they were not giving me a permanent position.

I asked if that situation was going to go on much longer. I was told that the theater was going to close!

I was rescued from this bad situation by chance.

One day, for the lack of anything better to do, I went to see a dress merchant who lived at 16 Faubourg du Temple. I told her my problems.

At her house was an elderly man with gray hair, deep-set eyes, a curved nose, silver-rimmed glasses, and diamonds all over his fingers. He was the owner of the house.

This man seemed to be listening to me with interest.

"I believe, mademoiselle," he told me, "that I can offer you employment. I am looking for horsewomen for the Hippodrome."[1]

"Oh," Mme Alphonse said to me, "that is just what you need. You will learn how to ride in no time. They are going to open a magnificent racecourse at Barrière de l'Etoile."

I asked how much I would earn.

"That will depend on your aptitude and what you will learn how to do. For now, I can give you one hundred francs a month."

"I must admit," I said, "that is quite tempting. And you will give me an engagement?"

"Right away, if you wish."

"When is my first lesson?"

"Next week. As early as tomorrow I shall introduce you to my son."

When he was gone, Mme Alphonse told me, "You cannot lose since you will be learning how to ride a horse from the best riding teacher in Paris. M. Laurent Franconi is quite a remarkable man."[2]

Everything was arranged and signed the next day. My play was closing at Beaumarchais. I left the theater.

NO MORE KIND YOUNG MAN (FROM TOULOUSE)

I was very cheerful. I rushed over to Lise's house. She had been released the night before. She was so ashamed, she refused to see anyone. I walked up to the third floor. She was in a tiny room facing the courtyard.

The key was in the door, so I went in without knocking. I found her stretched out on a small cot of painted wood.

"Oh! My dear Céleste, I know you have come by several times. I am worn out. You did not think that I had stolen anything, did you?"

"No, since I am here. But tell me what happened, because it seems like a dream."

"Oh," she said, "a bad dream. You know how I was taken away. My papers were checked, and nothing was found that could lead anyone to believe that I was an accomplice of these men. For some months there had been complaints that money mailed through the post office was not reaching its destination. A month ago a young man went to a post office to cash a money order. There was also a man present who, expecting some money, was filing a complaint. This man heard his name and was quite astonished to see the young man sign for him and hold in his hand the letter of advice that he was surprised he had not received. The young man was arrested and searched. He had several opened letters containing money addressed to various people. He finally confessed everything. They were a group of seven or eight. One of them was a postal employee. That employee would steal each letter containing a check, and then the accomplices would claim the payment. You must have guessed who the postal employee was. You can understand the judge's suspicions. It was believed that I was also an accomplice!

"The dates were checked, and it was evident that he was already doing these types of withdrawals long before he knew me. It is quite a tawdry affair. His father is one of the most important personalities in Toulouse. What is going to become of me? I can never show my face again!"

CAMILLE

There was a knock at the door. I opened. It was a tall young man with blond hair.

"Is it possible to see Lise?"

"Oh! It is you, Camille. Come in," said Lise. "Camille *is* no one," she told me, laughing.

"No," said the young man. "I am nothing, and I wish that were not so, because you would not be here. Anyway, you are free. I am going, my guardian is waiting for me. I shall be back soon."

And I heard him skip down the stairs taking four steps at a time, like a schoolboy.

"Who is this young man?"

"He is just a child. He is nineteen. Everyday he repeats, 'You see, Lise, I do not love you like everyone else. If I wanted, perhaps by pleading just right, I could have you. Well, I do not want that to happen; it would pain me to have to share you. I shall be your friend. Once I officially become an adult, I shall have a lot of money. Then you will be mine only. I shall make you so happy that you will not miss your past life!' "

"Is it true that he will have a lot of money?"

"Oh! He is the son of an extremely rich merchant. His father, on his deathbed, entrusted him to a guardian who will not let him have his money until he is twenty-one."

"Well! Your future is secured."

"Do you believe that?" She struck her chest, coughed, and said, "Do you hear that? I do not have long to live."

11

The Hippodrome

Equestrienne—The Reverse of Fame—The Baron's
Narrow Failure—Timid Léon—Coin Toss for Me

HAVING THE TITLE of equestrienne was just the beginning; now it was a matter of learning the skill. I had as many as two and three lessons a day, including one hour of French trot.

I did not have much time for my friends. Brididi was the one who suffered most from this neglect.

A song had just been written about Pomaré. It was attributed to a very witty man.[1] It was sung to the tune of Rosita's waltz:

Oh, Pomaré, young and beautiful queen,
Do not ever lose your zest and vigor.
May you forever reign over the cancan
And may Chicard grow pale under your gaze!
Adorned with flowers, your Mabille throne
Rests solidly on the shoulders of young revelers.
Better by far to rule here than on the island
Where our colors will cease to shine.

I too had my poets. Brididi sent me an epistle in verse. Unfortunately he was a better dancer than he was a singer.

My work at the Hippodrome was taking me away from the world where I had met him.

EQUESTRIENNE

Finally my big moment arrived. On opening day I was supposed to participate in three exercises.

The first one was a horse walk, the second a speed race, and the third a deer hunt.

I was the first to enter ahead of a row of four horses. I wore a Jewish-style costume like all equestriennes. I could hear my name making the rounds: "Where is Mogador?" "Oh, there is Mogador!"

There must have been at least eight thousand people present. All of elegant Paris was there.

The sun, which on that day was shining on the flashy decor, warmed everyone's heart and cheered the audience, which was applauding wildly.

I was trembling, afraid I would not be able to hold on to my horse. My body was leaning forward when I felt a sharp blow on my back, and I heard M. Laurent Franconi admonish me, "Are you going to stand like that? Straighten up, please."

I jerked myself erect.

"Good! Now we look like a broomstick," he told me. "Sit deep in your saddle, body straight but not stiff, elbows in, head forward. Press your fingers gently . . . good! And do not be afraid, you have a good horse."

He patted it on the neck, then, walking by some man, he told him, "This one is my student. She is doing fine, but she has been studying for only two months."

This compliment pleased me but did not stop my heart from beating so hard I thought I would stop breathing.

"Go!"

My horse took me away. I rested against his neck, like jockeys do. I spoke to him out loud and he speeded up. . . . I was about to over-take my companions, maybe even win the race! I made my horse swerve toward the rope in a curve. . . . I cut in front of the one nearest me and passed her! I let my horse take the lead and I spurred his left side. I squeezed my knees tighter. I went around one more time. I was stopped and handed the bouquet. I had won! My instructor shared my joy.

Once off their horses, my companions tried to pick a quarrel with me. They insinuated that I had almost knocked them over, that it was against the rules to cut in front. . . . I think they were right, but I dis-missed them and went to dress for the hunt.

I mounted a stable horse named Aboukir. I made him prance.

A deer was released.

This hunt attained the sort of success the organizers of this spec-tacle probably had not imagined. When the dogs were loosed, instead of rushing after the deer, they began to run in all directions, committing acts of impropriety on our dress hems and our horses' legs. We were doubled over with laughter. Finally the deer was put on the right track and the dogs followed the trail.

The deer, tired, retraced its steps and strode toward the dogs. Now they were being chased!

After the performance I was more triumphant than a conquering general. I was holding my bouquet in my arms so everyone could see it.

THE REVERSE OF FAME

Back home I asked my doorman to put up a notice; I could not live so far away. The next day I found a little fifth-floor apartment at 1 Faubourg Saint-Honoré. It had a room with two windows facing the front, a room facing the back, and a kitchen.

I started a little garden on the gutter, which jutted out about a foot.

I no longer saw Denise and Marie. Their lives were not any more moral than mine, they were just mingling in other circles.

During the worst time of my life, I had met a tall girl to whom I gave a bit of advice that I always practiced.

I know that an elegant life of vice is still a life of vice, but I always thought that, even when a woman is wicked, it is to her advantage to seek the company of cultivated men. The ideal would be to be good, but, when that is not possible, it is preferable to be the mistress of a man of good taste rather than a boor, of a witty man rather than a dullard. This discrimination has allowed me, in spite of my moral decadence, to enjoy the pleasures of the mind, the refinements of art, and to form among the upper echelons of each social group propitious connections and durable friendships.

The woman to whom I gave this advice had known how to put it to good use. She had met a wealthy man who, of the opinion that her neck and her arms were too long, covered them with diamonds to hide this deformity.

Under the pretext that we were neighbors, she invited me up to her place and spent the day showing me her valuables.

She had a great passion for actors and spent all her evenings in little theaters. It is said that she had dropped many a diamond from her bracelet in the dressing rooms of her favorites.

She invited me to have dinner with her and then see a play that night. She said she would lend me a shawl to keep me warm. This kindness touched me and I said to myself, "She is indeed a nice person!"

I was quickly disabused of this notion. She could not go to the theater alone; she had to have a companion. She could not wear all her shawls at once; she had to have a mannequin.

She took me to dine in a small restaurant on Rue du Temple. There were many actors, and they approached our table. We were served some soup. I was about to start eating when, holding my arm back, she told me in her boisterous voice, "Be careful, you are going to stain my shawl!"

I turned purple. That was her only reason for lending it to me.

She still continued to try forming a friendship with me. To further enhance this friendship, she even came up with the craziest and most eccentric idea: she would introduce me as her sister.

In reality, she latched on to me because my name was Mogador.

A few days later "my sister" asked me to accompany her to an actors' soiree. She generously put her whole wardrobe at my disposal. I refused. She then came up with a little scheme. She bought me what I needed and told me, "Here, all this is yours." So of course I thought she was giving it to me. The offer included a nosegay, long gloves, and a carriage rented for the night.

A few days later she handed me an invoice for one hundred francs! I made her wait. She became angry and made a scene in front of everyone.

One day I was at the theater in a loge with six other people. She asked to come in and demanded out loud, "Hey you, when are you going to pay me back?"

One of the persons there asked me how much I owed her and paid my debt for me. From that moment on, there was a complete rift between us.

She would go around saying, "'My sister' and I are mad at each other."

THE BARON'S NARROW FAILURE

I had learned some new routines at the Hippodrome. In particular there was an obstacle race that almost had dire consequences for me. I was riding a lovely and highly spirited chestnut mare. She would tremble a whole hour before going on, and when the gate was opened, she was already in a full sweat.

One day she had puffed herself up while she was being saddled. No one checked on her before the start. Once we had taken off, I felt myself tilt to one side. I wanted to stop, but I was right in front of a hedge. She jumped. I tried to throw myself to the side so I would not be dragged under her feet. I fell on the track, past the hedge. All those who were coming up behind me jumped over me as well as the hedge.

Those few seconds were frightful for me and for the spectators. I had sprained my foot.

There was talk of nothing but our bravery. We were forging on with truly frightening boldness. Often the audience would yell, "Enough, enough!"

Every day there were accidents that should surely have resulted in a death. Well, instead we would merely suffer a few bruises.

The ever growing number of my admirers represented a much more formidable danger for me. I was neither so kind nor so stupid as to give myself. I quickly realized that gallantry is like war; to win one must employ tactics. I have always been capricious and proud. Among the women who are prone to say "yes," no one enjoys saying "no" more than I. That is why the men who obtained the most from me were the ones who demanded the least.

Most of them would send me go-betweens. In a single week I was visited by countless numbers of women who would come tell me of my conquests and try to negotiate alliance treaties. But I refused to have anything to do with these women. And so, furious, they would go back down the five flights of stairs. When they reported on their mission, they were not believed, because, I blush in admitting this, the conquest of Mogador seemed so easy.

I was glad that I chose to act as I did. Opinions about me began to change. I was continually courted but now with more delicacy.

A young Dutch baron was among those whose emissaries were so poorly received. He told of his defeat to "my sister."

"Introduce yourself on my recommendation," she told him with her usual self-confidence. "You will be assured of an excellent welcome."

He believed her and came to see me.

It was at an inopportune time: I still held the flowers of triumph against my breast. But he handled the situation intelligently. Guessing my true feelings for "my sister," he admitted to me that he could not stand her, and he said so many bad things about her that I began listening to him. I held a few spiteful opinions that were begging to be uttered. With the help of malicious gossip, the baron left with my permission to return.

It is possible that once again, in spite of myself, I would have yielded to the indirect influence of "my sister." But the baron was abruptly called back to The Hague.

I went back to my work at the Hippodrome.

The fashionable young men, or those who aspired to be, had their own entrance next to the stables. One of them was attentive to me with stubborn perseverance. He was a thin, dark-haired young man, very meticulous in his dress. He was always staring at me but he had never dared speak to me.

I asked one of my friends, "Who is this young man who faints every time I miss a step?"

"My dear," replied Hermance, a pretty, petite English girl who wore a wig, "he is the son of a pharmacist."

"If you do not give him a little help," another one said to me, "he will never dare speak to you. He is very rich. His father is an important manufacturer of locomotives!"

I mounted my horse and entered the arena. My saddle was wobbly. I stopped in front of the large grandstand. While my horse was being girthed, I heard muffled sounds of compliments, always pleasing to a woman's ears. I spurred my mare and came in first by half a length. When I returned to the stables, I saw my admirer, who was very pale. He came toward me and said, "Oh! You scared me so much! Ten times I thought I saw you falling."

I had the unfortunate notion to reply that he was too kind.

From that moment on I could not get rid of him. He followed me to the door of my dressing room. I slammed it in his face. He came to see me the next day and finally would not budge. He was so in love that I was tempted to be lenient, in spite of my abhorrence of stupid people.

His name was Léon.

I had become a skillful equestrienne.

I filed a request for my freedom with the prefect. I was summoned and was told that there had not been enough time, and that if the Hippodrome were to close, I had no means of livelihood. Once more women came to me with propositions. I was afraid those women were sent by the police, and so I was even more unpleasant with them than the first ones.

COIN TOSS FOR ME

One evening I had gone to the Ranelagh with Angèle, one of my companions from the Hippodrome. A flower vendor brought me some magnificent roses.

"From these gentlemen," she said, pointing out two men seated a few feet from us; one was blond, with an ordinary face, the other, a handsome fellow, younger and more impudent.

I left the flowers on a chair without looking at those who had sent them.

They approached us. The younger of the two spoke up and was addressing me, "Do you like flowers? I regret to be offering you such ugly ones. If you would allow me, I shall send you some other ones."

I responded with a slight nod and a little pout.

"I see, mademoiselle, that you do not like to chat. That is sometimes a sign of intelligence."

And he came nearer, so near that he set his chair on my dress. I pointed the fact out to him and asked him to back off.

"No," he replied, "I tore it; I shall send you another one. The duke and I saw you riding and we both fell in love. We tossed a coin for you. I lost. The duke sent you one of his friends but you sent her away. Thinking that he had given up hope, I did as he did. I did not have better luck.

"And that surprised you?"

"Yes, we had bet fifty gold louis."

He said all this with such impudence that I took a dislike to him.

"There is certainly no more innocent distraction than this one. For the stakes to be interesting for you, you should have confirmed my consent, but that condition was missing from your wager. In fact, I shall admit that, if I had had to make a choice, I would have agreed with chance."

I did not realize that, in order to tell him something unpleasant, I was making an outright declaration to his friend.

The duke asked if he could come see me. I acquiesced, emphasizing loudly, "That would please me greatly," for his benefit, and the other little man left the place saying, "That comes from being a duke and having an allowance of three hundred thousand francs."

We were left alone, and the duke continued the conversation.

"What a difficult person my friend is! He is charming but a little conceited. He thinks that when I am preferred, it is because of my fortune. That has made me contentious, and I have come to believe it myself."

The provocation was direct, and I affably resigned myself to telling the duke that he was wrong to doubt himself this way.

He offered me his arm for a walk around the garden. That flattered my vanity, and it was a way to exasperate his friend, whom I resented for his cruelty.

The thought of revealing my failings makes me happier than I ever was at the thought of experiencing them. There must be some mysterious connection between decency and education to awaken a sleeping conscience in this way.

My liaison with the duke placed me in a totally new position.[2] . . . I became too elegant to avoid making enemies. I lacked nothing, not even the envy of my fellow equestriennes.

The duke was still on good terms with his friend, who never lost his self-confidence nor his hopes, and who would say to me, "You will come back to me!"

"Never!" I would reply.

And I was true to my word.

He consoled himself with Angèle.

12

Lise's Yellow Dress

To Appease Eulalie—Léon Becomes Bolder, but
Moderately—Help for a Despondent Man—Léon's Duel—
Lagie and Her Englishman—The Jewish Pianist—A Duke Does
Not Necessarily Bring Happiness—The Tenor Tormented by
Love—Vaudeville and *Bel Canto*—Flowers on a Cradle

WHENEVER SOMETHING good or something bad would happen to me, my great comfort was to go see Lise, so I could share with her my joy or my distress. Her landlady gave me her new address under condition of secrecy because Lise still refused to see anyone. Her apartment was on the fifth floor at 107 Champs-Elysées.

Lise was on her bed, a lit candle close by for her cigarette, a book in her hand.

"So, it is you! It is sweet of you to come by, but if the other one comes in, she is going to scream, she cannot stand you."

"Whose house is this?"

"But of course, you do not know. . . . You can imagine that after my arrest I did not dare go out; then one day I was told that a young woman wanted to speak to me urgently. If I had been standing, I would have fallen flat on my face. It was my sister. I was amazed by her elegance. I asked her,

" 'What do you want from me, Eulalie? My father is behind you, is he not?'

" 'Goodness, how stupid you are! He does not know where I am, so he could not have followed me here.'

" 'What, you mean you ran away?'

" 'Yes. Since your departure, everything has been going from bad to worse. Maxime took me away. Since he does not have much, I went to

112

work at the Hippodrome. I am staying at the Champs-Elysées, number 107. If you want, you can share my room.'

"Would you believe it? It hurt me terribly to know that my sister was a fallen woman, but I did not have the right to scold her, and in any case, it would have been futile.

"At the hotel I owed quite a bit of money and had no funds to pay with. In lieu of payment I had to leave my things, and I moved here with two chemises, some slippers, and the dress I have on. I said I was going to the country, not moving.

"Still, I must get out of this situation. I am dependent on my sister. She let me move in with her, but she regrets it. First of all, she is not rich and she is stingy. Yesterday she chastised me for buying a packet of cigarette paper!

"After every scene I pick up my two chemises and start to pack. Eulalie starts to laugh, and I stay, promising to be neat, something I cannot get used to. She follows me all day with a towel to wipe even my footprints. And so, as you can see, I stay in bed. . . . That way I do not mess up anything."

TO APPEASE EULALIE

I had to stifle a laugh, because the bed, the side table, the whole bedroom was a total wreck. Everywhere books, torn cigarette paper thrown here and there, tobacco, ashes . . .

"Oh, my dear," I said, "she is seldom pleasant, your Eulalie. I have often seen her at the Hippodrome, unaware that she was your sister, and I have already had one or two squabbles with her."

"Stay a little longer. She is not due home just yet. She is at Maxime's, and anyway, I know how to put her in a good mood."

She began to tidy up around her, wiping the table with her only dress.

"Well, my dear Lise, since you are so unhappy here, do you want a way out? I shall lend you all I can. If you want to come live with me—"

"No," she replied, "I prefer a friend to money. If I were indebted to you, we might have a falling out. . . . I love you very much, but your happiness, if you were happier than I, would end up distressing me."

The door opened. Eulalie seemed quite surprised to see me. Pomaré lost her composure. I was doubly surprised since I have known few women with as imposing a bearing as Pomaré!

Eulalie was an average-sized girl, plump, with a cold demeanor. Of another I would say she had a look of stupidity, but she was extremely clever. Even though she probably was no more than seventeen years old, she looked twenty-five.

"My dear friend, you seem surprised to find me here, but I had left the Hippodrome and as I walked by, I saw Lise at the window, so I came up."

She looked at me without greeting me and said to her sister, "I had forbidden you to open my window."

Lise was astounded by this autocratic tone. I went on most calmly, "Had I not seen Lise, I would have come up anyway. I wanted to ask you a favor."

"Me?"

"Yes, I heard you complain many times that you were not asked to race." She turned purple because I was bringing up a touchy subject. "Well! If you had the opportunity to be noticed in some steeple-chase, I am sure that you would be allowed to continue in Hermance's place."

"I know that well," she said, "but they will not let me try."

"I am offering you a way. I am leaving in a few days. I would like for one of my companions to do my routine for a couple of weeks."

She was beaming.

"I would like that," she said. "Just make sure they will consent."

"Oh, I have a way of forcing them. I shall not notify them. One day I shall not be there and you will be ready. They will have no choice."

"Oh my!" she said. "I must go see Maxime, who was not home earlier."

When Eulalie was gone, Lise told me, "You were saying a while ago that when she was on horseback you thought she looked like a water pitcher!"

"My dear, this was the only way. If I suggested her to them, they would laugh in my face. There is one hitch, however: I am not leaving. But I hope that in ten days you will not be here anymore."

LÉON BECOMES BOLDER, BUT MODERATELY

Once I was back home, I sent a note to the Hotel des Princes for a young man named Manby with whom I had spent several evenings at Lise's. He came right away.

"You are very kind to have come, my dear friend; I need to ask you a favor."

"Anything you wish, just so you let me kiss you."

"Now, now, no silliness! Lise is miserable. She wants nothing from me, but from you, she will accept everything. She must not continue to live with her sister who treats her like a dog."

"My dear," he said, "I surrender my fortune to you. I only have ten louis on me, and here they are. . . ."

The next day I ran over to Lise's full of joy. I was telling myself, "She is going to rent a room, give one hundred francs to her hotel, and she will be out of difficulties."

I told her what I had done. She seemed glad.

"Let us go do some shopping," she told me. "I have a lot of little things to buy."

I wanted to say "Go slow!"

We stopped at the Bayadères, on the boulevard. I waited for her in the carriage. She returned an hour later with a package.

"Oh! Look at the pretty color."

And she showed me some taffeta the color of corn.

"What is this?"

"It is a dress."

"Yes, and how much did it cost?"

"One hundred and sixty francs."

I thought she was totally mad. I decided that I was not going to take care of her anymore. I leaned back in the carriage.

Our cab was not going fast and we were renting it by the hour. I went to Faubourg Saint-Honoré and she to the Champs-Elysées.

"Are you going to leave angry at me," said Lise, "because I bought an apricot dress? I could not resist. I want to go to the Ranelagh Thursday. I am going to wear a short cape to match my dress and a straw hat. Everyone will think I have become rich. If I do not put on something flashy, I shall not be asked to dance."

I could not forgive her this extravagance, since until now, when I was ahead by twenty francs, I would buy ten yards of calico at twelve sous to sew some chemises.

"Now, let us make peace," she said as she was leaving. "Give me your hand and promise me to come by for me Thursday at eight."

"That means I have to go pick you up in a carriage. Well! We shall go, but do not get used to this."

I entered my alleyway and was about to go up my five flights of stairs when my doorman handed me a large bouquet of extremely rare flowers.

"Some people came asking for you, then someone came from the police."

I hid my face in the bouquet as if I were smelling it. He lifted his glasses and said to his wife, "How did he put it, the policeman?"

"He said that if by tomorrow you have not removed the flowers from your window, you will be fined."

I flew up the stairs like a bird. I wanted nothing to do with the police. I opened my window, looked at my little flowers growing so pretty.

"Dear sweet pea, nasturtium, and morning glory, must I destroy you?" I placed my beautiful bouquet next to them and it seemed ugly to me. I threw it in the bedroom and I kissed my mignonette and my pansies. The doorbell startled me. I threw myself on my garden and frantically ripped everything out.

The doorbell rang louder. I went to open the door.

It was Léon. The duke had forbidden me to see him, but in the spirit of independence, I did not comply.

"Oh," he said, picking up my bouquet, "I understand why you are plucking your garden; it is no longer worthy of you. Is it your duke who sent you this?"

And the bouquet went rolling once more. That did not please me. I picked it up. I have always taken up for those who are not present.

"I told you I wanted to be free, that I was not attached to anyone."

"You are mean, Céleste. Hermance asked me to go see her. . . ."

"Well, go! I am not keeping you."

My quarrels with Léon were scenes in three episodes. First he was impertinent, then he became smug, and finally he surrendered.

It was now the smug cycle.

He looked at himself with an air of satisfaction. He examined his trousers purchased in London, his tasteful vest, his impeccably cut frock coat. Pretentiousness and simpering airs in a man have always repelled me. I remained icily silent.

Meanwhile I had removed my crate, cut the ropes, and demolished my garden.

"Why do you work so hard at removing these flowers?" asked Léon.

"Because I received notice to remove them."

"From whom?"

"The police. I have my reasons for not wanting to be fined."

"You do not have any money? I would be happy to be your banker."

I told him I was going to the Ranelagh the next day. He sent a carriage for me.

I went to pick up Lise at the time agreed upon. She told me that young Camille had come to see her and that he was still the same.

"Well, good! I have confidence in him."

"Yes. He always tells me, 'I would not want you for anything in the world.' I tried once to make a liar of him, and he ran like Joseph."

"Try to hold on to that devotion!"

"By the way, what about you, what are you doing about Léon? Why is he not going out with you?"

"Because I do not want to anymore. The other day at eleven, I was going to the Hippodrome and he offered to accompany me. I pointed out to him that someone might see him, that it would not look good for his family. He put on an insouciant air and said he was not afraid. Once we were near Rue de Chaillot, he let go of my arm and began to run as if a thief were after him. A few people came up to me to find out what was going on. Since I was embarrassed, I also fled. Once back home, I found him on my doorstep, his hands in his pockets, and he was whistling. 'My dear,' he told me, 'I saw my mother and my grandfather walking toward me. I would have been in fine straits if they had seem me with Mogador on my arm!' That is why we shall not go out together anymore."

HELP FOR A DESPONDENT MAN

We made a splendid entrance. I did not have on a yellow dress, but my waist was so slender that everyone was remarking about it out loud. Since then Lise has been tightening herself because it really hurt her feelings.

The evening was filled with laughter. People were beginning to get used to us. The upstanding women looked at us without too much anger. The young lions were still shunning our quadrille and refused to pair up with us for fear, they said, of making a spectacle of themselves like Brididi. They would position themselves a little farther away. But they got bored, even stopped dancing under the pretext that the shouts prevented them from hearing the beat. They ended up vying with each other to dance with us.

A big dinner was organized. Several carriages followed one another, and we arrived like a wedding party at the Café Anglais, which rocked all night to the sound of our laughter, our cries, and our songs.

Pomaré would often glance my way with envy. I had a pretty voice and the charm of youth. She was hurt by the compliments I received.

At this dinner was a young man called Gustave whose preoccupied look I had noticed.

"But what is on your mind?" his friends would ask him.

"I am thinking about this poor Alphonse who is lonesome while we are having fun."

"And who is this Alphonse?" I asked.

"He is a man of talent."

"He is sick?"

"No, but he suffers from ennui."

"We must descend upon him."

"That is an idea. . . ."

The next day we received an invitation from M. Alphonse R——.[1] It had been suggested to him that he invite a few friends. He gave a tea party just to see us. He had been told so much about our joyous spirits that he let himself be coaxed.

We arrived with Lise at nine in the evening at Rue de La Bruyère.

The host was tall, thin, with pale hollow cheeks. He walked toward us, thanking us for sacrificing one evening to his shadow, invited us to sit down, and offered us fruits, cakes, and tea. Then sitting down in a chair, he remained motionless.

His friend Gustave was near him. A mother would not have been more attentive.

"Alphonse, what are you thinking about? You promised to be cheerful. It is time to get la Reine Pomaré to sing."

Lise heard him and, deeming this fashion of disposing of her a little cavalier, frowned. M. Gustave jovially went up to her.

"Mademoiselle, would you be kind enough to sing something for us?"

"No," said Lise rather dryly. "I am much less interesting than you think."

M. Alphonse R—— joined his friend in such a gracious manner that, in my opinion, it would have seemed in poor taste to require more coaxing.

"Oh," I told Lise, "you cannot refuse now."

"So it is for you?" she asked Alphonse.

She sang with incredible exuberance and verve. Alphonse appeared to be having a great time. Lise, who was as whimsical as the moon, had forgotten her moment of ill humor.

There was music. A short young man sat at the piano. Hearing his first notes, I detected a maestro. He was blond; his hair was frizzy and his eyes were blue. His hands were flying over the keyboard with incredible delicacy and nimbleness.

When he finished playing, unanimous applause rang out.

I took advantage of the noise to ask M. Gustave who this young man was.

"He is H—— the composer, H—— the young prodigy![2] I shall introduce him to you."

He walked over to him, took his hand, and brought him to me. I thought I saw M. H—— blush.

"I am grateful to my friend," he told me in a slight German accent that was not at all unpleasant, "for bringing me to you. Since the first day I saw you, and that was quite a while back, I wanted to get to know you."

I asked him with some concern where he had seen me.

"Oh, I saw you on horseback, and my heart has been racing with you since that day!"

He said good-bye and left.

M. Gustave told me quietly, "He has a lot of talent, but he would have even more if earlier his parents, who are Jewish, had not worn him out to exploit his aptitude. At the age of eight, he was giving concerts."

"What, he is Jewish?" I said with a slight feeling of revulsion.

I know that it is not debatable, and that I, more than anyone, have no business being prejudiced, but nevertheless as a child I hated Jews. There were many of them in the neighborhood where we lived. My mother always had reason to complain about them. When I lived Rue du Temple, a Jewish family lived on the second floor and I often played with the two children. On their Sunday, which is our Saturday, Jews must not touch money. They would ask me to start their fireplaces and do their shopping. The eldest daughter died. It was a Friday. I went in on Saturday as usual. I heard voices. I looked through the glass door and saw the dead girl naked as a worm. Her mother was washing her face and her chest. Her little sister was washing her feet. I did not understand the customs of this religion, but the event frightened me.

Poor H—— invited everyone to spend the evening at his house, Rue de Provence. Everyone accepted. To tease him, I told him that I had an engagement.

"In that case, let us do it another day," he said so loudly and so quickly that I regretted refusing.

"No, I shall cancel my dinner and I shall go to your house."

He implored me, "Do not miss it, that would hurt me greatly!"

There was only one child of Israel in this group, and he was the one falling in love with me.

M. Alphonse wanted us to come over the next day. Lise definitely had found a potion against his sadness.

LÉON'S DUEL

Léon came to see me; he was very pale.

"What is the matter?"

"Yesterday I had an argument at Tortoni's. I have to duel tomorrow."

"You!" I said skeptically. "And why must you duel?"

"Because . . . yesterday, there was talk of you . . . in terms that disgusted me. One of those men, whom I called a coward, had thrown a five hundred franc bill on the table saying, 'Here is the key to her heart.' I replied that I would use his bill as a weapon to smash his head."

"My dear friend, I do not want you to fight for me. He was within his rights to say this to you. I should have confessed to you what I have been. If you had known, you would not have replied."

I was overcome by deep distress. We spent three hours crying together.

"Farewell," he said as he kissed my hand. "If I am not here at eight, it means it is all over for me."

He closed the door behind him. I threw myself on the bed in tears.

"What a miserable creature I am! Oh, I am accursed! Léon! Poor child! He is going to be killed!"

I ran down the stairs. I went to see Marie. When I asked for her the concierge told me, "Her furniture was sold long ago. I do not know where she is."

I went home hoping that Léon had returned. I opened my window and I spent the night looking out, listening.

The clock struck six in the morning. I had a chill. I went back to the window and saw a carriage coming down Faubourg Saint-Honoré. I dashed down the stairs. I had reached the door as the carriage was stopping.

It was Léon!

I threw my arms around him. He pushed me toward the alley.

"Mad woman! It is cold and you are wearing only a chiffon robe."

"I am so happy to see you! How afraid I was!"

He entered, sat in a chair. He was in black evening dress, black trousers, black leather shoes, and stitched stockings. He was pale and he was cold. Finally, I asked him how it all went.

"Well for everyone. We were both such poor shots that the witnesses were more in peril than we were."

I asked him the name of his opponent. He refused to tell me, begging me not to speak of this encounter to anyone.

When I was completely recovered from my fright I saw several of his friends, who seemed to be totally unaware of this duel. I tried to get information. A quarrel in a public place rapidly becomes common knowledge. No one knew of it. I swore I would find out.

The Hippodrome was putting on its last performances. Dead leaves crackled under the horses' feet like ice breaking.

The day of the last performance it rained so hard that the clay soil turned to puddles of water at each end. There were few spectators, but when a performer is on stage, it only takes one acquaintance in the audience to encourage her. That day my friends were in the audience. I saw Pomaré. I wanted to win.

During the first round, we heard someone yell that a horse had just fallen. That did not stop us. I was in second place. The one in front of me was named Coralie. She was holding on tight to her reins and was not letting me pass. Her horse slipped up, but she went on. However, she lost half a second, which I took advantage of. We finished even.

There was a lot of applause. The others came out and we had to do another round.

I do not know which one bumped into the other, but in the curve both our horses collapsed. Coralie had fallen head first.

We were handed bouquets and we went back inside covered with mud and glory.

That evening I dined at the Café Foy with Léon and his friends. First we talked about my fall, then we teased Léon because we wanted to be funny at someone's expense.

"Well now!" I said. "We have dined together many times, and you always say the same thing. If Léon is not a master of the repartee, I want you to know that he is always master of the gauntlet."

There was laughter, but it sounded forced. The one who seemed to be most affected was a blond young man who wore around his neck, in lieu of a tie, ribbons that he obtained from women as souvenirs, but which in fact he wore to save money. He was often found at the entrance of famous cafés. He was never hungry, but he went in on the pretense that he wanted to say hello so he would be invited to dine, and then he ate enough for four.

As an office clerk he earned twelve hundred francs. Thanks to his stratagem, he lived as if he had an income of one hundred thousand pounds. He never tipped his hat for fear of wearing it out; he would simply wave.

A Palais-Royal actress fell in love with him. One evening she asked him for two francs to pay for her carriage. A week later, she put her money on the mantle. He helped himself to his forty sous!

Impatient that Léon was not replying, I went on, "My dear, instead of losing your temper over a vicious remark about me and fighting a duel, you would do better to spare yourself these tasteless witticisms."

We looked at each other. I saw him turn purple.

"Who? He had a fight! When? Where? With whom?"

"He never would tell me."

Léon was livid.

He became the laughing stock of everyone and left for the countryside.

LAGIE AND HER ENGLISHMAN

The duke was in Spain. I went places with Lise. The most enjoyable evenings were always the ones spent at Alphonse R——'s. His health and enjoyment were returning. I absolutely loved this circle of witty people.

I listened. My mind was expanding through this contact, and I certainly needed this because I was so thoroughly ignorant; sometimes I would stop short in the middle of a word for fear of saying something dumb.

But the women were impossible.

One of them remarked that Pomaré was not pretty and that her front teeth were rotten. Hers were not much better. I asked my friend Hermance the name of this skinny beanpole who was so tiresome.

"Her name is Lagie. She comes from Metz where the local garrison is going to miss her. She is totally fair regarding women; she maligns them all.

"Go tell her for me that I would like to meet her."

"Why?"

"To ask her if she wants war or peace."

After a week, I had so jeered, mocked, and annoyed her that she invited me to dinner.

A son of Albion was showering her with gold. Her dinners were lavish. She surrounded herself with a crowd of freeloaders who praised every stupidity she said or did.

That day there were a lot of people present. While the soup was being served, someone came to the door. She motioned to her guests to be quiet. She was afraid it was her Englishman.

Instead of heeding her request, a few pranksters began to sing at the top of their voices:

War on the tyrants!
Never, never in France
Shall the English rule.[3]

Reckless Lagie was singing along with them.

We heard a few "goddams!" coming from the landing. We laughed about the incident all night long.

But the next day we did not know how to pay for the dinner: the Englishman had left for good.

THE JEWISH PIANIST

We kept our promise to M. H——, and we went to spend the evening at his house. We played a game of lansquenet.[4]

H—— was seated next to me and was giving me advice. He was more interested in me than my cards.

My disdain did not repel him. His love was tirelessly persistent, even though I kept telling him, "I care deeply for you, but you are Jewish, and I could never love a Jew. And besides, you are better than I."

"I swear, Céleste," he replied with a gravity that did not lack wit, "that it is not my fault that I am of Jacob's race. If we could be born as adults and if we could choose our religion, I would become a Catholic to please you."

While I was teasing him thus, a new person had come in and was walking up to the man of the house to shake his hand. I lowered my head. The man standing in front of me, looking at me with dull eyes, was my host from Rocher de Cancale.[5]

He was going to say where he knew me from. All my friends would despise me. I leaned against H——'s shoulder, as if to say, "Protect me!" but, suddenly looking up, I looked the enemy in the eyes. He took a few steps and went to sit a little farther away, seeming not to recognize me.

"You know him?" H—— asked me.

"No!" I replied, so quickly that, to a jealous man, it seemed like a yes.

A few minutes later, he got up and went to speak to his friend. I lost my composure.

A young man came over and sat in H——'s chair.

"You are not very nice. Poor H—— is madly in love with you!"

"Oh, you are all alike! In your opinion, to be nice means you have to give yourself to whoever wants you!"

"But with him, it is different. His heart is wounded. He is so kind! He has a tender nature!"

Such is the world. Even the indifferent ones contribute to the encouragement of liaisons and attachments that fancy has formed and boredom will undo, and some will then end up in ruin, others in despair.

My love affair with H—— is a sad example of the dangers of passion. Thinking I was satisfying a whim, I might have altered his life instead.

It was time to part and all the guests had picked up their hats and coats. I remained seated. Lise asked me, "You are not coming?"

"No, I am staying."

I thought H—— was going to go mad with joy. So his guests would leave quicker, he was urging them toward the door.

I was leaning against a large piano covered with music notations. I looked at H—— when he came back inside. He wanted to kiss me but I stopped him.

"If you were sensible, you would take me home. . . . If you love me, I am going to make you miserable."

"I do not care, I shall give my life to have you to myself, even if it is just for one day."

His hand was burning, his eyes shining.

I pointed to the piano bench. He sat down and kissed my hand.

I stretched out in an armchair next to him; he was playing with so much soul and improvised such beautiful things that my heart melted.

"I am," he said, "between the two great passions of my life."

Little by little, he seemed to have forgotten me. I woke up at dawn in the chair where I had fallen asleep. . . . He was noting on lined paper the music he had composed during the night.

I was grateful for such a sweet and respectful affection. I promised him I would spend the evening with him.

His gentleness and reserve did not last long.

H——'s love grew each day. He followed me everywhere, would spend the night at my door. He stopped working.

"Have pity on me," he would repeat constantly, "have pity on me! Tell me that you hate me, and I shall kill myself."

Only in front of people was he sensible. Alone with me, he would drive me to despair. His skin was moist and he coughed often. They said he was ill.

When on rare occasions he played music, the music was melancholy and his piano sounded like a church organ.

"If I were not Jewish, you would love me, is that right? If I knew that, I would deny my God for love of you!"

One day I saw him going in the Church of the Madeleine. He stayed there two hours.

I was advised to break it off. It would be better to cause a great grief that would heal than to let him die slowly.

Lise decided she would tell him of the decision I had made out of affection for him.

A few days later I received a letter in which he told me that his life was not his own and he was putting his trust in God.

This letter was so lofty that I wanted to see him, to ask his forgiveness! . . . He would not see me. . . . I thought he had a mistress and I felt foolish for being naïve.

A DUKE DOES NOT NECESSARILY BRING HAPPINESS

The duke was back in Paris. He was nothing like H—— and did not tire me with his love.

I was in vogue. . . . He was rich. Novelties were his right. My apartment was so high, his feet so small, that to please him I had to move. I went to live on the third floor at 5 Rue de l'Arcade, twelve hundred francs in rent.

In my new apartment there was a living room furnished in velvet, and in this living room, a piano. This piano was the reason I got a tutor.

His name was Pederlini; he was Italian and patient. . . .

The duke came to see me every two or three days. . . . He would not say more than four words to me.

I really do not know why he continued these visits. It might have been because his friends would tell him, "When you become bored with her, we shall fight over which one of us will succeed you." To be contrary, he was making them wait.

Sometimes I went to the Opera where I was always bored. My piano teacher told me that one of his compatriots was making his debut there.

"He would like to meet you."

"Oh, yes! And what for?"

"Well, because he saw you at the Hippodrome! . . . He would like me to introduce you so he can talk to you."

"All right!" I told him after the lesson. "Bring me your singer. You can be the interpreter."

When I woke up, I regretted my consent, but the isolation the duke was leaving me in began to weigh on me. For a long time the duke had an old mistress who was fat and had an ugly figure. I would see her displaying her forty years in a beautiful carriage lined in blue velvet. She would grimace to appear cheerful. The whole apparatus was covered with a veil dotted with black.

Noon and the bell at my door rang at the same time. I went to the door myself.

My entranceway was dark. I saw the shadow of a body taller than my pianist by a head.

I invited them to sit down in my living room and I sat across from them. . . .

125

My new admirer was a tall, strong, handsome boy. His hair was jet-black and his eyes dark and shiny.[6]

He spoke to Pederlini, who translated.

"B—— says he finds you even prettier up close. . . ."

I began to play with the ring on my finger, just to keep my composure.

"What? You do not speak any French?"

"*Sì, un poco,* Céleste."

"Oh, you can pronounce my name?"

"I believe he can," said Pederlini, "but you intimidate him."

I wanted to reply that he was the one who intimidated me instead. B—— offered to teach me Italian, unless I would be good enough to teach him French. . . . He promised to be a good student so he could converse with me. I entreated him to hurry up, because we must have appeared rather silly. . . .

As they were leaving, B—— held out his hand and pressed mine with such force that it took me a few seconds to part my fingers, numb from the pain.

This B—— was quite a handsome man, . . . but the duke flattered my vanity. When his beautiful carriage stopped in front of my door, I was proud of what should have made us both blush.

He arrived just when I was still under the spell of their visit.

"I am bored. I would like to go out a little."

"Why did you not say that sooner?" he told me casually. . . . "Tomorrow, I shall send a carriage over to you."

THE TENOR TORMENTED BY LOVE

At four o'clock a lovely carriage with two horses stopped at my door. The coachman told me he was at my disposal.

I went out and did not come home until the streets were deserted. I was so tired I could not eat dinner. The fear of not being seen inside the carriage forced me to sit up straight on the edge of the seat, my face toward the window, my head bobbing up and down like a Chinese porcelain Barbary ape.

The next day I went for my ride earlier, and I was very sad to find the Champs-Elysées deserted. If the coachman had not announced that his horses were hungry, I would have stayed out all night.

Two days later this ridiculous and misplaced vanity had disappeared and good sense had returned; I pulled myself down a peg or two repeating to myself that all this pomp was transitory and this carriage did not belong to me.

One day as I was riding along Boulevard du Temple, I saw a girl I had met at the Théâtre Beaumarchais. I pulled on the carriage rope, called her over, and took her to dinner.

She was about twenty years old, tall, nice figure, pretty with a ruddy complexion. I knew she was not very witty, but she was sweet.

"Well! My dear Joséphine," I said, "are you happy?"

"No. I have a passion that is eating up everything. It began with my dresses and ended up with my furniture. I have nothing left, and *he* will not see me anymore. He says that my large feet and fat hands disgust him."

"Oh, my! Who in the devil are you so enamored of?"

"An actor! I took a job as a walk-on at the Délassements, out of love."

"Well, you must leave the Délassements, out of reason. Do you want to work at the Hippodrome?"

We had finished eating. I dressed her from head to foot and I took her to the Opera to see *Robert the Devil.*[7]

I introduced her to the duke and to his friends, who took us for ice cream at the Café Anglais.

B—— was making his debut.

I was having dinner at a friend's on that day. I arrived late at the Opera. The sound made when the door to my loge opened made my tenor look up. One of his lines in *Lucie* was "Celestial Providence!"[8]

I can still see him. His arms outstretched, he looked toward me and paused on the word "Celestial."

During intermission Pederlini came to tell me that I was going to unnerve him. I offered to leave.

"No, now it is done. He would look for you, and that would be worse."

"He is so handsome!" said my friend, dazzled by his black velvet suit.

She conveyed her compliments to him about his singing in the first act. He must have thought they were from me, because he seemed to be thanking me as he went on stage.

He tried so hard that he sang off-key.

He tried to make up for it in the third act, but his voice failed.

He was not booed, but there was laughter. He had an accent. They called him Gascon, Auvergnat.[9]

Being successful meant he could earn forty thousand francs a year!

Pederlini brought him over the next day. He did not seem very disconcerted. I pointed out to him the words he had mispronounced and made him repeat them several times.

"Since you have begun, you must continue," said Pederlini laughing. "I am sure he will make great progress with you."

B—— seemed to agree because he came for as many as two lessons a day.

For his second debut he sang better and, pretending that it was thanks to me, he would not leave me. He gave a big dinner in my honor.

The third debut was a success. B—— was on cloud nine.

VAUDEVILLE AND *BEL CANTO*

I had Joséphine hired on at the Hippodrome. We were rehearsing together. I was learning a new routine. There would be Roman chariots driven by women. Three of us were racing: Angèle, Louise, and I.

I felt perfectly secure, unaware of the dangers in store for me. Joséphine was a snake I was keeping warm wrapped in my cashmere shawl.

This dear friend could not think of anything better to do than to replace me in the duke's affection.

One morning she sauntered into my room to adorn herself with a shawl and a hat she borrowed from me and had herself driven to the duke's residence. At first he refused to see her, but she persisted so that he relented.

What she told him, I never found out. He was smart enough not to report gossip word for word.

She came back to my apartment after making him promise secrecy. She had probably received a few gold louis for her treason.

The duke came to see me at four o'clock. . . . He talked a lot about the Opera and singers. I understood that I had been on someone's tongue.

Joséphine did not flinch.

Once he was gone, she told me she had no idea how he could have known all that. However, I had seen her signal to him in the mirror!

It had never been in my nature to bargain with a situation. I could see that everything was over between the duke and me. I had no desire to humiliate myself in order to be in his good graces again, but I wanted justice from Joséphine.

I wrote to the duke to come talk to me the next day and informed him that he could withdraw his affection afterwards, but that I wanted one last meeting.

He was prompt, to the chagrin of my dear friend who, since the night before, was ill at ease. She wanted to go out, but I asked her to do nothing of the sort. Since she insisted, I forbade her to leave.

"You will leave in a few minutes, but I want to clear up a suspicion."

She straightened up with incredible assurance.

I did not have time to say more; the duke was coming in.

"It is very kind of you to come and I thank you. I do not want to thwart your will. It is possible that I did all that you were told. I could try to justify myself, but if your mind is made up, I would bore you without convincing you. I just want to know the author of all these lovely tales. . . . I see only one woman who is in a position to malign me in your esteem, and that is Joséphine, but I cannot believe that it is she. I met her when she did not know where to eat and was ready to stand on the street corner to offer her beauty to passersby. As you can see, she is wearing my stockings. She would be wearing my shoes if her feet were not so big. She wears my chemises, my dresses, my collars! I have been feeding her for several months. I found her a job. So if it were she, you must admit that it would be very bad and that I was right to ask you to come here."

Joséphine was not moving. She was certain of the duke's protection, but he had a fair mind and an honest heart. Seeing me pale with anger, he asked that we go into my room. There he tried his best to calm me down, then, ringing for the servant, he told him to send Joséphine away.

Once she was gone, he told me he had wanted to spare my feelings, that he would always be my friend, and that if ever I needed anything from him all I had to do was write him.

He told me he would be leaving for the country but did not say when he would return.

I was surprised to see the carriage appear the next morning as usual. The coachman told me that payment had been made for three months. The pleasure of going around in a carriage helped console me.

I was bored by myself. Almost every day I had dinner with B——. It was certainly not for the food because I have never liked macaroni, and that was the base for the dishes. I hate cheese, and there was some on everything, but I found lots of company there.

We sang and played wonderful music.

Even the police commissioner decided it was so good, he banned it.

B—— had rented a beautiful furnished apartment at 110 Rue de Richelieu so he could be near the Opera.

When he would sing with his friends, people would gather in the street and on the corner of the boulevard. There would be such a crowd, carriages could not circulate. He was asked to close his windows and not sing so loud.

Often he would show me letters he received about me:

How can you be so blind as not to see with whom you are in love, and to be connected with a woman who does not even have the respect of the horse she rides on.

I asked him curtly to keep his little love letters to himself.

The day the Hippodrome reopened, the Roman chariot races were a hit. The costumes were magnificent.

I wore a red Phrygian cap adorned with gold stars, a knee-length white tunic trimmed in gold, slit to the hip on the side, red sandals with buskins, an ample coat on my right shoulder, the sleeve pinned on the left shoulder with a cameo brooch.

This routine, in fact, was dangerous and tiring.

After the first one, I went home with a monstrous headache.

B——, who had come to congratulate me on my success, was a nuisance because of his attentions.

The doorbell rang. My maid entered frightened.

"Madame, the duke!"

"Oh! My goodness!" I said, startled. "I do not want him to see you here. . . . Go in there."

I showed him the door to a little cubicle at the foot of my bed.

He frowned and replied bluntly that he did not want to get in.

"Get in," I said sternly, "or I shall never see you again."

Just in time because the door was opening.

"You are making me wait in the anteroom," said the duke. "You must have had someone with you then?"

"No," I replied pointing to a foot bath still near the fireplace. "I did not want to receive you barefooted. . . ."

"What does that matter? You handled your chariot admirably! I promised my friends to have you dine with them tonight."

"I am sorry, but the excitement and the bouncing on the chariot gave me a headache."

"Oh, my dear! I promised. You must come."

"I must! . . . All you great lords are really amazing! I find 'you must' really charming! How do you know I do not have another engagement? I have not heard from you in two weeks."

"I am rich enough to have you go back on your word to others. Get dressed and be at the Café Anglais at six."

He left without waiting for my answer.

B—— got out of his cubicle, seething with anger and his eyes fixed on the door.

"To live like that, one cannot have a heart! . . . And I thought you had a big one! This man does not love you!"

"You are not telling me anything I do not already know, but what can I do? . . . I need a small fortune to achieve a goal I cannot tell you about."

"Why do you not settle down? This life is disgraceful. Go to this dinner. The order was explicit. . . . I shall accompany you there if you wish and then I shall take leave of you forever at the door."

Although it was said in bad French, the declaration touched me deeply, but it was not in my nature to give in.

"Take heed, my friend. You are saying that if I go to this dinner, you will not see me anymore. It is not because of this ultimatum that I give in. I am not going because I do not want or cannot go. I shall write the duke a polite letter."

And then I dryly asked B—— to let me rest.

The duke came the next day to check on me. He was cold and dour. Used to making everything bend before his will, he could not understand the word "impossible." I believe however that because of my nature and my frequent opposition to some of his whims, he grew to have a certain affection for me.

FLOWERS ON A CRADLE

I fell back into deep despair. Around me I could see rising and falling all those women whose fates I had envied from afar. The old ones are devoid of everything. The young ones have a gorgeous wardrobe that does not belong to them most of the time. If they were to die, not a single piece of fabric would be found in their armoires to bury them in.

A diversion arose to distract me from the discouragement I was about to let myself sink into.

Lise often went horseback riding.

She was quite happy. She had an apartment at 33 Rue Saint-George. She too had plunged into a courtly affair. Her new lover was Count de V——.

One day, coming out of the Hippodrome, I saw a lot of people in groups.

"Sir, can you tell me what is going on?"

"An accident, but the loss is not great."

"What happened?"

"Oh," he replied halfway laughing, "it is Pomaré who was showing off among the carriages. Her horse got spooked and took off."

Some other people who were coming from the fence came up to me to say, "Oh! The poor woman! She tried to jump off, her foot got caught in the stirrup, and the horse dragged her so far her head is injured."

I jumped in my carriage and went in the direction indicated. There was a gathering around blood stains. I told the coachman, "To Rue Saint-Georges!"

Her maid told me she had been gone since morning dressed in her street clothes. That did not mean anything because her amazon outfit was at the stables, Rue Duphot.

At the stables I was assured that she had not been seen all day. I was shown her outfit. I went home to change. I was drenched with perspiration. I was about to go back out, when the doorbell rang. It was Lise!

After hugging her tight, I told her the rumor going around and the fright I had. I did not leave her for two days.

The poor woman who fell off her horse died of her injuries.

Lise told me a lot of good things about her lover, that his name was Ernest, and introduced him to me.

Her sister was pregnant and had come to live with her to receive better care.

The four of us had dinner.

M. Ernest was a forty-five-year-old man, blond, and partially bald. He wore his hair long and brought it back over his head to hide the bare parts.

Eulalie was close to giving birth. She had Lise, who was going to be the godmother, knit her baby clothes. A cradle was purchased and Camille had requested to be the godfather.

She told me about a ball she had to attend at Passy and asked me to come by for her.

I told her I would, but that, since it was a week away, if she changed her mind to let me know.

After a week, not hearing from her, I went to see her at two o'clock.

"Well, are you still going?"

"Oh, certainly," she said. "Come in here, I am arranging the flowers for my hair."

I entered her dressing room. I saw burning candles. Her sister was lying on a sofa that doubled as a bed.

"Are you sick?"

"Yes," she said, "but it is nothing."

"Look," said Lise, "I am going to wear these pomegranate flowers."

I saw other flowers strewn on the cradle. I felt something like the head of a child, and I saw a little cross and blessed palms.

"What does this mean?"

"My sister miscarried last night. It is a girl. She will be buried tomorrow."

I backed out of the room and said, "Come by for me if you wish, I shall not be coming back here."

She arrived that night, all set, seemingly unaware that death resided with her.

13

A Chariot Race

An Accident—"Why would I give you
a raise?"—Quarrelsome Deligny

IT WAS EARLY July and the heat was unbearable, making my task at
the Hippodrome very unpleasant.

I had already had two or three falls with my horses. Twice I had to
be bled. All that had exhausted me.

I earned very little. I decided to ask for a raise. Would I get it? They
had more women than they needed because many offered their services for free to make a name for themselves. They had never received
any training, but what did that matter to the administrators, so long
as they made money? They despise the ones who make them rich. If
it were not for the police keeping an eye on them, they would get four
out of ten killed. No effort was made to avoid accidents. We were given
lame horses who fell when pushed. While performing the Berny Cross,
an Englishman and his horse fell in the center ditch, which was about
twelve feet deep. The man passed out. His teeth were broken and he
had a large gaping wound on his forehead. The doctor ordered him to
lie down. One of the directors, more concerned about the possibility of
the routine being banned because it was dangerous, said, "Put him on
a stretcher and take him to the hospital."

"How disgraceful!" I said. "That is the fate that awaits us if we have no
other resources. Not only is our pay docked when we are sick, but those
who take a fall like this, if they are not killed on the spot, are forced to
die in misery. Take this poor man to my apartment. I shall take care of
him and put these callous hearts to shame."

One of the directors admitted I was right and ordered the wounded
man taken to his house. He was a good soul with exceptional generosity.
The name of Ferdinand Laloue has stayed in the memory of those he
has helped and those who have known him.

To perform this routine, one has to be a good jockey. Since the good ones are expensive, they hire shady characters who cannot stay in one place and who are almost always tipsy.

Two weeks earlier I was asked to try out a steeplechase horse. To train him I was provided with two jockeys to sit by me. They were dead drunk. They took off at such speed that my horse got excited and made me go around eight or ten times. I jumped over twenty three-and-a-half-foot hurdles. My hands were bleeding.

It was not out of pure enjoyment that I endangered myself in this way. If I could have done otherwise, I would have quit the Hippodrome with no regrets.

AN ACCIDENT

The race promised to be impressive. The chariots were taking turns passing each other. I had overtaken Louise and I was about to overtake Angèle. It was the last lap.

In the curve near the stables, out of the corner of my eye I saw Louise riding very close to me. I was about to whip my horses to spur them on when I felt a powerful shock.

Louise had gotten her wheel tangled with the back end of my chariot. If she had stopped immediately, the cramp could have pulled out of the rims, but she whipped her horses to pass me, and, dragging me with her, caused me to whirl around. My chariot's shaft jabbed my horse on the right; he reared against a post, emitting an earsplitting whinny, then fell over backwards dragging the other horse down with him, which, trying to get back up, pulled sideways and overturned my chariot.

I was still holding on to the reins, but one of the struggling horses hit my shoulder. I let go, stunned by the pain. I could hear jumbled sounds.

"She is dead!"

The horses were dragging me face down in the dirt. Twice something ran over my leg.

Someone stopped the struggling horses. One had a broken leg and had to be destroyed to put an end to its cries of pain.

The scene must have been excruciating for the spectators. Some women were crying, others had fainted. The audience had climbed on top of the fences and was questioning the doctors who surrounded me.

I opened my eyes, I got on my knees, then stood up. I ran my hand over my right thigh and pushed people away. I wanted to walk to make sure I had no broken bones! I managed to walk but with agonizing pain and leaving a trail of blood behind me.

To reassure them, I saluted the spectators who had just displayed such a keen interest in me. I took a few steps with some help, then I collapsed.

I was revived, then bled twice. The blood was not coming out. They bandaged me and placed me in a barouche.

Once I had been taken upstairs to my bed, I was seized by a fever.

To prevent the chariots from skidding in the curves, studs had been put on the wheels. One of these wheels had run over my thigh and had left a purple ring of flesh around it as wide and thick as a hand. My knee was dislocated and water was building up on the cap. Over the bone was a two-inch gap that must have been caused by one of the horses' shoes as the animal was struggling.

The Hippodrome doctor prescribed compresses and rest. I survived his prescription for six days without improving.

A young man came to see me. He had witnessed the accident, and although he did not know me, he had been checking on me. He told me that I was not receiving proper care and that he would send over the best surgeon in Paris.

The next day at nine in the morning a fat man arrived. He went straight into my bedroom. I asked him what he wanted.

"Come on, remove the bandages on your leg. I was sent by M. Gustave de Bel. . . ."

He pressed on my knee so hard I screamed. He examined my red swollen wound, which had partially closed up.

"Who is the idiot taking care of you?" he asked placing two fingers on each side of the scar.

I thought he was going to squeeze. I took both his hands in mine.

"Now, do not be childish. Do you wish to keep this beautiful leg?"

My bedroom door flew open, and I saw my mother in tears.

"Maman!" I said, forgetting the doctor who, taking advantage of my distraction, parted the flesh that was starting to close up.

He was handed a towel, which became stained with dark blood. As soon as I had caught my breath, I pulled my leg away.

He began to laugh at my anger and told me, "You really hate me, right? Well, I am not here to be liked. I want to make you well. Now, I must check the bone and burn the flesh."

"Never!" I told him. "You will never touch me again. I would rather die."

"Now," said my mother, "be brave!"

I was ashamed of my weakness, and I placed my foot on his knee. He picked up a scalpel, spread the flesh apart, and lightly scraped the bone.

"That is enough for today. We shall continue day after tomorrow. You need to put an oilcloth under her and a wooden rod on top of her knee. Then you need to go get a still. Fill it with ice, which will slowly melt on her leg, night and day."

My mother saw him out. I asked her how she got my address and who had told her I was sick.

"In my neighborhood there is a woman who sells seats at the Hippodrome. One day she gave me two tickets. I wanted to see if this Céleste everyone was talking about might not be my daughter. Every other day I received news of you, but the last six days I could not stand it anymore. Rosalie told me that your leg would have to be amputated. Here I am. Do you mind?"

"No, on the contrary."

"WHY WOULD I GIVE YOU A RAISE?"

My mother moved in with me. I did not dare ask about her personal life.

My companions came to visit me. Angèle was one of the most solicitous.

My fat surgeon was true to his word; he came to burn me a second time.

During his last visit he told me, patting my cheek, "Well, my child, the wounds are pink. You are saved. It is so hot, I was afraid gangrene would set in. If at all possible, give up this profession."

"Sir," I said, "how can I repay you for the care you have given me?"

"You do not owe me anything. I am no longer practicing. It took an incident like this to get me out. I am too fat; I cannot climb stairs anymore."

He left without giving me his name, and I never learned it.

My mother was advising me to quit the Hippodrome. And B——— was urging me to give up such a dangerous profession.

I promised them to quit at the end of the season if I did not get a raise.

I began by walking around my room, then I went downstairs. I rode to the Hippodrome in a carriage. I had been replaced; they barely remembered me!

This infuriated me so, that I insisted on being given my costumes and my horses for the next performance.

As I climbed into my chariot, mended as I was, I became very emotional. I was much applauded. I lost my head and stopped at the second lap.

That almost caused another accident. The chariot behind me was about to climb over mine.

I told my mother that if she wanted, as soon as I had a little money, we would go hide out somewhere. She agreed.

The season was over. I asked for an appointment with the director to find out if he wanted to hire me for two years and give me a raise.

"Why would I give you a raise? Do you not manage *your own affairs?* What do a few hundred francs more or less mean to you? I plan to decrease the personnel; I have more women than I need."

He did not hold me back as I went home in despair.

My mother was consoling me and said, "Was there not a fire? . . . Maybe it is financial difficulties that make them ungrateful."

I dried my tears and took a carriage to go pick up my things. Until the last minute, I had hoped they would keep me on. But nothing, not even a polite good-bye.

QUARRELSOME DELIGNY

To distract myself, I went out into the world. Sometimes I would go see Lise, sometimes, Lagie.

Several times I ran into a short blond man with a ruddy complexion who gave himself military airs, swore, drank, bantered, raged, quarreled, and was rarely polite. His name was Deligny.

I disliked him so much that I never went in anywhere without inquiring whether he was present so I could avoid him.

He noticed my aversion and tried every way he could to run into me so he could pester me.

And so, whenever he gave a dinner party, I would be invited and I would not be told he was there. We would quarrel all evening.

He bragged that he had never fallen in love and that he was rough with women. They say that love often arrives holding hate's hand. That is what happened.

He would drink less in front of me and would almost become charming. He was teased a lot, but his feeling was becoming strong enough to overcome the gibes.

One day my mother suggested, "You should open a business and I would run it. It would give you a position, and I could stay near you without being a burden to you."

I liked the idea. I gave notice to the landlord. My mother looked for a shop and found one at 2 Rue Geoffroy-Mary.

I rented a residence at number 5, almost across the street.

While we were packing up, I received a letter from The Hague. It was from the baron, the man my fake sister had sent to me.

In this letter he explained that he had just been very ill and my presence would speed his recovery better than all the help from the medical community.

A trip to a foreign country seemed like an excellent preparation for the business career I was planning to start. My mother accompanied me to the railroad station.

14

Travel Impressions

Cold Season, Icy Welcome—Love in Puritan Country—
Boredom Worse than Winter

MOST MEN ARE courteous when they travel. Yet there are many who, when they see a woman in a coach, flee, saying, "Let us go to another, we would not be able to smoke."

Two young men, about to enter the coach where I was, closed the door to go look for another one. After searching the train, they came back because they did not find any empty seats. I could see by the faces they made that they wished I would go to the devil. I could have reassured them since I smoked cigarettes, and cigars did not inconvenience me in the least. But I took pleasure in teasing them.

One of them tried to soften me up by telling a racy story. I replied with sharp yeses and noes. He was put off and did not address me anymore.

My companions spoke quietly to each other, then settled in to sleep in their corner.

I was not sleepy and I wanted them to keep me company. This was just the moment I had reserved for a grand way to cheer them.

"If you gentlemen wish to smoke," I told them, "please do so. I like the aroma of tobacco."

All at once they rummaged through their pockets and did not thank me until they had broken off the small end of their cigars with their teeth.

To show their appreciation, they went so far as to bring me sweet water and cookies back to the compartment I had not wanted to leave.

At first they were intrigued about my identity. Then, once they recognized me from the Hippodrome, they became cheerier and less hesitant.

My maid was snoring louder than the locomotive. She kept falling over on her neighbor, who finally wedged her with his cane and coat.

It was bone-chilling cold.

Like everyone who has never traveled, I was all decked out, corset and all, as if I were going to a wedding, so that by morning I was dead tired.

I went to the Hôtel de la Poste in Brussels. I slept for several hours.

After lunch I walked around the city. I had imagined that Brussels would have a certain cachet. I came back to the hotel disillusioned, and then I took the wrong train to Antwerp.

I arrived very disconcerted. I asked where I could find the steamboats that go to The Hague. I was addressing a tall puffy-cheeked man who let me repeat my question three times, then finally indicated that he did not understand.

An employee came to tell me that the steamboats were not running because of the ice and that they would start up again in a couple of weeks. I took on airs of importance and said that I was expected for business that could not wait.

"Lady! There are some carriages, but you will be very uncomfortable."

He pointed out the Hôtel du Cheval-Blanc.

I was shown to a room with two beds for me and my dimwit maid, whom I had to wait on.

A fat girl came in to light the stove. Imagine, a coal fire in the middle of a bedroom. The stovepipe was stopped up, and I spent the day with the window open, dancing the polka to keep warm.

I ordered some food, and I was brought some beer.

I had reserved two corner seats on a hackney. A man as tall as a small leaf came to join us.

We had to switch conveyance ten times. We would leave one carriage to get into a skiff that would slide between ice breaks. We would get on another crate, then another small craft amid dangers and commotion.

The small craft we got on was a sort of large raft with pointed edges in the front and steel-shod like an ice skate.

We had just picked up another traveler. He was in a carriage made just like the vans that take money to the bank here.

He got out of the front compartment, helped unharness the two horses, and had the carriage carefully loaded on the skiff. He was speaking Dutch with the sailors. We started to move. We could hear only the cracking of the ice.

My maid was dead with fear and cold, and I was not very confident.

"Come on, be brave!" I said. "You only die once. This vehicle reminds me of a casket placed here for that purpose."

141

The young man said in very good French, "Mademoiselle is right, it is a casket, but it is not empty."

"Not empty?" I replied. "But does that mean we are traveling with a dead man?"

"My father, mademoiselle," he said, removing his travel cap.

I was ashamed for the lack of restraint I had shown and for my cheerfulness. I did not dare move anymore.

Swearing, our sailors picked up some steel hooks and worked at pushing back enormous ice blocks.

Once we had returned on land, we got back in a carriage.

Two horses were harnessed to the young man's vehicle and he walked ahead of it with reverence.

We went through Rotterdam. All I saw were road markers, chains, and fences. The countryside was flooded, and the water that covered the fields was frozen. Here and there children were ice skating. A few leagues from The Hague, the scenery became livelier. The meadows were covered with skaters. The women were carrying round baskets on their heads, sweaters in their hands, and were gliding like swallows flying low. That is how they travel to visit each other from one town to the next. How lovely! I was enchanted and I wanted to try.

We stopped at an inn. I sent for some skates, and there I was, trying. For my first attempt, I fell flat on my face. For the second, same thing. I had to give up. When it was time to sit down in the carriage, I regretted not having given up sooner.

Finally we arrived. I went to the Hôtel de l'Europe. The Hague is a very gloomy city. French women traveling alone are not very welcome unless they are sixty years old.

People looked at me and hesitated. I almost did not get a room.

LOVE IN PURITAN COUNTRY

I was led to the second floor to a very clean room. Another, plainer one was connected to it. Each one had a little stove waxed like a pair of boots. I made them turn red.

I wrote a note to my friend, who was feeling better. He was on duty and could see me for only a short while that evening, and then, with great precaution.

He arrived looking over his shoulder like a tracked man, had me speak softly, and begged me to remain incognito.

The next days I visited Scheveningen.

When I arrived on the beach, I walked in the fine yellow sand as close to the water as possible. When I turned around, I saw maybe two hundred men all dressed alike: yellowish trousers and jackets, wide-brimmed hats, like our market porters. I had heard that women had been abducted in boats; then, after their belongings were stolen, they were thrown into the sea. Thank goodness a golden-haired Dutch woman appeared and I felt emboldened.

The men who had frightened me so lined up to let us by. Some of them saluted me. I left the beach laughing at my fright. They were oyster fishermen.

The next day was a beautiful icy day. The sun was pale but cheery.

I was told I should visit the park. I put on a black velvet dress, a matching coat, a white pinwale corduroy hat with roses pinned underneath the brim, and a veil, more to keep my nose from turning red than to hide. This park was magnificent. Nearly tame stags and deer roamed freely.

I saw coming toward me a tall blond woman whose hair was curled English-style.

Several people were walking alongside her. The passersby were saluting her and she would reply with a smile. I could hear, "The queen!"

I saw my baron coming out of an alley on a superb gray horse, but when he saw me he did an about-turn!

I went back to the hotel for dinner.

The baron came to see me for a minute and said that indeed during my morning walk I had run across the whole court. I understood why he ran off; he was chamberlain.

He sent me some theater tickets. *Count Ory* and *Figaro* were playing. This theater does not have loges but a balcony divided in several places for chamberlains, ladies, and the king. The most important persons of the city go to the orchestra pits. I made a long face when I was shown my seats.

My white hat interested many of the young men seated in the balcony.

Unfortunately, I had not counted on the nuisance of my fame. During intermission two curious men positioned themselves right in front of me.

"Oh, it is not possible!" said one of them. "But, yes, it is, it is Mogador!"

The two of them left, but they came back with reinforcements. I was seized by the irresistible desire to cross my eyes.

"You must be wrong," said a newcomer.

"No, no," said his debater, "I know her well. She is slightly pock-marked; that is she. In fact the baron can settle this for us."

Thank goodness the curtain went up. They did not dare come back down.

I left my seat before the play was over. I had hoped that I could get to my hotel, but they had left their seats at the same time as I, and they were lined up in the hall.

I saw the baron at the entrance. He turned his back to me, motioning for me to get into the waiting carriage. A man pushed me. I heard someone speak to the coachman, but I could not make out the words. We left posthaste. We had been riding for a good while, when I began to worry because I should have arrived a half hour earlier.

I figured that I was lost and was being taken to a wood. I was in dire circumstances. He probably thought I was rich and he was going to rob me and kill me.

The carriage stopped and I recognized my hotel.

"The fool!" I said getting out. "He got lost."

"No," said the baron who was waiting for me at the door. "I ordered him to take a detour, otherwise you would have been followed. Do not go out and do not look out the window!"

"Well, now, am I in prison here?"

"I am saying this for your own good. One of your compatriots, Mlle Hermance, supposedly because she was attracting too much attention, has just been sent back to France."

I rose early and tried to find some amusement, but in vain, and four o'clock arrived after much yawning. I was relaxing until all my fibers were loose, when I heard several voices coming up the stairs.

I thought the baron was bringing me some of his friends. I opened the door and saw five young men, but no baron. I quickly shut my door. I listened; they were talking about me. One was saying, "I knew she was staying here."

A door next to mine opened. It led to a room where they were going to dine. They knocked on the wall and sang songs composed for me.

BOREDOM WORSE THAN WINTER

At eight o'clock there was a knock at the door. Since I did not recognize my friend's voice, I did not open. A note was slipped under the door. This is what it contained:

I do not dare go see you. Your hotel has been invaded. Go out at ten. I shall wait for you at the corner of the place and the Café Anglais.

When the appointed hour arrived, I wrapped myself up like a conspirator and we slid along walls like two shadows.

Since there was a lot of frost, we progressed slowly. My maid slipped and fell. I began to laugh so hard that I had to hold on to a wall.

A watchman was pacing quietly. He stopped to listen to us and yelled, probably, "Who goes there?" I did not know what to answer, and I was afraid to take another step. The watchman was still yelling. I replied, "It is we!"

Apparently that was not enough, and if the baron, noticing my tardiness, had not come looking for us and had not spoken to the sentry, he might have shot us.

"You must change hotels. Since we have a dearth of women as beautiful as you, when one of them arrives, a revolution ensues."

"My dear, your country bores me. I shall not change hotels. I am leaving tomorrow without fail."

I returned home as laboriously as I had arrived, and I saw Paris with exuberant joy.

15

Acts of Desperation

A Muffled Sound, Something Falling . . . — The Carriage
for Indigents — A Solution That Destroys the Problem — Stars in
Those Days Did Not Take Advantage of Their Botched Suicides

MY MOTHER FOUND everything completed for the move. Our shop
was ready. I had saved a little money, but it was not enough. I sold my
jewelry, some cashmere garments, and I paid off some small debts.

I was not planning to become a prude, but I wanted to leave this life
of subjection to the pleasures of others. I wanted to laugh only when I
felt like it and for my own personal enjoyment.

I was recalling the Sundays of my childhood. In those days I would
check on the sun four days ahead to find out if it was going to rain. That
is not a custom of the beautiful people from high society. What does
Sunday mean for most rich people? A day of boredom.

Take as an example those strollers who come home on Sunday night.
They have walked four leagues in the country to pick wild flowers. They
are tired, dusty, but they have had enough fun to last them a week.

I would compare these pleasures from my childhood to those of the
dazzling gilded young people I frequented, and I found the first ones
superior.

What did all those young people, who thought they were so original mixing anglomania with the traditions of the Regency, do for fun?
The more creative ones had ridden tall skinny horses, had raced either
through the Bois de Boulogne or the Champ-de-Mars, had lost money,
had dined every day in restaurants, had played games all night long with
mistresses, had gone to dances, to their clubs, and they had been unable
to find ways to have fun.

I had seen the two lifestyles. The life of the idlers seemed more genu-
inely enjoyable, and I made the decision to return to them.

My shop was very pretty. My mother had made it look elegant. She hired some good workers, and the opening of the fashion shop was set for the *twentieth* of the month. This was the *ninth*.

The apartment I had rented was on the third floor, facing the courtyard.

I had hired a new maid, a girl from Nantes named Marie. She was short, had gray, cat-like eyes, a big nose, and a dumb but honest look.

At that time I had a pretty little white dog with black spots that I had raised. I was afraid of losing her because she was coughing. One of the workers suggested I give her a powder that was touted all over Paris to prevent illnesses. I gave my little dog the dosage prescribed. An hour later I could hear moaning, and I heard my maid forbid the dog to leave the room. The poor creature ran between her legs and collapsed at my door. I had poisoned her with too strong a dose.

I have always been superstitious. The death of my dog seemed to be a bad omen. I did not like my apartment any more. It depressed me.

We had several employees. When one of them quit, my mother asked me to go see a woman who had applied for a job. She had said her address was on Rue Coquenard.

I put on a shawl, a hat, a veil, and I left by way of Faubourg Montmartre.

I had reached the corner when I heard a muffled sound, several voices yelling, and I saw everyone rushing. I drew near. Several persons were around something on the ground. A blond woman with unfastened hair was being lifted. I let out a dreadful cry.

"Marie!" I yelled, kissing her.[1] "Marie! Wake up. . . . Oh, God! How horrible! She is not dead, is she?"

An elderly man who was feeling her forehead replied as he removed his hat, "It is all over!"

She was brought up to her room, a furnished garret. I followed this sad procession. She had left only a letter with a request that it be sent to its address without opening it.

I could see that poverty had led her to this. She was laid out on her pallet. A doctor said she had broken her back.

I knew the man the letter was addressed to and I promised to go see him. But in the meantime, I immediately sent him the letter by messenger.

The woman she was renting from was asked if she had been renting from her for very long.

"No, just two months. I had given her notice because she is registered with the police. I have a *demoiselle* here, so I could not keep her."

"Did she ever have any visitors?"

"No, I think she was sick the whole time."

I gave her Marie's last dress. I sent a bedsheet and a bonnet with recommendations that her hair be attractively done up. She was so proud of it! I remember one day she said to me, "I hope I never, ever die in a hospice; I am *afraid* they would cut my hair."

Her lover lived on Rue Racine. I had a carriage drop me off in front of his house.

I checked with the concierge. The first thing I saw on his table was Marie's letter. That meant he was not in!

The doorman did not seem eager to go get him, but his wife, who was nicer, told me that he was at the tavern next door. I spoke to a waiter there and he was paged in the billiard room.

"Tell whoever it is to wait for me at my house," he said. "I am finishing a betting pool."

I waited for him at the concierge's. I waited for more than an hour. Finally he arrived, disheveled and full of wine.

He was a fifteenth year student, still young and rather handsome.

"Oh! It is you!" he said to me. "Why did you not go in? You could have had an absinthe with us. I won the pool."

"Do not laugh my friend, I have some bad news. Read this letter."

And I pointed to Marie's letter still on the table.

"Again!" he said. "If that is why you came, you could have stayed home. Good grief, shall I never be rid of her? . . . I do not want to read her letters."

"Read this one," I told him. "It is the last one."

"She told me that a hundred times. Upstairs I have ten of them that I have not opened—"

"That was wrong, you could have prevented a terrible thing. . . . She is dead!"

"Dead!"

"Yes, dead! She threw herself out the window."

He picked up his key, asked if there was heat in his house, and invited me up to his room. Once inside, he removed his cap, threw his hair back, and opened the letter. It was eight or ten pages long. He lit a candle and read. . . .

During the reading he moved his head a few times but never shed a tear.

Finally he told me, "It is an irreversible tragedy. I cannot do anything about it. For a year now I have had another mistress whom I love very much. At first I kept that fact hidden, but Marie would follow me, and she found out. After that there was a lot of weeping and crying. I began to hate her. One night she came over, determined to kill me. . . . She had a knife! I told my mistress to go upstairs, and I locked Marie in an empty room. Since she was making a racket, I went out to spend the night elsewhere. Once I had left, she was let out and was told that if she returned and made so much noise again, the guards would be called to arrest her."

"What you did is mean. You have no heart."

"You should have been there. . . . I do not know a worse torture than having near you a person who torments you with an unrequited love. . . ."

He read the letter one more time without any more feeling than the first time. There was a knock at the door. . . . He had removed the key.

"Who is there?" he asked.

"It is I," said a woman's voice.

He set the letter down and went to open the door. I saw a small brunette with an upturned nose enter.

"Oh!" she said. "You are entertaining Mogador? You should have had someone tell me not to come up."

She turned to leave. He hastened to hold her back.

I understood then that poor Marie must have been quite miserable. I picked up the letter so this woman would not see it. This letter would end up being the instrument that would avenge Marie!

THE CARRIAGE FOR INDIGENTS

In my haste to leave, I had inadvertently taken this poor child's letter with me. Here are a few fragments:

At least read this letter to the end. Do not laugh. I have told you this many times because I always hoped that you would have pity on me.

My crime is to have loved you too much; forgive me; I am going to pay for it dearly. I have never had much strength when I was faced with giving you up. Repeatedly I came back and asked your forgiveness for the pain you caused me. . . . You would have me sent away! I would send you my soul and my tears in a letter that you would burn without answering, or that your mistress would personally return to me with an insult.

You will miss me, even if just for love of her. When I shall be no more, she will leave you.

Leave the Latin Quarter. Go back to Bretagne where your mother is still waiting for you. . . . I was present when you received letters from her in which she bemoaned your abandonment.

You have been in Paris for fifteen years now, and this life of billiards and taverns has ruined your conduct and withered your face.

Leave! There is still time. Later, all you might get to see is the tomb of your mother, that saintly woman, who has no one but you.

Oh! If she had been able to see deep in my heart, she would have loved me because of the love that I have for you. If you had been willing to keep me near you, by dint of devotion I would have come out pure from the abyss where I have fallen. How I have loved you, how I love you still! You have been my first and my last love!

If I had enough money to buy coal, I would be able to tell you whether death is as painful as your abandonment. But I have nothing, only my window or the river.

My friend, I forgive you!

In just a moment, on the edge of this window, I am going to kneel, join my hands together, and I shall say, "God, forgive me! Let me die! . . ."

Marie

That last prayer was answered.

The next day I did not go out, waiting for the person I had visited the day before. When by four o'clock I had no news, I thought maybe she had gone to Rue Coquenard. I went there, but there had been no one!

Marie's body was removed at two o'clock. The welfare office had sent its carriage for indigents. No one accompanied her.

A SOLUTION THAT DESTROYS THE PROBLEM

My mother and I had begun our important commercial endeavor.

The shop was open. We had plenty of customers. All the women I had known came to us to buy clothes.

However, we were not on the road to making a fortune, simply because these women bought on credit. I could not refuse.

My mother made me understand that we could not make any money this way, and she took charge of refusing new accounts.

My apartment was between two courtyards. At the entrance, there was an anteroom; on the left, a living room and a bedroom, and across from that, a cabinet where the servant slept. In a corner on the right was the door of a right-angled hallway leading to the kitchen whose window faced the window of the cabinet.

One morning someone rang the doorbell. I was not up yet and told

Marie who was going to see who was there, "I do not want to see anyone. Have whoever it is go down to the shop."

From my bed I heard someone ask, "Mlle Céleste!"

"She is not in. If you wish to see her mother, she is at the shop—"

"No, she is the one I want to see. She has been making me track her for too long. I know she is here and that she is hiding. I have orders to pick her up."

"I do not know what you mean. If Madame were here, I would have told you so."

"Well! Tell her that if she does not go to the prefecture before noon tomorrow, I shall have her picked up by the guards!"

I hid my face in my hands. I was embarrassed in front of this girl.

"Oh! Madame, what can they want with you?"

"I do not know," I replied. "He must be mistaken. Do not tell anyone about this."

What was going to become of me? I could not run away. The little I owned had gone into this shop. I could no longer go downstairs without risk of being arrested, maybe even sentenced to a month for having missed the summonses that had been sent.

What about the neighborhood? Everyone will know this story and I shall not dare show my face again. There is nothing I can do until tomorrow.

I thought about Marie. Tomorrow was Sunday. I could not be arrested tomorrow; the offices would be closed. My maid would be out all day, and my mother would not open the shop.

I spent the evening writing letters. At eleven o'clock, my mother came to tell me good night.

"Oh, you are writing to suppliers."

"Yes."

I did not even think to kiss her.

I knew she was seeing Vincent again. She was hiding the fact from me, but the first salesgirl had described him to me and I recognized him. She told me that, often, when I came downstairs, Vincent would go out the back door to Rue de la Boule-Rouge.

From deep in my heart, all my anger toward him and my indifference toward her had surged.

Once I was alone, I straightened up everything and sealed a few letters to my friends.

I rose early. Around ten, it began to rain a mist so fine it resembled fog. I called Marie.

"Come on," I told her. "Get dressed and go for a walk. It is your day off."

"Oh," she said, "the weather is too nasty."

I did not care, it was imperative that Marie leave. I placed a piece of blank paper in an envelope with some name on it.

"I need for you to take this to Avenue de Saint-Cloud," I told Marie.

She had a friend from back home on the Champs-Elysées; she would take advantage of the opportunity to go visit her, and she would stay there long enough for me to execute my plan.

I sent her on the errand, and I called her back in the stairs to tell her that I was going out and that she could stay at her friend's until eleven o'clock.

I closed the door and went into Marie's room. I moved all her things into my room. I put white sheets on her little iron bed. I went to the kitchen and looked under the stove. There were only a few pieces of coal.

In those days we wore large pelisses. I had a black silk one, which I put on and went downstairs.

The sidewalk was slippery and the sky dark. Most of the shops were closed. For a moment I was a little concerned, but I breathed easy when I saw that the earthenware shop was open. I bought two clay stoves, which I brought home hiding them as if I were carrying a treasure. I went back to get some coals. I lit both stoves in Marie's room and I locked myself in it.

I had even plugged up the key hole.

I sat on the bed and asked God and all those I had hurt to forgive me, and I waited.

The flames were behind my head. I did not look at it but I could see rising above me a diaphanous beam that was coming down.

"Oh," I told myself, "if I do not die, tomorrow I will be arrested."

Perhaps I had not put in enough coal.

I got up and felt my body sway in spite of me. I knelt down to put in more coal. The bluish flame drew me and I remained transfixed with my mouth open.

Then a metal ring encircled my forehead and the fire seemed to be in my chest. . . . Laboriously I got up, leaning on a table to help me. I looked at myself in a little mirror.

How horrible! My head was puffy, the veins in my forehead were swollen, my lips were blue, and my hair was standing on end! . . .

That is when a terrible struggle began. Death was scaring me. I wanted to call for help, but my voice failed me. I wanted to run, but my strength faltered.

I was dragging myself on the floor. I could not see anymore. . . .

STARS IN THOSE DAYS DID NOT TAKE ADVANTAGE OF THEIR BOTCHED SUICIDES

When I came to, I was on my bed and my room was full of people. Two men were rubbing my arms, two others, my legs, so hard that I thought I was burned.

"She is saved," said the hairdresser whose shop was next to our house, and who was one of the first to come to my rescue.

My mother was near my bed.

It all came back to me, even the threats from the police. . . . I began to cry, to struggle. I wanted to do it again.

The two doctors proclaimed that I was delirious and that I should not be left alone for one moment.

My mother sensed that her presence was irritating me, so she left. Probably Vincent was waiting for her. It was Marie who watched over me.

"How was I rescued?" I asked her.

"Oh, madame, if it had not been for me, you would have been lost. The weather was so bad that I took the omnibus going and coming. I did not find the person you had sent me to, so I came back to tell you. I did not see you in your room and thought that you had gone out. I went in the kitchen and I saw so much smoke in my room that I was afraid it was on fire. I tried to enter, but something was holding the door closed; it was you, who had fallen behind it. The doctor said you fell with your head facing the space under the closed door providing you with a thread of fresh air, and that without it, it would all be over."

"My poor Marie, you do not know. . . . This man who came the other day. . . ."

"Do not worry, madame. If he returns, I shall tell him to arrest me, if he must take someone. And besides, no one will be allowed to come upstairs!"

I begged all those around me to keep this misadventure quiet. When such things are attempted, it is better not to fail or ridicule ensues.

16

Lise's Return

The Beautiful Baker and the "Table d'hôte"—Hemoptysis—
Waiting for Ernest—When the Courtesan Has Nothing
Left to Sell—Two People, Including the Coachman

FOR ME EVERYTHING was going from bad to worse! The women to
whom we had refused credit were not coming anymore.

The rent was due. There was not one red cent saved. The goods had
been sold and we had to pay for them.

I was going to be sued, my property seized. I was going mad. Every
day I cried for having failed in killing myself.

Lise was in Italy. The only friendship that gave a little comfort to my
despair was Deligny.

When I left for Holland, our relations were still very bittersweet.

I have already stated that he was quarrelsome and made fun of every
woman. He and his friend Médème, a tall, pale, blond, thin man, vied
with each other to see who could drink the most, have the most quarrels,
change mistresses most often. . . .

Because of his personality, he could not have remembered me very
clearly. Therefore I was very surprised when I received his visit.

I was in such a state of mind that only something extraordinary could
have reconciled me with a desire to live.

Deligny could not accomplish this miracle. But he was witty, amusing,
and my life was so sad, so isolated, that I welcomed him with pleasure,
finding in his visits some distraction from my worries. . . .

Our first meeting was short. He had conceded on every point. That
could be considered a victory over such a willful nature.

We spent a few evenings together. I kept him from getting intoxicated
and from swearing. He reluctantly obeyed, but he obeyed.

His father had an income of fifteen or twenty thousand pounds, but he had four children and could give his son only a modest pension, which his cabaret life ate up and then some.

He did everything he could to help me. I could have abused his generosity. He would have signed bills of exchange, notes for whomever I wished. I used my influence only to make him leave this life and this society of people who, wealthier than he, were ruining him.

THE BEAUTIFUL BAKER AND THE "TABLE D'HÔTE"

One day I saw a woman stop in front of my shop window. That sort of thing happened all day, and yet I let out a cry.

I opened my door to see her better. She walked by without looking at me, crossed the street, and went in at number 7, right across the way. A little while later the mezzanine window opened and I saw her looking out, standing next to a fat woman named Fond.

This Fond was one of those former beauties who, after wasting their lives, sell youth and beauty to others.

This woman hid her odious business under the name of "table d'hôte."

I was about to go back inside, still wondering, "Where have I seen this face?" when a maid came over to say, "Would you be kind enough to take two or three bonnets up there, on the second floor?"

I was led into a small red living room. The small woman came toward me as she was removing her hat. Once her hat was off, I recognized her immediately. She was the pretty girl from Bordeaux Denise had pointed out to me at the reformatory, the one a man had married so he could sell her.

I wanted to ask her all sorts of questions. We were not alone. I showed her what she had asked for, telling her if there was anything else she needed, to please come see me.

She promised she would and was true to her word. The next day she came to order a hat. She told me everything.

In Paris she was called the Beautiful Baker. I had heard of her. A man had kidnapped her, and her husband, who was not getting anything out of the affair, had him arrested. She had turned her husband in to the police and was separated from him to come live with Mme Fond.

Now she never passed by the shop without coming in. She was living across the street. Two or three times she had invited me over. To please her, one evening I accepted, and I did not regret it.

There is quite a study to be made of these so-called *table d'hôtes*.

After dinner a game is played. The regulars arrive. They are inscrutable people whose names are seldom known. The mistress of the house baptizes them. One is named the Major, another the Commandant. They all try to get a few hundred sous from each other. The women borrow the smallest amounts, up to fifty centimes.

The old mistress of the house calls everyone "darling." She charges a fee on the cards. Whatever the outcome, she always does well. Yet these women have practically nothing. Those who should have been very rich were destitute. Why? They bought the love they could no longer inspire.

If a newcomer joins this world, the mistress of the house is very friendly to him. First, she entices him to play a little game. The stranger is amazed at so much politeness and reserve. For three francs he has been served a dinner that is worth ten francs a head. He admires this miracle of order or generosity. But champagne is brought out and heads begin to turn!

The poor stranger loses everything he has on him, sometimes more, and he realizes too late that he has been duped.

Around the main female character flutter other women, sometimes young and pretty, who serve the mistress either by bringing people to her or by baiting the players.

Pitiful flunkies who make small profits. They are gamblers, and when they do not have any more money, in exchange, they give the key to their room.

I pointed out to my new acquaintance that she was in very wretched company.

"I know," she told me, "but my husband can come back at any moment, and I do not know where to go."

She was right. . . . A few days later her husband came to get her and beat her senseless. She came to tell me about her woes.

"Have you no friends?"

"No," she told me in tears, "I am quite miserable. I have been leading this life now for six years. If I could go back to my parents', I would leave right now."

I asked her if she had written to them.

"No, I have not dared."

I entreated her to do it so she could leave once and for all.

This woman had had her day in the sun. Then she could be seen every evening in a shop, on the corner near the Opéra-Comique. A passerby could think that she was happy. She was covered with jewelry, lace, and silk. That is what leads so many poor heads astray.

One morning she came to tell me that she had found a way to make a little money so she could return to her village where her brother was waiting for her. She wanted to organize a ball at the Frères-Provençaux and charge twenty francs a ticket.[1]

I mentioned the idea to Deligny who sold a few of them to his friends, Médème and others.

HEMOPTYSIS

One day a servant with stripes on every seam of his uniform looked in at my door.

"Is this where Mlle Céleste lives?"

"Yes."

He went out and motioned to a carriage, which pulled up in front of our house. It was a pretty surrey with two horses. An extremely elegant lady gently got out leaning against the servant. She motioned to the footman to wait for her outside, lifted her veil with one hand, and extended the other to me.

"Lise!" I said drawing back, she was so pale.

"So, you think I have changed? . . ."

"Yes," I said, somewhat recovered. "I am surprised to see you; you are so beautiful!"

"Oh! If that is the case, good! You see, everyone thinks I am ill."

I invited her to sit next to me. She could barely stand up.

"I have just arrived from Nice. I had caught a cold. . . . Ernest is so good that he took that very seriously, he loves me so much!"

"Ernest, that old wrinkled-up count?"

"Yes, I know you do not like him. For an excuse to visit me, his doctor convinced him that I was sick. Ernest would not let me go out, and I was bored. That is what he mistook for illness." She coughed and continued, "Ernest ordered a traveling coach and took me with him, passing me off as his wife. He forbade me to see you, but he is away for a few days."

When she walked in she was pale, but as she spoke, her color came back and her eyes shone. Yet, there was something different about her.

"Oh," she said laughing, "I had all my upper teeth pulled, and these are the pretty ones that replace them!"

I winced thinking about what she must have suffered.

She told me, "I have adopted a little girl from the foundling home."

"What!" I said. "I thought one had to have proof of a certain position."

"That is why she was not given to me but to Ernest, who committed himself to provide an income for her, even if he were to send her back to the orphanage."

At that moment the Beautiful Baker came in to publicize her dance tickets.

Lise bought two, jingling gold coins in a pretty little net purse. She was wearing diamonds on her ears and fingers.

I asked her what she intended to do with her tickets since I did not think she would go.

"What am I going to do with them? Well, go with Eulalie, and you, if you want to come also."

"So Eulalie is still at your house?"

"Yes, I have taken her everywhere."

"And Camille?"

"He is still the same. Farewell. I shall come pick you up Saturday."

That Saturday I was told that a lady was waiting for me downstairs and that she could not come up. When we arrived at the Frères-Provençaux, everyone let out a general Oh! . . . Under the lights she looked ashen. She was leaning against me to keep from falling. I made her sit down.

"You see, it has been a long time since people have seen me; they are surprised."

Afraid is more like it. People would walk by whispering. She was wearing a pink domino, trimmed in *broderie Anglaise,* and a black hat with roses.

"Can you hear what they are saying?"

"No," I replied. "Probably they are saying how stylish you look."

"Come, now," she said, "tell me that I am nothing more than a shadow of myself."

"Are you mad, my poor dear Lise?"

"I am so afraid of dying."

And as she watched the dancers twirling, her eyes brightened. She was following them with her soul. She seemed to be inhaling the lives of others.

"I want to waltz."

I did not dare prevent her and asked Médème to invite her to dance. I recommended that he hold her tight.

"Oh! I cannot do it," she said leaning against the wall.

After a dry cough, blood began to flow from her mouth.

"How could you have allowed her to go out?" Deligny said to me. "She is finished!"

"She is fainting," said Médème.

He picked her up in his arms and took her downstairs. No one noticed except Lagie who said when she saw her go by, "There goes Pomaré putting on airs."

WAITING FOR ERNEST

I took her home. She had a fever. She would not let us take her clothes off. She wanted to return to the ball, to dance.

We had to turn on all the lights. I stayed with her most of the night. Finally fatigue took over and she fell asleep.

The next day I went to see her. She was up, paler than the day before.

"Oh! There you are," she said, her lips tight. "So they think I am dead? What treason!"

I thought she was mad.

"Are you not outraged?" she told me angrily.

"You have not told me what is wrong with you."

"Well! Eulalie is Camille's mistress. They were both deceiving me. In a few days he will be an adult. She ran off with him. She is pregnant and wants to marry him, but I know his uncle, his guardian. I shall write to him; I shall go there if I have to."

She burst into tears. I tried to comfort her.

"Now, am I not your friend? I shall not abandon you. . . . Your lover, this count, has he not amply proven his affection? Those ingrates, forget them."

"Forget! Yes, you are right. For one thing, I am seeing my mother again. She visits me on the sly. I give her things for my brothers and sisters. Eulalie was her favorite! She is going to defend her. I cannot talk to her about this. I wish Ernest would come back. I am expecting his doctor today. I shall not tell him that I went out yesterday."

We went into her bedroom. This room was decorated in yellow, like the one on Rue Saint-Georges, but better furnished. There were two windows in the front with white and yellow curtains. Between the two windows stood a light wooden stand holding a plaster Virgin Mary covered with a lace veil. Through it, one could see pearls and flowers.

"The doctor!" announced the chambermaid.

"I shall leave you."

When I returned, her mother was there. She would not let me in. I came back a few days later. She tried to send me away, but I insisted and went in.

Lise, who did not leave her bed anymore, scolded me for staying away so long. Her mother was looking at me; I did not dare say that I had been sent away.

"I wish Ernest would return," she told me dejectedly.

I made her repeat, because this Ernest she was still waiting for I had seen the night before.

"Being sick is so expensive! I already have a lot of debts. It looks like everyone is afraid I am going to die; they are all bringing me their bills."

I took leave of her. Her mother led me into the dining room and said to me, "You probably know that this M. Ernest is in Paris? Word has been sent to him several times, but he never replies. The doctor he had been sending does not come anymore. Day before yesterday, they came from the Mère de Famille shop to repossess some items. I asked for some time. It is a matter of three hundred francs for a pink domino. They will be back in a few days."

"This must be avoided. I shall go there."

I went to the shop to say I was taking responsibility for the debt. I returned to see Lise a few days later.

"You who love her, scold her," said her mother. "She spent the whole night writing."

"Yes," said Lise with a strange smile. "Yes, that made me feel good."

Her cheeks were hollow, her lips red. I could hear her breathing was hoarse. I wanted to cry. Her eyes never left me. I figured out that she had something to tell me, but we were never alone; her mother never left the room when I was there.

She picked up a little blue enameled watch from the night stand and handed it to her mother telling her, "Here, send this over there, it is my last piece of jewelry. How I wish Ernest would come back! Not a single letter from him!"

Her mother left. She pulled me closer to her bed and said, "I wrote Camille's uncle. He wanted the boy to marry his daughter, so he will prevent this wedding. I am avenged. You will tell her, tell Eulalie, if you run into her, that it was I. . . ."

Someone was coming. She put her finger to her lips. Her mother entered.

I told her how unhappy I was that I did not have any money to give her so she could avoid these transactions at the pawnshop.

A few days later her living room, dining room, and boudoir furniture were repossessed. I was able to keep everyone out of her bedroom.

What had been taken was ample enough to cover the five hundred francs requested.

She asked who was walking next door. I replied that people were looking at her apartment. Every day she was saying that she wanted to move; she was not surprised.

"Yes, I am going to leave this place, and I shall go live in the country."
Then her eyes would fill with tears and she would continue, "Yes, in the
country, at the Montmartre Cemetery."

When she would tell me about her hopes, I was sadder than when
she would talk about her approaching end. I advised her to write to a
few friends. No one came.

M. Ernest had stopped taking care of her. No efforts could change
his mind. He sent a reply that he did not want to make new sacrifices
for a woman who had only a month left to live.

Each time I left this poor girl, I would tell myself, "Let us hope she
dies before they come for her bed!"

WHEN THE COURTESAN HAS NOTHING LEFT TO SELL
She had asked me to get her some good wine, some grapes, asparagus,
and those were not in season. Even though I had very little money, I
bought what she wanted.

I arrived with my arms full. Eulalie was the one who opened the door
for me. I almost dropped everything on the floor! She took me into the
dining room to tell me, "Do you know what she did to me? Yesterday,
Camille's uncle had him come over, presumably to talk business, and
he whisked him away in his carriage, almost by force. She is the cause
of all this. This morning I received a letter at the hotel. Camille is bid-
ding me farewell. He declares that he will send me some money and he
repeats that he wanted to marry me. I want her to wake up, and I shall
tell her what is on my mind."

I begged her not to do anything of the kind, but to be considerate of
her sister's last moments.

"What do I care? I wish she had died a month earlier."

Her mother, who seemed to have a marked preference for Eulalie,
appeared to have taken her side.

Lise rang.

Her sister opened the door, leaned against the door frame and, with
her arms crossed, said, "Well, it is I. Are you surprised?"

I saw Lise, barely awake, rise on her elbows, smile, and fall back down,
saying, "Finally! . . ."

Eulalie came closer.

"You are pleased with your work, you devil's daughter. Instead of
repenting, you are evil to the last moment. Look at yourself. You are
half dead, so you will not be able to enjoy your triumph for very long. I
have been abandoned and so have you. Your Ernest, he is in town and

he does not want to see you. You thought you were loved by everyone! Where are all your lovers?"

Lise closed her eyes without replying. I saw tears slip out from under her eyelids. Her mother was tugging on Eulalie and motioning for her to be quiet. She was probably going to continue.

"Oh! If you are the mother of both of them," I yelled, "take her away! And you, Eulalie, leave!"

I pushed her into the next room and locked the door.

Lise pressed my hand and said, "If only you could stay near me! Of course she is right, why would he come back?"

She showed me her emaciated arms and hands.

"The life I have led, it is a business. I was bought for a kiss. I have nothing left to sell, so no one comes anymore. The honest woman is taken care of by her companion from her younger days until the end. For us, nothing but mockery and insults during and after. Hand me the rosary that is at the feet of the Virgin Mary. Remove the veil covering her and put her near me, on this table. Send me a priest or ask my mother to."

She rested her head on the corner of the nightstand. The glow from the night light and the reflection on the white Virgin Mary lit up her face. I asked her mother to go get a confessor.

The next day, I went back to see Lise. I had dreamed about her all night. I saw her dressed up for a ball. Her flowers were black.

When I went in, I questioned her concierge with my eyes. He nodded in a way that meant, "It is not over, but it will not be long."

I went up the three flights of stairs breathless. I was going to ring, when I heard laughter and talk. I knocked. Her sister opened, a napkin in her hand. I entered the dining room. I saw oysters and white wine. They were having a cheerful lunch.

"Does this mean she is better?" I said looking over this feast.

"Yes," replied her mother, "she is resting."

"Did she make her confession?"

"Yes, she saw her priest yesterday. That made her happy. She asked her sister for forgiveness."

"It is about time," said Eulalie. "I shall never forget what she did to me."

TWO PEOPLE, INCLUDING THE COACHMAN

I went in Lise's room. She turned to look at me with her dead eyes, made a sign of recognition, and sighed without saying a word.

I sat in a chair near her and asked her how she was feeling. She motioned that she was fine. She had wrapped her rosary around her arm. Her prayer book was next to her.

"Oh," she said. "Listen."

I leaned over because her voice was weak.

"I ordered my portrait from a poor artist. It is almost finished. No one will want it. Go get it and you can keep it!"

She barely had time to tell me the name of the painter, Montji. Her voice failed her again. She pointed toward the Virgin Mary and kissed the cross of her rosary. She wanted to be alone.

The next day, when I returned, all the doors were open. Her soul had departed and a candle was keeping watch over her body. All those around her had dry eyes.

I kneeled at the foot of her bed, then I kissed her on the forehead, closed her eyes, and cut off a lock of her hair.

I did not go back home. I went to see Deligny, who, seeing my distress, did his best to distract me and comfort me.

The next day it was pouring down rain. I took a little surrey to Rue d'Amsterdam. Once I had arrived at Lise's door, I heard the nailing of the coffin.

Her body was displayed at the door. The street was deserted in that area, the weather was horrible, and no one was going by. There were two people in her funeral procession: me and my coachman. When the last clump of dirt was thrown on top of her, a cross with her initials was dropped in.

Deligny was at my house. He chided me for going through so much trouble. I was crying for her and for me.

A week later I went to the cemetery, hoping to find a stone, several people. Nothing. And yet her mother, by paying fifteen hundred francs of her debts, had inherited some fifteen thousand francs.

I came back ten days later. The dead woman was as neglected as the sick woman had been.

I ordered a metal enclosure and a marble tombstone with these words: Here lies Lise . . . born 22 February 1825, deceased 8 December 1846. Her friend, Céleste.

I went to see Montji. He let me have her portrait for two hundred francs instead of three hundred, which was the agreed upon price.

That is the portrait that hangs in my house.

These expenses inconvenienced me a lot, but I made them without regret. Deligny helped me.

A few small newspapers had the nerve to make a few jokes about this sad and forsaken ending: "Much will be forgiven her because she loved so much." They should have stated: "She might be forgiven because she died as a good Christian and because she suffered so much."

She had indeed suffered much. I have never known anyone who was so afraid of dying. Because of her religious beliefs, however, she wanted to face her coming end. But nature won over her will. Often during the night she would call out for help. She would cry, "My God, let me live!" And then her feeble hand would reach out to no one in particular. The poor girl who was waiting on her, who was actually quite attached to her, asked for her severance pay so she would not be a witness to these agonizing scenes anymore.

Alphonse, who had recovered his desire to live, his cheerfulness in the company of this will-o'-the wisp, took the news of her death grimly. He is probably the only one she did not send for. He is the only one who would have replied.

17

Dinner at the Café Anglais

Daddy Longlegs's Rudeness—A Young Man Named Lionel—
First Stammering of a Tumultuous Love Affair

THEN I GOT SOME rather odd news that affected me even more since it had some bearing on the ideas, feelings, and doubts painfully resonating within me since Lise's death.

This bit of news had to do with the poor pianist who I had accused of unfaithfulness and myself of gullibility.

I was told that after our separation, H——— had been miserable and became ill. He left for Rome, became a Roman Catholic, and entered a monastery. It was difficult for me to believe that this decision could have been as a result of our separation. In any case, I replied to the person telling me this story that if I cursed all my friends as I had cursed him, the Church would owe me a reward. Deep down inside, I was more moved than I wanted to appear.

I hated my apartment, and, to avoid being there, I spent my nights out.

DADDY LONGLEGS'S RUDENESS

Deligny had returned to his dissipated life. I went along with him and was loud so I would not hear my sadness. My health had been acutely affected by my suicide attempt. One does not ingest the fumes from a bushel of coal without some consequences. I had a cough and a burning in my chest. I drank champagne to extinguish it.

Such a state of mind did not produce an even temperament. I bullied Deligny. To his demonstrations of tenderness, I would invariably reply, "Today you love me, or so you say. But if I become ill, you will abandon me like a dog; if I die, you will not accord me one regret."

In the end I would have benumbed myself to all feeling. One dinner followed another. I no longer slept but found rest in memories.

In the chaotic midst of this crazy life, I had become friends with a small woman who had come to the shop. She was nice, witty, and unconcerned about tomorrow. This woman was Frisette, Brididi's mistress. She had come to see me out of curiosity and had become attached to me. That way she could keep an eye on me to make sure that I was not involved with her dear Brididi, who, I believe, had totally forgotten me.

What I particularly liked about her was her kindness. She did favors for whomever she wished and hid the fact to avoid thank yous. If she had only six sous to take the omnibus, Frisette would give them to a poor person and would go about her shopping with a song on her lips.

I am not sure which one of us took the other to a dinner at the Café Anglais. I went out of idleness, not allowing myself to have fun. I had no idea that this evening would have a decisive influence on my life and would probably engender its denouement.

At this dinner I was in familiar surroundings. I recognized several people I had seen at Lagie's.

My attention was first drawn to a tall, skinny, dark-haired and pale young man who seemed to be about thirty years old. His forehead was absurdly wide and high; his face was long, thin at the chin, his eyes were large and black, his nose was pointed, his mouth medium size, and his teeth rotten. . . . He was master of the feast and gave orders like a commander. He would reply to the women around him with the air of a protector.

While waiting for dinner to be served, he sat at the piano. He was a good musician, but he would contort his body and grimace too much. His bony hands looked like spiders.

During dinner he picked on me. He was clever, but he was always talking about himself. According to him, he did everything better than anyone else. His title was the best, his fortune the largest; no one was as brave as he.

All this bombast was getting on my nerves. I had not replied to his provocation, but my anger was building up, and already I had given him a nickname, which I whispered to my neighbor. I called him Daddy Longlegs.

What increased my bad mood was that I was seated next to a very handsome man who was quite pleased with his own person; he was a dandy. Focusing on Daddy Longlegs's sarcastic remarks, I was not paying attention to my neighbor's pantomime, and that put him in a very bad mood.

Things were off to a bad start. I had not opened my mouth yet and I already had two enemies.

I was the butt of all of Daddy Longlegs's jokes. Anger finally got the best of me.

"Sir," I told him, "would you be kind enough to leave me alone? I have had to listen to your foolishness now for an hour. I am not afraid of spiders, but they disgust me, and when they come near me I squash them. So, you big Daddy Longlegs, put an end to this preoccupation with me!"

The epithet of Daddy Longlegs immediately put the jokers on my side. They understood that the attacks at my expense gave me the right to a certain latitude.

My foe became furious. He did not expect such reprisals from one of those poor girls who usually lower their heads under the yoke of opulent self-conceit.

"And who brought," he yelled," this . . . ?"

There was a deep silence. Everyone knew this was going to be entertaining.

A YOUNG MAN NAMED LIONEL

It so happened it was the fad that during the dinners organized by this Daddy Longlegs there would be a victim to whom he could spout his vulgar diatribes. I had been chosen by him for that day. But with my disposition, he was out of luck.

My handsome neighbor was siding with my enemy and supported him with his eyes and gestures.

Frisette was the only one not amused by the scene. The poor child knew that a huge storm had been brewing in my heart. She came over to me and, in a low voice, begged me to leave with her. I replied out loud, "Why would I leave? The gentleman is at the end of his tether. If it were not for women like us, where would he be . . . at the zoo? . . . I have paid my dues by listening to him."

Without realizing it, during the heat of this discussion, I had gained an ally who, touched by my courage, became interested in my cause and took up the cudgels for me.

He was a young man whom I had not noticed named Lionel.

"Now really, gentlemen," he said in a soft and proud voice, "will you not stop this? There are two of you ganging up on a woman! One would already be too many."

And, addressing Daddy Longlegs, whom he seemed to know quite well, "Dear friend, today I can recognize neither your usual good taste nor your generosity."

"Now," continued Daddy Longlegs, who could detect in this notion a means for an honorable retreat, "if I have wounded Mademoiselle's ego, I am more than prepared to make amends. Since you have pledged yourself as her knight, you decide on the ransom."

"Fifteen louis!"

"Fifteen louis, so be it. She will have them tomorrow."

"Tomorrow! That is quite late," said my champion.

"I do not have them on me."

"No problem! Vesparoz will lend them to you."

There was no backing down. Daddy Longlegs's ego was on the line. He rang.

Vesparoz, the café's head waiter, came.

"Bring me fifteen louis."

A waiter arrived carrying a tray with the sum requested on it.

"Give this money to Mlle Céleste."

Of course I refused to take it.

But my champion would have none of it.

"Bring me this!" he told the waiter, and he put the fifteen louis on the table next to him. Then turning toward me, "My dear child, come sit next to me."

I went willingly.

"Take this," he told me. "It is yours and you could not refuse it without offending me. Those are the rules of war. And now," he added, addressing Daddy Longlegs, "you can continue all you want, at the same price of course."

He must have thought this was good advice because he got up and extended his hand to me. "Let us make peace," he told me.

There was no reason to hesitate anymore, and I graciously placed my hand in his.

FIRST STAMMERING OF A TUMULTUOUS LOVE AFFAIR

When we left the table to play some music, dance, sing, Daddy Longlegs called me over to a corner near a window and confessed that he had caused this ridiculous scene just so he would have a pretext to make up with me. I responded coldly.

He became tender, caring. He was promising me the moon.

As for me, I had no desire to make up to that extent. I listened to him distractedly, but at the same time, I watched my ally with interest.

The latter noticed that he was the object of my attention and drew near us.

I then began to repeat out loud the tender words Daddy Longlegs had just told me softly. I intended to adorn myself with my victory, and in order to really confirm it, I replied to Daddy Longlegs, "I can see that you are more yourself again and I believe you are sincere. But I have known you only since yesterday, and I see no reason to continue our relationship."

And I left him in the corner.

He picked up a bottle of champagne and drank it almost in one swallow.

Lionel did not take his eyes off him. As for me, I was following all of Lionel's movements. When he was speaking to a woman, I wanted to place myself between him and that woman.

I sat down next to Frisette, and I got her to talk to me about him.

He was a twenty-year-old man, rather tall, of good and well-proportioned size, with a round face and lovely brown hair with a fine white part. His forehead was of medium height, his face was oval, his eyebrows were thick, and his mustache compact. His brown eyes were of ordinary size, but the look in them was deep and piercing. He had elegant manners and was impeccably dressed but without the rigid, awkward bearing many young men have.

His mind was quick. He gave me the impression of having a fierce nature, but one he knew how to tame, and that he could tone down his ardor with charming manners.

"Without him," I told Frisette pointing him out, "I do not know how this quarrel would have ended. I am not sure that I thanked him."

I wanted him to come talk to me . . . but he did nothing of the kind. Dancing began, but he did not invite me to dance; yet he was looking at me.

The tall handsome man, my table neighbor, came up to me and loudly asked me if I wanted to escape with him. I got up without replying.

Daddy Longlegs was no longer speaking to me.

This little game of eye and heart because of Lionel was getting tiresome. I went straight up to him and I asked him if he wanted to take me home.

"Yes," he said looking at me as if he could read my mind. "But first, I would like to dance with you."

A waltz was starting. He had me twirling on the dance floor before I could answer. I was nimble and his arm was tense. I felt a flash of happiness that passed through me quick as lightning, but which I can still remember.

I came back to Frisette, radiant.

She knew Lionel, or had just asked questions about him, because she said to me, "You have been dancing with the Count of C——." [1]

That name was quite lovely, quite removed from me.

"Are you coming?" said Lionel. "I shall take Frisette home first, then you."

"I am really sorry to put you through so much trouble."

"It is a pleasure. I would not have dared ask you. I did not want to be the third one to persecute you."

He promised he would come over that evening at four. I went home, my head and my heart filled with his image. How foolish of me to have lost hope in life! And I was twenty years old!

18

Lionel

"Just who is this Zizi?"—Deligny Chooses Africa—"Do not
let go of this, Céleste!"—Maids, Too, Have Their Troubles—
Letter of Reason and Death Certificate—For the Heart:
Digitalis and the Sound of a Doorbell

FOUR O'CLOCK took so long in arriving that, to make the time pass
more quickly, I went down to the shop.

A few days earlier I had written to my friend in Holland. He sent me a
note for two thousand francs to be cashed at a bank on Rue d'Hauteville.
With these two thousand francs and my three hundred from the night
before, I was rich.

I stood in the doorway. A jumble of carriages was obstructing the entrance. A pretty phaeton led by two beautiful black horses was waiting
to turn on Rue Geoffroy-Marie. The restless horses reared and one of
the servants got out.

"Leave it, leave it," said the young man holding on to the reins. It was
Lionel.

He appeased his horses and disengaged his carriage with considerable ability. When I saw he was out of danger I crossed the street to go
up to my apartment, but he saw me.

"How pale you look!"

"I got scared when I saw you jammed in with all those carriages on
the corner of Faubourg Montmartre."

He started to laugh and offered his arm to accompany me upstairs.

I was ill at ease next to him. I did not want to lower myself, yet I felt
so beneath him that I did not dare stand in front of him. My unease was
even more ridiculous because he was unaffected, charming, and gallant.

"I shall never again come with my horses," he told me, "since I scared
you. I do not know this neighborhood well (I live on Rue Grenelle-
Saint-Germain), but, if you will allow me, I shall come often."

I was reserved in my replies. However much a woman is or has been lost, when she is in love, she can retrieve a trace of modesty and virtue from her past. I loved him.

"JUST WHO IS THIS ZIZI?"

I wanted to elevate myself in my own esteem, but that was impossible. The scene from the night before had reminded me even more forcefully of who I was and what my life was. I had absolutely nothing to give.

"Perhaps I am intruding?" he said rising to leave.

"No, no, please stay."

"Céleste, are you aware that I have known you for a long time? I have often seen you at the Hippodrome, and each time I admired your dexterity and your courage."

It comforted me to think that he had found some merit in my courage! Yes, I had some, since I was deathly afraid of horses. I did not know then that all my efforts would eventually be rewarded with one word from him.

"Would you like to dine with me this evening?"

"Yes, if you have nothing better to do."

"Be ready at six."

He came for me in one of his carriages. It was a lovely surrey lined in blue silk, so small that the two of us barely fit in it. I sank back into the cushions.

"You are afraid of being seen?" he asked me.

"Yes, by you."

We dined at Deffieux. I was morose. This love seemed like an illusion to me.

He took me home and we spent the evening together. I was uncomfortable. I loved him too much to lie to him. I told him all I had done, all I had been.

"Others would have told you," I said, "enemies. You might have been sorry. I love you and I shall love you for a long time. A reproach from you would hurt me. I wish I could redo the past, but that is impossible. Do you want the present?"

His answer was a kiss. It felt as though another woman had just awakened inside me.

He did not like the neighborhood where I lived. He thought I lived too far away. I decided to rent an apartment at Place de la Madeleine and I gave the shop to my mother. At the risk of making a big dent in my resources, I paid two months in advance so I could move in as soon as my new lodgings were ready.

Sometimes Lionel liked to gamble. He gave a party in an apartment he owned on Rue Bleue. Lagie came with me. The dinner was splendid. Several times a reference was made to a woman called Zizi.

"Just who is this Zizi?" I asked Lagie.

"She is his mistress. We are at her apartment. He sent her away to the country."

There was a buzzing in my head. We had just gotten up from the table. I went straight to Lionel and asked him if what I had just been told was true.

"Not exactly," he replied. "It is true that a woman I have known for a long time lives here. But you are in my apartment. I intend to leave her, and when I do, I shall let her have all that is here."

The game had begun, and the stakes were high.

For a long time I remained buried deep in only one thought: he had a mistress! For the last two weeks he had been giving me his spare moments.

Lionel lost a lot of money. I was glad.

One of his friends near me was saying, "That Lionel is crazy. He has a lot of debts and his father is young; he will be ruined before he inherits."[1]

It pleased me to hear that. A secret presentiment told me that his ruin would bring him closer to me.

The next day there were races in Versailles. We did not even go to bed. At six in the morning, a landau with four horses was at the door along with some other carriages. There was one barouche still empty.

"Do you want to come?" asked Lionel.

I felt like refusing, but I did not have the courage.

Once the races were over, he told me farewell. He was leaving for Saint-Germain where he had some business. His friends, who knew quite well what sort of business was drawing him, decided as a joke to invite Lagie and me to dine in Saint-Germain.

We arrived at the Henri IV pavilion. When he saw me, Lionel took off. Those who were with me began to laugh.

"Now why would he leave like that?"

"Well, it is because he is between two fires. Zizi is here, but it does not matter, you will dine with us. I shall say that you are my mistress."

I bitterly regretted coming.

Lionel was told that I knew everything. He came over to hold my hand, which remained stiff and cold in his.

We sat down to eat. I was not hungry, but I was dying of thirst. My mirth was turning into cynicism. I let my neighbor kiss my hand and my neck.

He came to stand right in front of me, stared into my eyes, and motioned for me to step outside. I obeyed.

He took me far into the garden, had me sit down, and, taking my hands, said, "What is the matter, Céleste? You seem to take pleasure in torturing me."

"Do you not have a mistress? Do you want me to cry in front of her? I am free, I want to forget you—"

"To forget me! Why? Is it my fault that before meeting you I had a liaison? I cannot abruptly leave her, without a reason. Be patient!"

During the night I listened for his door to open. Zizi stayed in the country and I brought him back to Paris without taking my eyes off him. I was afraid I had made him angry. I must have been wearying him with my excessive love.

He liked everyone, and he often went dancing or to parties with young men. I resented the fact that he would not sacrifice his pleasures for me.

DELIGNY CHOOSES AFRICA

One day Comte de S—— invited me to a ball given every year at the Frères Provençaux by the Jockey-Club.[2] He made me promise I would go.

It so happened that it was the same day that Lionel had announced he had to attend a friend's party. I thought he was lying to me. I volunteered to sacrifice my dance invitation if he wanted to stay. He refused.

I waited, hoping that he would change his mind. The doorbell rang. I went to open the door: it was Comte de S—— coming to get me with one of his friends.

It was my first time being invited to this ball. Not every woman who wanted to go, could. Only actresses and kept women were invited. They all used the occasion to tear each other apart.

If they had been told in advance, "We have invited Mogador," they would have all raised their voices saying, "Pooh! How horrible! We are not going." But they had not been warned. It would be a surprise for them.

When I walked in, widespread clamor erupted. The women retreated to the corners of the room; the men drew near me. It was difficult to find a vis-à-vis for me. If it had not been for a girl called Brochet, who remembered that before her life under gilded ceilings she had been a washerwoman, I would have had to dance facing two men. The other women had gathered together and were whispering, "Mogador! A circus rider from the Hippodrome! A woman who has danced in a public dance hall!"

That was all they knew about me and they found me unworthy of them.

Among them, however, was one who was less patrician. I liked her a lot. She was called Chouchou.

"It pains me to see all these silly geese putting on airs," she told me. "Look at those two sisters. Just a year ago they were only too glad to share the dinner and small iron bed of some poor boy who had picked them up on the docks. They were hired in theater where they were given a letter to wear so they could show off their youth. And this Verveine! She is grinning from behind her fan to hide her bad teeth. Four years ago she was a servant at the Passage des Panoramas. I can still see her in galoshes washing the outside of the store in the morning."

Chouchou was ebullient. She went on for a long time and told me about the lives of all these women.

I had hoped to make Lionel jealous by going to this ball, but to no avail. He asked me if I had a good time.

One day I had gone to Enghien with Lionel; we heard a lot of noise coming from upstairs. Geniol, who knew me, came to ask me to leave. He told me that Deligny was on the second floor with several of his friends, that he had seen me in the garden with Lionel, he had been drinking and partying, and he had just been overcome by a fit of anger and was breaking everything. We left.

The next day I sent for news of him. I was told that he was sick. After having tried very hard to forget me, seeing that he could not, he had enlisted and left for Africa.

When he returned from the campaign, he rushed over to my apartment. I told him honestly about my liaison with Lionel. He did not blame me.

"It is my fault," he told me, "I did not know how to make myself loved. I am getting what I deserve. Many are the poor girls who have loved me and whom I hurt. They would tell me, 'Your turn will come.' They were right."

I had not seen him again until the day Geniol told me, "Leave, he is breaking everything!"

I often talked about him. Lionel wished he could have torn me away from this memory, which made him jealous. I was aware of it, and, to incite Lionel's love, I would bring it up repeatedly. The heart is like that.

I wanted to make myself as big as the world so Lionel would love me. I was investing my life in him. I wanted to erase the past. When I would wait for him, I would worry, I would invent a thousand stories, I would imagine him with another woman. He was amused watching my growing attachment to him. Without actually having a fortune, he spent a lot of money and incurred many debts.

I had no part in his follies.

Early in our acquaintance, he had given me a ring. But it was he I loved. Sometimes we would go out together in the evening. I was proud and happy; I would snuggle up close to him. I loved him too much for him to love me or to notice.

Lionel took advantage of it. Several months went by like this. I loved him more each day.

My botched asphyxiation had left me with a serious bronchial inflammation.

"You should take care of yourself!" he would tell me.

"Pooh!" I would reply. "I shall live longer than your love."

One morning, his valet came to get him at my apartment.

"M. le Comte must come at once. Monsieur le marquis is very ill."

"Oh, no! My father!"

Several days went by without news. In the evening, I would go to the door of his house and look; I knew he was there and I would go home calmer.

I wrote to him to tell him how worried I was.

Finally, I received a letter.

My dear child, I thank you for your concern. I have just suffered a terrible loss. Although I had been expecting it for a long time, I did not believe it was so near.

You can understand that certain sorrows need solitude.

It was a farewell. I felt as if life were slipping away.

"It is not possible," I said to myself. "It cannot be all over between us. . . ."

I went to see my mother. She had closed the shop and had left with Vincent.

I went to see Frisette. She comforted me, saying that at times like these, with a death in the family still so recent, Lionel could not be with a mistress. He had duties to fulfill.

Two of Lionel's friends came to see me a few days later.

"Well," one of them told me, "Lionel just inherited. That is good for you!"

"For her? That is not certain," said the other, whose name was Georges. "He is going into mourning in the country, and now he must think about getting married."

"You have seen him?"

"Yes, at church," replied the first one. "He really loved his father, but nothing better could have happened to him."

"Is it ever a good thing when one's father dies?" said Georges looking at him.

"Sure, when a person has debts! His father had an income of four hundred thousand pounds, but he is leaving four or five children. . . . Do not let go of this, Céleste."

First of all, I had understood one thing only, that he was leaving. The last sentence brought me back to my senses. I straightened up to tell them that I did not love him for his fortune. They laughed in my face and left saying, "Still, do not let go of this, Céleste!"

I was stunned. To take one step toward him was not possible without seeming to have an ulterior motive. And yet, I had moved because of him. I had furnished a new apartment. To please him, I had gone to considerable expense. He did not know that, and I would not have told him for anything in the world.

He left town without saying good-bye. I was devastated. I did not even know his address. I only knew that he had retired on some land that he wanted to keep as his inheritance.

MAIDS, TOO, HAVE THEIR TROUBLES

I went back to see Frisette. I told her, "I want to forget him. He is an ingrate. Come with me, let us party and have a good time."

We spent our nights gambling.

Georges came back. He found me so sad, so changed, that he felt sorry for me. He told me, "If you love him so much, write to him. Here is his address."

I started ten letters, which I tore up. No, I would tell myself, when I shall have money, lots of money. If he came back and saw the destitution around me, he would think that it was out of need. He would throw me a few louis coins and leave again.

I gambled everywhere, at other women's houses, at *tables d'hôtes*. But gambling did not agree with me. I met a young, handsome, rich, kind,

Russian prince! He loved me, even though I did not hide my indifference toward him.

When I had paid off my most urgent debts and had a little money put aside, I wrote Lionel:

My dear friend, in writing to you thus, I do not wish to level reproaches at you so you would pay attention to me. I have loved you, and a love like mine is most insignificant. You had a right to trample it.

You trod on my heart. Since your departure, I have been losing myself in gambling establishments, killing my memory of you by wearing myself out.

I was mad to love you so much. I knew you could not keep me. With a little reasoning on my part, I could have healed myself. Heedlessly you crushed me. That was mean! I have a better opinion of myself. I did not know I was capable of so much love.

I need nothing. I am almost rich now. I wish you all the happiness in the world, and I forgive you your neglect.

I sealed this letter and posted it. I began to count the number of hours it would have to travel. I placed my hand on my heart at the instant he was to receive it the next day. I hid my weakness from everyone.

I spoke of him only with Marie, my maid, this girl who had saved my life.

I had not requested a reply but I was waiting for one.

The next day Marie came into my bedroom. There could not possibly have been an answer already, yet I looked at her hands.

"Oh! Excuse me, madame, this is what is happening: I have a sister who is seventeen. She came to Paris to learn a trade, but she ran away. I do not know what she did, but she has been arrested. My mother sent me a power of attorney to secure her release from prison where she has been locked up. She is coming out tomorrow. She wanted to enter a house. My mother would not let her."

"She did the right thing."

"I wanted to ask madame if it would be all right to let her stay in my room until my mother comes for her. She will to go back to work at Choisy-le-Roi."

"My poor Marie, I have no objections. But she must never come down to the apartment. My situation is too shaky for me to receive openly a woman in an irregular situation."

Augustine—that was her sister's name—got out the next day and came over. She was tall, thin, almost blond. I thought that maybe cooped up alone in a cabinet on the sixth floor she would be bored to death. I told Marie to keep her in the kitchen during the day; she could do some mending; I would give her so much a day and she would be fed as well until she could find a position.

We received a letter from her mother announcing her arrival very soon. I would be glad to see Augustine leave. There was something dishonest and impertinent about her, and she was lazy. I had bought some Indian fabric for dresses. We had a devil of a time getting her to make hers.

LETTER OF REASON AND DEATH CERTIFICATE

It was Augustine, returning from an errand, who brought me Lionel's letter that the concierge had handed her.

My dear Céleste, I did not reply to your letter sooner even though I wanted to very much. You must not hold it against me. I have to take care of matters too serious to neglect. I must sacrifice my current pleasures to my future position. I am happy to hear you are affluent. I know the one whose happiness I am condemned to envy, but he will never be as happy as I was with you.

If, as you state, you have some affection for me, you will take good care of your health; it is dear to me.

I am waiting for one of my friends. My old manor will frighten him, it is so dismal. Nature and the countryside are magnificent, but I believe these are beauties he will have little use for.

I am living in one of the old towers of Château Magnet. My window looks out on lovely meadows in bloom. Through them runs the Indre River. The horizon all around is closed off by splendid woods and forests.

Anyway, my dear child, my life is now quite different, and I am trying to forget a past that is too enticing.

Adieu, my dear friend. Take good care of yourself. Save a nice corner for me in your memory.

All my love.

Lionel

This letter was burning my fingers and my eyes. I searched for a tender word, but all I found was indifference and reasoning.

Marie came in and announced that her mother was arriving in two days.

Her sister had gone out without telling her. She had taken Marie's prettiest bonnet and her silk pinafore. Marie was worried, and for good reason, because Augustine did not come home. Her mother arrived. I believe it was her arrival that had made Augustine flee. The poor woman, who had not seen her daughter in a long time, left downhearted for Choisy-le-Roi where Augustine was expected.

Three days later Marie brought me a letter that she had just received. On the outside were the words "To Mademoiselle Marie, care of Mademoiselle Céleste." The return address was "HOSPICE DE L'HOTEL-DIEU."

Mademoiselle, would you please come by within the next twenty-four hours to identify the body of a person named Augustine . . . who died yesterday at four in the evening.

We hired a cab. At l'Hôtel-Dieu, I presented the letter.

A young woman had been brought in two days ago and had died the next day.

We walked through a glassed-in terrace and went down a few steps. As the crypt was being opened, I could hear a strange sound. The waters of the Seine were lapping against the rampart; it sounded like voices whispering. The door was open and a damp cold met our faces. The guard lit a weak candle on the stairs. Only one side of the crypt was lighted by a basement window. On the right as we came in, here and there on both sides, were what looked like stone beds. Some were flat, others formed rather high domes.

"This way," said the guard, his hand cupping the flame to protect it from the draft.

At the fourth bed the man stopped, handed me the torch, and lifted the dome. It was a wicker lid covered with an oilcloth.

"Oh! Madame," exclaimed Marie, squeezing my arm, "this is not my sister."

I brought the light closer to the corpse of a woman dried up by disease. She was a skeleton covered with an almost blue skin.

"I am certain she is here," said the man, "I made a mistake."

He lifted another lid and said, "Look at this one."

Marie let out a loud scream. She had just recognized her sister! She picked up the young woman in her arms and was talking to her. I wanted to take her away.

"No, leave me, I do not want to leave her. Augustine! Sister!"

She was shaking the corpse whose head was limply bobbing. It was a gruesome sight. The body was covered with large black blotches, her hair, cropped short, made her look like a boy. I could not get over the sight. I motioned to the guard to pull Marie away from there. I led her away from the crypt in spite of her reluctance.

I asked where she had died. I was sent to Sainte-Marie. I wanted to know what her ailment had been. A nun walked up to me and drew me into a corner.

"I did not want to relate in front of a relative how this poor creature was brought to us. She was picked up by a sentry at the Ecole tollgate. She had been forced to drink and had become mixed up in a brawl during which she was beaten. She came down with erysipelas and I had to cut her hair. She gave me your address saying she was a servant in your household."

We left. Marie sent for her mother and arranged to meet her the next morning at ten at l'Hôtel-Dieu to see her daughter Augustine, who has been "very ill."

The scene was even worse than the night before. The mother was waiting for us at the entrance. I whispered to Marie to bring the clothes and to speed up the arrangements. I was trying to save time. A young boy came down, probably using some other stairs, and asked me, "Madame, do you wish to see the young woman before she is nailed up?"

"Who is being nailed up?" said the mother.

And she followed the boy before I could stop her. They were closing the lid when she arrived.

She threw herself on the man doing the work, pushed him aside, and tore her nails trying to remove the planks. They did not stop her, since, after all, she had a right to see.

Marie had her sister taken away, asking me not to abandon her mother who, at times, suffered from epilepsy and had just had an attack. I took her away and she remembered nothing.

FOR THE HEART: DIGITALIS
AND THE SOUND OF A DOORBELL

All these events had affected my health. My heart palpitations were getting worse. I had to send for the doctor. He prescribed rest and strong doses of digitalis syrup. I did only half of what he recommended. Instead of resting, I stayed up many nights. Winter had arrived, and I became seriously ill. I had to be bled. I took to my bed.

One night that I was thinking about Lionel, I picked up the bottle of digitalis tincture. Instead of drinking a few drops, which always soothed me, I swallowed the whole bottle. It did me great harm.

Everyone was saying that I would not last long, that I had been affected by Lise's death. The people who came to see me attributed my decline to that. However, it was not the only reason.

Lionel

I knew that Lionel had rented a house for Zizi at Saint-James, and that, if indeed he had left her, he was still taking care of her. I wondered what this woman had that she was so fortunate! . . . One day that I was sitting in front of a fire in my room, trying to warm my body and my spirit, a double ring at the door shook the flames in the fire.

19

In the Country

To Berry—At Magnet—Disenchanted Return—
A Passport for Le Havre

"NOT A MOMENT TOO SOON," said Lionel, who was followed by a young man. "I was going to ring again! . . . We are frozen! . . ."

Lionel took me in his arms, kissed me, and drew me inside saying, "Permit me to introduce you to one of my country neighbors, one of my good friends, Martin."

"I am startled by your sudden arrival, I had no idea . . . !"

He gave me a sidelong glance and continued, "You are dining with us tonight? I am warning you that I am spending three days in Paris, and I am hiding out at your apartment. Do you still see Frisette? We must invite her so Martin will not be bored. Do you still love me a little?"

He must have seen my reply in my eyes.

"There is someone at the door," he said laughing. "If it is my replacement, I am going to throw him out."

And in fact it was Jean. They had met while traveling. Lionel greeted him in the most casual manner, offered him a chair, played the part of the host, rang for Marie, ordered like the master of the house. Poor Jean did not know how to leave. Standing near the fireplace, I did not know what to do with myself either. Finally, Jean departed as if he had come to visit a friend. Lionel was laughing his head off.

After dinner I left the room to give an order. I really wanted to know what he would say about me and could not resist the temptation to listen at the door.

"What do you think of her?" asked Lionel.

"She is fine," replied Martin. "I like her better than the one you took me to see yesterday."

Curiosity is always punished! So, he had gone to see another one before coming to see me. He was exhibiting his mistresses to a friend from the provinces. I did not want to admit that I had listened in, but I could not hide the change that had just occurred in me.

"What is the matter, Céleste, you seem strange?"

"Me, strange, me, strange. . . . You are the strange one. What kind of provincial manners have you brought back from your province. You throw my friends out the door, and you say I am strange! I assume you can act like this when you are with Mlle Zizi, who is in your pay, but with me, it is rude!"

He looked at Martin, thinking that he might have been indiscreet. The poor man's eyes replied, "I swear I have not said anything!" Lionel said that since he had arrived at night, and not really being man of the house, he would go to his own domicile. I did not argue anymore, but I had the feeling I loved him less. The slightest annoyance gave me palpitations and caused me to spit up blood! My doctor came the next day. Lionel asked him what I had.

"What she has is a stubborn head. She does the exact opposite of what she is told to do. I am not coming back."

The doctor also said that if I could be taken away from Paris and away from this bustling life I was leading, he was sure that my health would return.

Lionel and Martin conferred with each other. They seemed to be struggling with an idea. Lionel delayed his departure by a few days.

"All right," said Lionel, "I do not want to be coaxed to be made happy. Céleste, pack a trunk, I am taking you to the country. I shall hide you the best way I can. If you are spotted, people will assume you came for Martin."

I could not believe my ears. I understood nothing except that I was the happiest of women and that never had illness caused so much joy. I threw my things haphazardly in my trunk, putting high-top shoes on top of flowered bonnets. I left my apartment in Marie's care. She began to cry. I thought she was silly.

I left, happy as a lark. If Lionel was taking me with him only out of pity, I actually gave him a great opportunity to change his mind, because joy had already cured me.

Martin would offer his arm to help me down at the stations. He was gallant. Lionel would approach us from time to time to make sure Martin was not taking his role too seriously!

In those days the railroad went only as far as Vierzon.[1] Magnet was still twenty-five leagues away, so Lionel had left his highway carriage at the hotel. His valet had ordered two post horses. Lionel and I climbed in the surrey. Martin, probably so as not to intrude on us, took a seat in the back with Joseph, the valet.

It had snowed the night before. The evening was cold and dark. Lionel closed the windows. Our breath formed a curtain against the curious. The postilion cracked his whip and the eight-spring carriage clattered off.

Night was descending. The lanterns were lit.

The postilion was cursing for having to be out in this weather. The roads were bad. I pressed Lionel's hands and then fell asleep on his shoulder. Suddenly I woke up. He was yelling, "What is the matter with you, postilion? You are going to make us tip over!"

The replies to this call were protests. Lionel jumped on the horses the moment they were about to go into a hole. Martin, comfortably tucked away in the hood, had fallen asleep with Joseph. Both of them got out and walked over to the postilion, who was lying in the snow, twenty feet away. The poor man had fallen off with the porter. The carriage had run over his legs. We were near the post house. Lionel unhitched the horses and went for help. He came back with a makeshift stretcher and a doctor. He gave a few gold coins to the injured man, and we left with another postilion.

AT MAGNET

We had left the highway and were now on a bad road and our carriage was bouncing over enormous bumps. The night was pitch black. I could see huge trees that met over the road forming arcades. I felt a jolt and at the same time I heard a shout: "The door please!"

The moon had just emerged from behind the clouds, illuminating a beautiful château. The towers were majestically and somberly silhouetted against a gray backdrop. The ground was covered with snow.

A door opened and a man came toward us with a lantern. The horses' breath was wrapping us in a cloud.

I was led into a large room where the fireplace must have been eight feet tall. Martin was taken to his room in the right wing. I followed Lionel. He went up a stone staircase in a large tower on the left.

We entered a large room where a servant was lighting a fire. There were four lighted candles. This room, which must have been thirty feet square, with red brocade curtains, was adorned at the top, below, and in each corner with carved wooden gilded columns.

185

There were beveled mirrors in magnificent frames, paintings on the doors and on the fireplaces; there was a gilded bed trimmed in silk to match the drapes. On the ceiling was a gilded flower basket made of wood draped with silk gold-fringed curtains; lacquered rosewood furniture adorned the room. Large red and gold wingback chairs completed the furnishings. The bed faced the fireplace.

Terrifying shrieks drew me out of my gaping wonderment. Lionel started to laugh. He told me that at the tower's peak was a nest of owls. I replied that I was sorry about that because they bring bad luck!

A fire was crackling in the hearth; the resinous fir was cracking. The owls were quiet the rest of the night, and in the morning, when I woke up, it took me a long time to recognize myself. A bell sounded to announce lunch. Martin came to get me. We walked through the large room I had seen the night before, then a billiard room, an enormous living room, a small living room, and finally we arrived in the dining room. After lunch Martin made me visit everything. A vine was entwined around the towers, and the green trees in the park brightened a little the dreariness of the winter. The château stood above an enormous valley stretching out in the distance. The snow was partly melted.

The stables were magnificent. The first one held ten horses. Each stall contained a horse worth at least three to four thousand francs. All had hoods emblazoned with Lionel's coat of arms. Six splendid carriages were parked under the shed. We went out into another courtyard. The hounds, hearing the master approach, came to stand at the fence. I had never seen any so beautiful. They were light orange.

I picked loads of violets. I was dazzled by all this. I had met so many people: coachmen, stableboys, cooks, a gardener, stablehands, a valet, farmhands, grooms, hounds, stewards, keepers, that I was thinking, "My goodness! What a fortune it must take to pay for all this!" I had not been there more than four days when I realized the truth of it all. Lionel could not maintain this style of life if he did not marry a rich woman. He had lived in a home where four hundred thousand pounds were coming in. This was split six ways. This land, which was his whole fortune, was not worth more than twenty-five thousand pounds in income, and, well administered, would barely bring in two percent.

He had fallen into the clutches of Jews and usurers who had brought him very little, but to whom he had given a lot. Rather than break off with these people who were duping him, he was letting himself be taken in by new offers.

The Jews from the Champs-Elysées always had an excellent horse ar-

riving from London for him. Some pursued him all the way to his château. During my stay I saw an antique dealer who had made a special
trip to Berry from Belgium.

Lionel did not know how to get rid of all these leeches. He had seventeen horses. . . . He loved hunting . . . , another very expensive recreation.
He was blindly rushing toward his ruin. His was too generous at heart
to keep count of his money. He was kind, and yet he had moments of
cruelty. He would say unkind things to me, which I could have avoided
had I not replied.

DISENCHANTED RETURN

The first day, I was not pleased to have some tall butler following me.
It was not so bad when he was behind me, but when he would stand in
front of me, I would not dare eat. He would take my plate at the same
time as the others. When dinner was over, I was still very hungry.

We would spend two hours at the table. One time, I started to get
up. Lionel told me sharply, "Where are you going? The general rule is,
no one gets up from the table until the master of the house does." I was
livid! When a farmer or a peasant came to discuss business, he would
send me away, saying, "Go to your room, I do not need to have everyone
see you."

I received a letter from Marie that read:

*Madame should come back. Everyone is saying that she is dead. Several
of her friends have dropped by to see if it was true.*

I mentioned it to Lionel, who was in a bad mood. He replied, "Who in
the devil do you think will take care of you? Your friends from Mabille?
I would like to think you care very little for them."

"That is where you are wrong. It does not matter whether my friends
are from Mabille or elsewhere, they are thinking about me and I am
grateful to them for that. . . . You see, you brought me here and you
regret it. Well! I shall leave tomorrow."

Deep in my soul I was hoping he would say no. He did not. The next
day I just knew he would tell me to stay. The next day, he dolefully said,
"I do not regret bringing you here, Céleste, since you are feeling better.
I love you very much, but I must get married. One of my relatives wrote
to me on that subject. That is why I am letting you leave."

My heart was heavy, but I had to concede that he was right. The next
day he took me to Châteauroux with my trunk. When the carriage went
through the gate, all my courage left. I wanted to ask for his forgive-

ness, beg him to reconsider. When I arrived in town, I bought a ticket on a coach going to Vierzon. Lionel kissed me and left abruptly, but quick as his turning around was, I still had a chance to see that his eyes were damp.

What a contrast between my return and the journey I had made a few weeks earlier! The delights of happy love and gratified vanity were followed by the coldest, bitterest, deepest disappointment. With a thud I had fallen back into the mediocre reality of my bohemian life. Instead of the splendid carriage, in which I rode so softly on fluffy cushions next to him, I was alone, being jostled in a rickety coach. At the same time I had lost the cause of my happiness and the cause of my pride.

Today, many years after these feelings, I am glad I experienced them. When such abrupt transitions do not completely unnerve the heart, they lift it and strengthen it. They give you a mastery over yourself that you later learn to use over others.

My anguish was doubly painful because I could see my situation clearly. I had not lost my head; I still had my common sense. I did not blame Lionel, but the thought that a woman would take her place near him burned me like a hot poker.

A PASSPORT FOR LE HAVRE

All over Paris there was a rumor that I was dead. Adolphe, back from Metz, where he had been living since our separation, had gone to my apartment, pale and in disarray!

"I really loved her, you know! And I love her still," he told Marie.

"Monsieur is right," said Marie, "but Madame is fine. She is in the country and wrote to me yesterday."

He kissed her he was so happy and departed leaving his address.

I had barely gotten settled when a policeman from the Madeleine district came around asking for me. He was told I was not in. He left saying he would eventually find me. Marie warned me. I immediately made up my mind.

I decided to go on a trip. I went to the police chief of my neighborhood. I got a passport witnessed by two people, and I had Jean informed that I wanted to go to Le Havre. I asked him if he would accompany me.

He agreed. My passport, with a visa for Le Havre, was a guaranty I would not be punished if I was caught. I could prove that I had been away. We left that evening.

20

Gust of Wind at Le Havre and Masked Ball at the Opera

The Old Man, His Son, and the Sea—"Mogador? Do not know!"—
Golden Youth—One Plucky Girl—The Panther Hits
the Mark Every Time

ONCE IN LE HAVRE, I figured out that I had been unaware of one of my reasons for leaving Paris. It was a pretext for writing to *him*. Postmarked Le Havre, and motivated by a journey, my letter would appear more natural.

My dear Lionel, the reasons for our separation are so good that you saw I was resigned to it. However, one must not require of human nature what it cannot achieve! I think of you more than ever. Thanks to your good care, I have regained my health. I have reclaimed Jean's friendship. I shall be here for a few days. If you were to have something to tell me, you could write to me. Keep me in your thoughts.
Céleste

Jean asked me if I wanted to go for a boat ride with some other travelers.

"No," I said pulling my coat tighter around me with a nervous gesture of apprehension. "I would rather walk."

I took hold of his arm and we walked outside.

I bought a ton of trinkets. A gust of wind hit us so hard, my purchases and I were almost lifted in the air like balloons.

The sky got so dark that it looked like nighttime at two in the afternoon. We returned to the hotel without incident. I displayed the little knickknacks I had just bought on a chest of drawers. Whistling furiously, the wind was beating against the walls and the window.

"What weather!" I told Jean. "I was right not to go for a boat ride! What will those poor people who went do in such a squall?"

"Oh! They are not in danger. . . . They must not be far away!"

The waves were rushing in like mountains, then breaking on the beach. Others came after them, seemed to crush them, and then receded with a roar.

At times I thought I could see the poor little skiff and it was no more than a black speck.

"There they are!" I would say. . . . "They are going down!"

"No," Jean would say, "it is just the waves!"

Ignoring the cold, we opened the window. There were many people at the entrance below us. Each one, neck craned, was trying to spot the boaters. In the crowd, an old man was moaning, "My God! Why did I allow my son to go? They are lost!"

I was the first one to see them. I was so shaken that I almost fell off the balcony to tell the poor father, "There they are!" I invited him to come up near me so he could see better. We had gotten some opera glasses, but they were of no use to him; his eyesight was too poor to recognize anything.

When I would say, "They are coming!" the poor oldster would laugh and press my hands. When I would lose sight of them, he seemed to blame me, as if I were impeding their progress.

"There they are! I can see them again! They are struggling!"

"Look, my child, look carefully!"

A hundred times I thought they had sunk. Two hours went by in this anguish. Finally they arrived, broken with fatigue and fear.

The old man left my side to go kiss a handsome young man who must have been twenty-five years old. I told myself as I watched him leave, "Ungrateful like a child! He does not thank me for sharing his terror."

But that evening at the host's table, he came to sit next to me. Instead of one conquest, I had two. The father did not stop talking about me! He thought I was charming, adorable, pretty! I told you he had poor eyesight.

The son must have been in the habit of thinking like his father. He became more unremitting in his attentions, and after two days, he admitted frankly that he was madly in love with me.

Jean could see this little game, and what is really odd is that he was assisting him by standing aside. He hated Lionel and would have given in to any of my whims to make me forget one name, one memory.

My shipwreck survivor was not very witty and was beginning to bore me greatly! He would write me such funny letters that I could not help laughing in his face. He spoke of nothing but marrying me, certain, he would say, that his father would forgive him a love that he had helped give birth to.

I told Jean that I wanted to dine in my room. He asked me why. I replied that the father and the son were mad, that they were plotting an abduction.

"I thought that amused you," said Jean.

"I never laugh at the expense of those who love me. If I hurt someone, it is unintentionally."

I looked at him as I said these words since they were meant for him. He did not reply.

Jean had a friend at Le Havre. After dinner he asked my permission to go see him. He had barely left, when the door opened. I thought that it was he returning; I did not even look up from my reading. I heard the lock turn once; I turned around and my shipwreck admirer was there.

"Why did you not go down to dinner?" he asked me with a look of alarm. "You are avoiding me?"

He really looked frightening. I told him I had a headache.

"You did not come down to hurt me. You are a coquette, like all Parisian women. You make people fall in love with you so you can torment them. I love you and I shall not get over that. I have seen your passport; you are unattached. You are going to leave this Monsieur and follow me, or I am going to seek a quarrel with him."

"MOGADOR? DO NOT KNOW!"

This was beginning to take a worrisome turn. Jean could enter any minute.

"Now, my friend, do not work yourself up this way! You meet a woman with a man who is not her parent, that must not give you a good opinion of her. . . . Instead of listening to reason, you want to take her away, marry her, fight a duel. But for whom, I ask you? . . . You have no idea! . . . I shall tell you. . . . For a girl who has wasted her youth, who is not worthy of anyone's interest, who gets picked up and dropped. In other words, for Mogador!"

I thought this name would frighten him. He said, "Mogador? I do not know what it is. But I love you! It does not matter what you have been; I love you. I do not live in Paris; you will be able to hide your past in my province."

"Well," I said, "wait a few days. The person with whom I came to Le Havre is going to leave. Once I am alone, we shall see."

He seemed quite content. Jean came home a few minutes later and said with surprise, "Oh! You have already packed your trunk?"

"Yes. We are leaving tomorrow, at dawn."

I had stayed away only ten days.

GOLDEN YOUTH

My heart was beating fast as I was approaching my apartment. Perhaps I had a letter from Lionel! . . . The concierge handed me one.

I did not even notice Jean leaving. I was devouring my letter as I climbed up the stairs. Lionel was congratulating me for the way I had come to terms with losing him. He added that it was not so easy for him, because he had no one to console him.

I read this letter several times. He was jealous. A flash of joy sprang from my heart to my brain! I had a hold over him. I was filled with tremendous joy because, for the first time, I became fully aware of my power.

"To bring him back at my feet," I told myself, "there is only one way: to torment him." And since I loved him very much, I was merciless.

My letters might have left something to be desired when it came to style or spelling, but I insist they were masterpieces of coquetry. A week later he was more smitten than ever, and he wrote:

My dear child, I am coming to Paris for two days. I shall be at the Hôtel Chatam.

It was a Sunday. The boulevard was full of people, and I wanted to hurry but managed only to be jostled by pedestrians. Once in front of Lionel's door, I tried to compose myself so I would appear calm, cold even. He kissed me.

"Céleste, do you not love me anymore? . . ."

"Yes, I do," I replied, "but I have to get used to the idea of not seeing you anymore since you are going to get married."

"No," he said almost cheerfully, "I am not getting married. Without realizing it, I was about to make a foolish mistake. A chamber maid told me some things about my fiancée. . . ."

"Is that why you are back?"

"Yes, partly, and a lot because I love you."

We spent a week together. He was not letting me out of his sight. I had written to poor Jean to avoid an encounter. Then Lionel had to return to Berry.

"I am taking you with me," he said.

He did not have to say, "Do you want to come?" I spent two months with him. He received a letter that one of his relatives was coming. For me, this letter meant I had to leave. I understood. He broke the news to me with great care.

"Go back to Paris for a little while," he said. "As soon as I am alone, I shall come get you."

I had a feeling that this visit meant some new marriage plan was afoot. I looked for the letter and had no difficulty finding it. It announced an intended union that would be arranged through a family friend.

I went back to Paris and wrote to him that I was not taken in by what he had said. It was a while before he answered.

Something told me that all these marriage plans would fail. I proceeded resolutely down the path I had traced; I was waging a terrible war against Lionel's heart with my follies and eccentricities. I went everywhere: balls, concerts, performances. Every night after the theater we almost always dined at the Café de Paris. Its beautiful rooms decorated with gold vases filled with flowers glittered in the light. The meals seemed to be out of fairy tales. The diners were young, rich, and elegant. Their names were the greatest names in France, but their lives were frivolous, their temperaments capricious and flighty.

Léon and his friends, all sons of very honorable merchants, very honest bourgeois, were pedantic and arrogant. They ranted against the nobility, but it was out of jealousy.

What I liked best about my new hosts was that they were almost all connected to Lionel. That way I made sure that not one of my extravagances would escape him.

ONE PLUCKY GIRL

Amid the tumultuous life where I was once more whirling, I was making new acquaintances every day. I became friends with a woman older than I. Between this woman's personality and my then-state of mind there were certain analogies that made me want to study her carefully. Two years earlier or two years later, had she passed through my life, I would have probably not paid much attention to her, but at this precise moment, she was exercising a sort of influence over me. She had been one of the fashionable women. She was rich and was looking back over her past life with contempt. Perhaps she had been a maid and it was because of mean treatment that she had become mean, something that often happens. In any case, she cut up her dear female friends with such enthusiasm that only their bones remained. "And those I do not touch because they are foul."

This Panther, so ferocious toward everyone, had, for some reason, become attached to me. One evening I wanted to take her to the Opera.

"No," she replied, "it would be a waste of time!"

"Why?"

"Because clever people do not go there anymore, and, if they do, they put on a false face."

"They will remove it for you!"

"Five years ago I gave away my black taffeta domino to some poor girl in mourning for her mother."

"We shall rent one."

"All right, you win."

After dinner her eyes were shining. If she had drunk only one glass, it was a tall one! At the entrance of the Opera she stopped a man who was following several masked women whose coats he was carrying.

"Not so fast, Gerbier, how about saying good evening to your friends!"

The man, who must have been about fifty years old and stuttered a little, told her to be quiet, that he was not alone! "Oh! Monsieur is with his family today. We pick up the little one at the boarding school, and we take her to the Opera to shape her heart and mind."

The man threw himself in the crowd to escape her.

I asked her, "Who is this man?"

"An idiot! At his age, he is playing groom to an actress. I hate actresses. But for a few exceptions, the stage is no more than an exhibition."

"They are not all like that. . . ."

"Oh! No, I exclude the old ones, and, if you wish, one out of one hundred among the young ones, but the rest live off the collective resources of European fortunes."

We had arrived at the foyer entrance.

"Hello, beautiful mask!" a man coming out said as he grabbed me around the waist.

"Well," she asked him, "has your servant been behaving himself?"

"Why do you ask me this?" said the man, who was trying to place her.

"Indeed, you told him on New Year's Day last year, 'François, I am giving you this old boot! If you are a good servant, you will have the other one next year.' Does he finally have the pair?"

Everyone laughed. We went into loge 21 that Jean had let me have. There were two people already there. One woman turned around. I saw her eyes gleaming through her domino, then I heard her say, "Oh! How dreadful! There is a snake in here. Who let these women in?"

"Ladies, this loge is rented."

"Yes," I replied, "it is mine."

"You must be mistaken! . . ."

"No, ask the usher; I just gave her the ticket stub."

She called the usher over. There was indeed an error; their loge was the one next to mine, and they had to leave. During the discussion, Victorine had been looking at the domino, and, unfortunately for the woman wearing the mask, she recognized her.

"Yes, it is she! . . . So, I am a snake, am I! Well, you are going to hear me hiss."

The mask did not reply, left, and entered the loge on the right. When she was seated, Victorine asked me, "Do you want me to tell you why I am called the snake? The story will amuse you and our neighbors also."

There were a lot of people in the loge on the left. The domino turned toward us and looked at Victorine defiantly.

"Believe it or not," she told me, "I was loved by one of the most fashionable men in Paris. He loved me very much, but he circulated among high society. A highborn woman stole him from me. I would not hold such a grudge against her if she had not been a titled woman and if she had been more generous toward others, but in all honesty, she was too cunning to be interesting. My lover returned to me. She wanted to take him back. This was annoying. At his home I found letters from her, and I sent them to her husband after I had made the addressee's name illegible. You see Céleste, in this world, one half of the population steals from the other. I yelled: thief! And that is why she calls me a snake."

The domino did not expect so much audacity. Her exasperation was evident by the movements of her fan. After a few seconds, the lady complained of the heat, left, and never came back. To top off the affront, the Panther spit out her name. I chided her for saying it so loud.

"And why not? Because she has a husband and children? She does not respect them; why should I respect them?"

"Come on, let us take a walk through the foyer."

THE PANTHER HITS THE MARK EVERY TIME

She stopped in front of a young man whose back was resting against a post.

"Good evening, de J———. How is your father?"

"You know me?" said the young man.

"Obviously."

"Well, my father is better."

"Oh! Now I understand why you seem sad! The price of money is going to go up. You poor boy!"

Then she burst out laughing. I asked her why the price of money was going to go up.

"It is going to increase for him. Several years ago he wanted to borrow from a usurer and write letters of exchange. He told him, 'My father is sick and I am certain he has not much time left, so you will be paid on time.' If the father is doing better, payments will be higher! All this is a little bit the fault of the fathers who do not rear their children well. When they are small, they are taken care of by foreigners. Later they must eat with governesses, then they are sent off to school, far from the family, and they get out when they are seventeen or eighteen. Love takes hold of them before they have thought about loving their parents. They incur debts and their fathers do not pay them. The better ones wait for the end, the worse ones wish it. Oh! There you are," she told a man we came across. "You were in your wife's way, so she sent you to the Opera?"

"What do you mean?" said the man.

"Now, now," replied the Panther, "do not get upset. Horns are like teeth, they hurt when they are growing. Once they are out, they can be used to eat with. You are a living example of this, since, thanks to your wife, you have a position that allows you to live."

The man frowned. I pulled Victorine away, dragging her through the crowd.

The hour was over and I did not see Jean. My companion guessed my thoughts.

"Why is he not coming?" she asked me.

"I do not know. He let me have the loge I asked for, but I suppose he is pouting. If Lionel knew that he would be delighted."

"Your Lionel will adore you," said Victorine. "You are doing the right thing. My first lover, a painter, would make me sleep on the tile floor in January. When he left, I felt the cold. I took revenge on my first lover with my second, on the second with my third, and so on. I was called Panther, Snake, but I was loved. Now I am hated. I never have good thoughts; I do not know how to have a good word. I am thirty years old! A titled woman would be young; I am old."

"Why did you not keep some friends instead of making yourself be hated?"

"Friends! But honest people do not have any. How could I have any? I do not lend money!"

21

Hooray for Reform!

The February Revolution—Châteauroux's Nonexistence
and the Crudeness of the Berry People—A Tree of Freedom
and a Quart of Wine

THE NEXT DAY I went for a walk with Frisette. There were many people
in the streets, all whispering. I approached several groups and listened,
and did not understand a word they were saying.

Once we reached the boulevard, the crowds were bigger. All we could
make out amid the noise was the word "reform!" I stopped a young man
and asked him what that meant. He replied, "We want reform."

"Oh! And what kind of reform?"

He shrugged his shoulders and walked away without answering.

We were on the Boulevard Bonne-Nouvelle, in front of the Café de
France. There were many young men at the windows. Some of them rec-
ognized us and began to yell, "Hooray for Mogador! Hooray for Frisette!
Hooray for reform and beautiful women!"

The curious and the strollers gathered around us. The air was charged
with peril. I went into the house at number 5. I knew Madame Emburgé
and asked her for permission to wait at her house until there were fewer
people outside. She opened a window and we saw this blue-speckled,
black stream called the populace march by. It reminded me of Lyon.
However, since everyone must dine, even those who want to wage war,
around six o'clock the streets were more passable.

"Have dinner with me," said Frisette.

THE FEBRUARY REVOLUTION

I accepted. It was ten o'clock when we parted. When I reached the Rue
Le Peletier, I heard an explosion.

"Where are you going?" a man asked me.

197

"But, monsieur, I would like to get home on the Place de la Madeleine."

"Well, then, take another route. They have just fired on the Ministry of Foreign Affairs."

I took the Rue Basse-du-Rempart. It was empty. I continued quietly. I was thinking about Lionel. "A revolution," I was telling myself! "A revolution, which ruins and forces the nobility to go into hiding. . . . Oh! If only Lionel needed me, needed my life!"

At the corner of the Rue Caumartin, the pharmacy had been transformed into a temporary first aid post.

When I got back home I wrote Lionel about everything I had seen, telling him for the first time, "Do not come."

I could not sleep. Everyone in the house was up. At four o'clock in the morning, someone knocked on the outside door.

"Open, open!" I told the concierge. . . . Him, him, at a time like this! . . . "Oh! Lionel, why did you come to Paris? I was happy to know you were in Berry!"

"I can leave if I am in the way!"

"In the way! . . . Oh! Now really, am I not allowed to have a good thought?"

"My dear child, I did not know what was going on! I left Châteauroux yesterday. When I got to the station, I could not find a carriage. I brought my suitcase over my shoulder."

The day after his arrival he joined the first legion of the National Guard. The Madeleine post was set on fire! Powder and loaded guns that had been left there were exploding every minute. Lionel came home at five, black with dust and worn out. He had helped tear down the barricades.

There was a commotion under my windows. Approximately a hundred men, nicely dressed, looking rather reasonable, had gathered and were talking. Finally they all went to the carriage station and set fire to the little shed used by the watchman.

They were the neighborhood coachmen having some fun, just like in Lyon. Only there, it was because of the tariffs.

CHÂTEAUROUX'S NONEXISTENCE AND THE CRUDENESS OF THE BERRY PEOPLE

The next day we left for Berry. At Etampes I began to breathe easier.

I had not dared ask him about his marriage plans. He was the one who told me that he had been rejected.

Lionel, young, elegant, with a name and a fortune, should have succeeded at anything. But he had one fault that was a constant obstacle in his life: he was not emotionally stable. I thought I had detected a great strength of character in him, but I was wrong; he had a violent temperament. He did not know how to restrain his passions and his desires. He loved me, and I must have been the reason for many of his uncertainties. I could not rise to his level, and he blamed me for having to come down to mine. And yet, out of affection for him, I had changed.

The château, which had become his in the division, was dilapidated. Only one room attested to a past splendor. The whole estate was three hundred years old. Everything, the château and the rest of the property, needed repairs. The farmers, already in debt, were not paying. The creditors became demanding. Lionel borrowed sixty thousand francs at twenty percent on a first mortgage. There was a revolution. Even though money was for sale at these prices, it was not easy to find. The Belgian farmers told him they wanted to go back to their country. Berry is unhealthy. There are risks of fevers that are difficult to avoid, the work is strenuous, the farm hands are slow because they are not well fed. They can make ends meet only if they deprive themselves. Many of them sell their wheat and eat potatoes or chestnuts. The Belgians could not get used to this poverty. They had been brought there by Lionel's father, who was hoping to take advantage of the vast lands called heath.

Lionel let them leave. He even gave them some money because one of them had lost his whole harvest in a hail storm. Another had seen three of his relatives die. Others had been sick. The best lands remained vacant.

Châteauroux does not exist. It is the sort of hamlet one goes through looking for the town. The inhabitants are crude. Some of them are so crude, they are no more than savages. When the uncultivated nature of peasants rebels, they become brutal. In the surrounding area there had been some atrocious crimes committed, and several châteaux had been invaded. The caretaker in one of these châteaux had been cut with a scythe. The Villedieu château had been partially burned. The area where we lived was calm, and besides, Lionel was liked. I had gone to Châteauroux in one of his carriages. I heard children yelling. There was a carriage ahead of mine. The coachman made his horses turn around and told me, "We cannot pass. See, they are pelting the carriage of Madame de —— with stones."

I begged Lionel not to go out, or if he did, to erase the coat of arms off his carriage.

He took this badly, telling me that it would be cowardly.

I spent the night wide awake. I was afraid that my presence in the château would make him lose the favorable consideration he enjoyed in
the region. One day I saw some forty men armed with rifles and pistols
in the garden. They were coming toward the château.

Lionel was in the billiard room with Martin. I walked in shouting,
"Flee! Hide! Or you are lost."

"What is the matter with you?" asked Lionel.

"The matter with me?" I said. "Armed men are out there, yelling.
Flee, go down to the basement."

And, certain that he was following me, I ran toward the stairs leading
to the basement. It was huge. I turned around, and I saw that he had
not followed me.

"Yes! Yes!" voices were yelling. "That one! Let us take that one! It is
the most beautiful one!"

Suddenly shots were heard. With each discharge, I could feel myself
getting weaker. I wanted to hide inside the wall. Finally, I went back to
the stairs. The shooting seemed to recede.

"Where did you just come from?" asked Lionel, who was calmly lighting a cigar.

"Where I have just come from? From the basement. What did this
little skirmish mean?"

"Listen, and you will find out."

And in fact, I could hear these words: "Hooray for M. le Comte!
Hooray for the republic! Hooray for the trees of freedom!"

We were on the terrace. A man came back, removed his hat, and said
to Lionel, "I hope you do not mind, M. le Comte, if we plant a tree of
freedom? If it offends you, then I do not wish to do it; we just want to
have some fun and drink a glass to your health."

"No, I do not mind," said Lionel, "since I let you have it along with a
quart of wine, and, as long as you do not plant it in my garden, it does
not matter to me."

I had been receiving one letter after another from my maid. I had
debts, bills to pay. Lionel, in spite of his great fortune in lands, was
poorer than I. I could not, and would not, ask him for anything.

I let him know that I had to go to Paris.

He raised the lid on his writing desk and rifled through his pockets.

"My poor Céleste, I have nothing. I am going to borrow two hundred
francs for your trip."

22

Roulette

The Gambling Demon—
It Is Safer to Pay One's Debts before Playing Again

BACK IN PARIS, I was in a bind. I did have a few pieces of jewelry that Lionel had given me, but to part with them seemed impossible.

One evening I was at a dinner with Lagie and Frisette.

"Come gambling with us," they said. "We play roulette every night. There are several roulette games, but the best is the one on Rue de l'Arcade."

"But," I said to Lagie, "there must be risks. Gambling houses are illegal."

"Yes, but there is nothing to fear. Not everyone is allowed in. Precautions are taken."

All I had was one hundred francs. I decided to go in spite of my fear of the police.

Once we were on the Rue de l'Arcade, our carriage stopped in front of a large and beautiful house. We climbed stairs painted red, lit from a distance by little lanterns.

We went up to the sixth floor. Lagie rang. A doorbell sounded three times. A servant came to open. His livery was flashy.

From the anteroom we went into a living room. We were welcomed by a woman in her thirties who probably used to be quite pretty, and who would still be if her pale, skinny face had not been framed by a forest of black hair in long curls that gave her a wild look.

"You have not been her before, mademoiselle?" she asked me.

"No, madame, it is my first time."

"Oh! Are you lucky with the red and the black?"

"I do not know."

She got up and went to speak to some other people. Lagie told me,

"She is the mistress of the house. I mean by that, the rent is in her name. The man holding the bank is some sort of amphibious animal. No one knows where he comes from or what country he is from. He put the house in this woman's name. If the police came, she would be the one taken away."

I examined her and tried to discern on her the desire for luxury that drove her to her destruction. She dressed simply; her silk dress had been mended; everything about her seemed destitute. Each time the bell rang she would jump off her chair, and she would stare anxiously at the door.

THE GAMBLING DEMON

"Why do we not start?" said a tall young man.

"The banker has not arrived," replied the mistress of the house, who was watching the clock. "He will not be long; it is almost eleven."

"*You in a hurry* to lose your money, Brésival?" said a fat girl called La Pouron.

I went up to Lagie and asked her who this man called Brésival was.

"Oh," said Lagie, "he does not have much to do with women; he likes gambling too much for that. He is married and has adorable children. He will end up gambling their baby clothes away."

A few minutes later a man appeared; he had just let himself in with a key.

The newcomer must have been about forty years old. He wore a black suit and a white tie. His complexion was tan, his hair, brown. He looked a little bit Italian. He spoke to the mistress of the house to give her orders and make reproaches. He looked at me for a long time.

The servant opened both flaps of the door, and I saw a large, well-lighted room, a long table covered with a green cloth, a roulette wheel in the middle, and chairs around. Everyone went in. I stayed near the fireplace in the first room.

"You are not going to play?" asked the mistress of the house.

"No," I replied, "I am not used to gambling. Besides, I do not feel safe. Are you not afraid?"

"Oh! Yes," she said, "but I cannot let my fear show; yet, I am in great danger."

"So you make a lot of money?"

"Me!" she said, with a sad laugh, "I am barely fed."

"So you must really love the man who just entered?"

"Me! Love him! I hate him, I despise him, but I am afraid of him."

Some people came in the room where I was to smoke, so it became impossible to talk. I got up to go to the game. The mistress of the house, who was called La Pépine, said to me softly, "You do not know how to play? Bet on the hand of this old decorated gentleman over there; he is lucky at the game."

I took a gold louis coin out of my purse and put it on the red near his money. The banker was yelling, "Place your bets, gentlemen, place your bets! No more bets!"

He was turning a device that everyone was intently looking at.

"The black loses! The red wins!" the banker proclaimed.

"So you are playing now?" Lagie told me.

"Yes, but I have only five louis!"

"And ten that you have just won, that makes fifteen," said the decorated gentleman. "You have let it ride twice, and look, red is winning again. You have twenty louis. Are you letting them ride?"

I really felt like picking them up, but I was being called a coward, so I let them ride.

"No more bets!"

I turned my head so I would not see. My poor twenty louis were swallowed up by the black. I met Pépine's eyes. She gave me a faint smile and retreated behind the red wool portiere.

She had just appeared to me like the devil. Well! I am ashamed to admit this, but I invoked Satan so he could help me win my forty louis back, and when I heard, "Black loses, red wins!" I made such a jump, I almost knocked two people over.

I went into the other room to count my winnings.

"Go back in," said La Pépine in hushed tones, "and continue playing, but bet very little. . . ."

I went back to the game.

"Are you taking your winnings?" asked Lagie.

"Of course not!"

Mlle Pouron congratulated me on my lucky streak, because I continued to win. I had before me two thousand francs, in gold, which was rare at that time. Then the exchange rate was a louis and ten centimes. I was very pleased and not at all sleepy. The candles were beginning to go out. Everyone looked tired and haggard. The rouge on some women had faded. The men who were losing, and who up until then had not spoken to me, hoping to be winners, were letting their bad humor show. I won four thousand francs. I felt sorry for Brésival. I could see him searching through his pockets, placing his hand on his forehead, and looking at everyone. I pitied him, because he seemed to be in horrible pain. I asked him if he wanted a few louis. He did not just take what I was offering him, he grabbed it. In a matter of five minutes he had lost what I had just given him. I was probably going to give him more money, when La Pépine, who was bringing chocolates to the players, stepped on my foot. I stopped looking at Brésival, who continued to eye covetously what I had in front of me. Suddenly he furiously banged his fists on the table, producing a dull sound because the table was covered with several layers of cloth. He threw himself on the roulette wheel and tried to destroy it saying he had been robbed and he wanted his money. I had fled into the other room holding on to my money, which I certainly intended to keep. In the first place, I had not won it from him.

La Pépine was gazing at the scene with glee.

"Thank you very much! I am leaving."

"Where do you live?"

"At 19 Place de la Madeleine. I would like for you to come see me."

I took off, giving ten francs to the servant who opened the door for me.

IT IS SAFER TO PAY ONE'S DEBTS
BEFORE PLAYING AGAIN

I spent the next day dashing to all my merchants to bring them money. I paid them periodically because the thought of being in debt was unbearable to me. I used them when I needed credit. I knew that they charged me double, but I liked to buy, so I said nothing.

In those days, actresses and kept women could get credit only from a few special merchants. If I had gone to Ville de Paris to buy a dress and I had said, "Deliver this to Mlle Céleste, equestrienne," the parcel would definitively not have left the store until full payment had been made. Today all the department stores, like Ville de Paris, Chaussée d'Antin, Trois Quartiers, Siège de Corinthe, deliver to your residence, and, if your purchases get there while you are out, they are left and you do not get the bill until six months later.

They use all forms of temptation. If I had not been deterred by a sense of rectitude, today I would have debts amounting to three hundred thousand francs; cashmere fabric, jewelry, carriage, furniture merchants—all used to make me offers of unlimited credit.

And so I brought money to my tradesmen, in person, in 1848!

I bought a few dresses, some undergarments, and best of all, a travel bag trimmed in silver.

My gambling profits were going to my head. All I could think about was winning more so I would have a lot of money when Lionel came back.

23

La Pépine

A Handsome Sort of Ruffian — Money Is Scarce, but
Gold Is Flowing! — The Lover from Le Havre — The Italian Woman
Leaves Avenged and the Le Havre Citizen, Contrite

THREE DAYS HAD gone by since my evening on Rue de l'Arcade, and I
was continually torn between the desire to go back and my better judgment, which told me not to. The fear of being caught at this house or
of losing was stopping me, but the lure of winning drew me.

At eight o'clock in the morning I was relaxing when Marie and her
big nose came in to announce that a lady wanted to speak to me. At my
house it was not yet customary to wait patiently.

"Am I disturbing you?" said La Pépine sitting down next to my bed.

"Not at all; I was thinking about you. I won a lot the other day."

"Why did you not come back?"

"I admit that it would not be a bad idea to go back. All I have left is
five hundred francs."

"That is too much. Never bring that much to my establishment. You
must bring only one hundred francs, and, if you lose that, stop playing."

I had been wrong; she was not trying to help the banker get his
money back.

"Would you like to have lunch with me?"

"Yes," she said, "only do not let any one else in; I must not be seen at
your house."

A HANDSOME SORT OF RUFFIAN

I had a very elegant dining room with carved oak furniture and stained
glass windows. It looked a lot like a crypt.

We sat down to eat. I was afraid of this woman. No, not really afraid
that she would hurt me, but afraid of her as a person.

"I am so skinny!" she said showing me her neck. "Oh! The life I lead is killing me! Staying up every night! Trembling with fear every time someone rings at the door!"

"Why do you do this kind of work?"

"It is because I have no choice."

"What! You are forced to do it?"

"Yes."

"By this man who runs the games?"

"Yes."

"But what has he done to you?"

"I met him in Italy, in my country, where my mother had a shop. He was living under an assumed name with a woman, still beautiful in spite of her age. I was eighteen then, and pretty. I fell in love. This woman found me at his house and told me, 'Poor wretch! You are ruined. Do you know who this man is? He is a swindler. He pursued me because I was rich. He ruined me, tortured me. Today, I have nothing left, so he has to get rid of me. Watch out, if you have nothing, he will sell you!'

"My lover was so successful in persuading me that it was just jealousy making her speak this way that I believed him.

" 'Listen,' he told me, 'we cannot live like this anymore. I do not have any money. If I had some, I would take you with me. If someone could lend us money, we could leave together. Or, if I had some money, I would give some to this woman to get rid of her.'

" 'My goodness,' I told him, "if I had some, I would lend it to you, but every week my mother sends her earnings to her business manager.'

" 'Oh!" he said. 'Are you not the one who runs the shop, keeps the books, the one who signs?'

" 'Yes.'

" 'If you wanted. . . . But you do not love me enough . . . and besides you do not trust me.'

" 'Yes,' I replied, 'yes, I trust you.'

" 'Well then, go get the money in the name of your mother; it will be handed over to you; then I shall give it back to you in a month, you will take it back, and no one will know the difference.'

" 'If it were a small amount . . . , but maybe you need a lot.'

" 'Yes,' he said with a sigh, 'at least ten thousand francs.'

"My mother called to me early in the morning. She was not well. I went to see my lover at noon. His trunks were packed. I told him to wait until the next day. My mother had not gotten up. Encouraged at the thought that she might not be able to get up for a few days, I went to see my mother's banker and told him she had a purchase to make and would need ten thousand francs.'

" 'Has your mother given you a receipt?'

" 'I shall give you one, that should suffice.'

" 'For the boss, possibly,' said the cashier, 'but he is away. I must go by the rules.'

" 'Away for long?'

" 'For about a week.'

"I went to see my lover to tell him of my defeat. I told him to wait until the next day; I would try to reach my mother.

" 'Do not do that,' he said, 'all would be lost. Just sign the same name as your mother's, but add *widow* instead of *daughter*. . . . I shall have returned the money to you before she gets well.'

"I went up to my poor mother's room. I asked for her signature to pay a bill someone was requesting downstairs.'

" 'Whose is it?' she asked.

"I gave her some name chosen at random.

"An hour later, I was back with my money, which he took from me before I had a chance to give it to him.

"On his doorstep, I saw the woman I had met a few days earlier. She said to me, 'Listen to me, you poor child! He tells you I love him and you believe him because you see me on his doorstep. He is fooling you. I want him to give me back some jewels he has that are mine so I can sell them to pay for my trip. I am stranded here at the hotel where I am living. I am waiting for this scoundrel's charity to get what belongs to me. Watch out for yourself!'

"My mother was feeling better. He said nothing about returning my money, and pretended he was waiting for news from Paris. My mother told me she would be able to go downstairs the next day.

" 'I am going to take you to Paris,' he told me. 'We shall return when I have what I need.'

"For ten years now I have been dragging my miserable life yoked to his. He has me do all sorts of work. I implicated myself to protect him. Sometimes I get the urge to kill him. . . ."

"Why," I asked, "have you not left him or turned him in?"

"How could I have? When I arrived in Paris, I did not know a word of French. Turn him in? Was I not even more guilty than he?"

"Does he cheat at the games?"

"He is quite capable of it," she said in hushed tones, "yet I do not know. The old man I recommended to you is a promoter; he often brings people in, and he wins a lot."

"Why do you not leave him?"

"Oh!" she replied, "because I have no resources, but soon. . . ."

MONEY IS SCARCE, BUT GOLD IS FLOWING!

We finished lunch and went into my bedroom.

"Listen," she said, "I liked you the first day I saw you. Would you like to do me a favor?"

"With pleasure, if I can."

"When I escape from this man, I want to take my things with me. Would you let me send them to you a few at a time? You will not say anything, will you?"

I promised.

"Come this evening," she told me.

I arrived at midnight. There were even more people than the first time. The game was lively.

Money was so scarce that the government had just allowed people more time to pay their debts and had opened national workshops. Landlords were reducing their rents by a third, pensions were worth fifty francs, pawn shops were no longer lending anything above one hundred francs, and commerce was ailing! Well! On this table were mountains of gold, silver, and bank notes. The rate of exchange for gold was fifty francs per one thousand. Every day emigration was making it even more expensive. Where had they all gotten this money, with what difficulty and at what price had each one obtained it?

Present were some old beauties from Frascati who thought all this seemed pitiful compared to what they had known. One of them, called Blais, told me, when she saw me thrilled to have won a thousand francs, "Why, little one, you rejoice over so little! During one play I have had one hundred thousand in front of me. I used to have a carriage and magnificent diamonds, and I do not remember experiencing as much joy as you over these few louis. Women are really degenerating!"

"You should have kept some of your riches," I replied. "I hope that when I am your age, although I have possessed less than you, I shall have more left. You should keep quiet about these treasures that have not served you well."

This woman was living in abject poverty. She had a son in the navy who sent her the little bit of money he earned.

My gaze met Pépine's, and her eyes were telling me to play cautiously.

I had won three thousand francs. I wanted to leave, when the sound of the doorbell made everyone jump.

"It is the police!" the gamblers said all together.

"Open!" the master of the house told a servant, and at the same time he triggered a spring. The table opened down the middle and all the money disappeared into a false bottom.

Laughter drew us out of our stupor. It was a group of young men who had forgotten that there was a special signal to be let in!

THE LOVER FROM LE HAVRE

The next day I was walking down the boulevard when someone touched my arm and said, "Finally it is you; I have found you."

It was the shipwreck survivor from Le Havre whom I thought I had left on the coast for good.

"Oh my!" he said. "Where have you been hiding? I have been in Paris for a month; I am not a boy from the provinces anymore. You did not deceive me. Your name really is Mogador. I was told all sorts of bad things about you, but I do not care. Where do you live?"

I did not want to give him my address, but he would not leave. Since I had to go home, he followed me. At the door I said to him.

"Until next time."

"What do you mean, next time! Do you think I am going to leave you like this? In my province, people are friendlier than this."

I went up the stairs, and he followed me. Once in my apartment, we talked for a long time. He made extravagant declarations of his love for me. It was five o'clock, and I was dining at a friend's house. I asked him to let me get dressed. He left, but at ten o'clock the next day, he was back. I told him that I loved another, and that I was too forthright to deceive him.

One day I was sad and he asked me why. I unburdened my soul, and I let him see the black mark on my life. He left without a word. The next day he returned triumphant.

"Yesterday I wrote to the prefect asking him to scratch you off the list. You shall be free. You owe me your freedom. Now do you believe in my affection?"

A flash of joy sprang up from my heart to my face, and then I became thoughtful again.

"You doubt my accomplishment," he said. "Well! You will see. I shall have a reply in six days. I shall not come see you until I have it."

I received a nice letter from Lionel telling me to be patient. I had only two days left to wait when a messenger brought me a trunk and a case.

"Mademoiselle Pépine asks you to keep this until she can come for it."

I did not dare refuse; I had promised. Yet, at a time when I needed most to be on my guard, seeing this woman, receiving her belongings, seemed unwise.

I was about to write when a carriage stopped at my door. I saw Pépine enter. She was dressed all in black and held her veil close to her face.

I told her as I opened the door, "Oh! I was about to write to you. I cannot keep these trunks without knowing what they contain."

"It is not necessary, I am coming for them," she told me. "I am leaving France tonight; I am going back to my country. Tomorrow he will be arrested."

She kissed me and had the trunks taken down by Marie. I breathed easier when I heard her carriage leave.

A week had gone by when I received a long letter from my shipwreck survivor:

My dear Céleste,

I am too distressed by my defeat to tell you about it in person. I was called in yesterday, but unfortunately! . . .

I was asked what my relationship to you was. I said I was your friend.

"Do you intend to take her with you or to provide her with a pension so she can be assured of an honest life?"

I admit, my poor friend, that I was disconcerted because you would have refused to follow me, and my resources are intermingled with my father's.

I left truly sad, my dear Céleste. I am departing dispirited. Forgive me the mad hope I have given you.

I began to laugh. I felt sorry for myself. I had deluded myself with this illusion!

24

The June Insurrection

"You cannot pass!" (We Pass Anyway) — Mogador
Would Have Had the Suffragettes Whipped —
Is It the Right Departure?

SUMMER WAS COMING. Lionel finally returned to Paris. In spite
of the ominous rumors going around, everything seemed lovely and
cheerful to me. It was becoming clear that there was going to be more
fighting.

Lionel could not pay his succession taxes. He was receiving no rent
from his farms. He had come to try to put his affairs in order. The June
insurrection broke out. Terror became intense. A shop in my building
had just been transformed into a post for the antiriot soldiers. Lionel
had returned to the National Guard. I was standing at the carriage entrance with other tenants picking up bits of news. Our neighborhood
was quiet. The streets were too wide to set up barricades. We began to
hear a muffled rolling sound.

A detachment from the line brought some young mobile guards who
had been disarmed at their post. They were foaming at the mouth with
rage. They wanted to fight. They were given something to eat and drink.
There were twenty of them; the youngest was twenty years old. They
started beaming when someone came to get them for combat.

One of them came back the next day to see his mother. He was wearing a black armband: his brother and ten of his companions had been
killed.

The Marais district was under siege. Whole houses had been put to
the sword, windows had been shot out.

"YOU CANNOT PASS!" (WE PASS ANYWAY)
"Marie," I said to my maid, "quick, get me a shawl and a hat. I have to
go see my mother."

211

"Where do you think you are going?" the young guard told me. "You cannot pass anywhere. There are orders posted. The artillery is camping on the boulevards."

"I shall say that I want to see my mother."

"You need a laissez-passer from the captain."

The captain's office had been transferred to the ministry's office. On my way there my passage was barred some twenty times. But I pleaded, insisted, and I reached it. The captain knew me because he had seen me at the Hippodrome where he had been detached.

"Monsieur, I have come to ask you for a laissez-passer to go see my mother on Rue Saint-Louis."

"But that is impossible. They are fighting in that area."

"Oh! Please, monsieur. I shall make it, if you give me a laissez-passer."

In his office there were also two gentlemen who wore similar embroidered ribbons in their lapels.

"She is brave," one of them said, "give it to her."

"Here," said the captain as he handed me a paper. "Be careful. Use the streets."

Downstairs I found Marie who had followed me. Every minute someone wanted me to turn back. I would show them the paper and I would be allowed to go on. On Place de la Bourse, squads of men in gray were leading others dressed like them; they were prisoners.

The young mobile guards, black with gunpowder, were on guard duty on Rue de Vendôme.

The battle had gone to their heads. They were handling their loaded guns in a careless and dangerous way.

I passed near two guards who were arguing.

"There is only one way to come to an agreement," said one. "The one who will bump off the other will be right."

A shot was fired. They all pounced on their firearms and lay down taking aim at each other, not knowing whether the attack had come from among them. It was awful to watch.

I had taken refuge by a carriage entrance. Marie was huddled against me.

When they saw that it was a false alarm, they put their rifles down. A second shot was fired in our direction. I saw the spark come out of the barrel and the bullet lodged itself two feet above our heads.

Firing was continuous. There was canon fire from Faubourg Saint-Antoine.

I could see the house where my mother lived and that renewed my courage. We had to climb over a tall barricade that stretched across Rue Saint-Louis, at the end of Rue des Filles-du-Calvaire. We had barely come down on the other side when someone began to fire on some runaways coming toward us. They managed to go into a house. My mother's was partially demolished. The concierge had been killed the night before. His wife and their three little children were standing around his bed.

"Where is my mother?" I asked, disregarding the sorrow I was intruding on.

I had not finished my sentence, when Vincent showed up.

"Well, well!" he said. "It is you, Céleste. Your mother is upstairs . . . go on up. She is fine, thank God."

Seeing him and hearing his voice reawakened my hatred.

"You are not going upstairs?" he asked again.

"No, I found out what I wanted to know."

MOGADOR WOULD HAVE HAD THE SUFFRAGETTES WHIPPED

We had to go to Rue du Temple, and there we were allowed to pass. The stores were closed, except one or two here and there that served as temporary first aid post. The boulevard pavement was covered with hay, canon parts, ammunition, and stacks of rifles. A few wounded men, whom the surgeons had bandaged, were there, amid the gatherings, listening.

"Well, no, I am not mistaken," said a young man wearing a surgeon uniform as he was barring my passage, "it is Céleste!"

I had recognized Adolphe's friend. I pressed his hands and kissed him.

"I have just returned from getting news about my mother. . . . Do you still see Adolphe? How is he?"

"Oh! You did not see him where you have come from? He was over there, at the Bastille. I was told that some doctors were wounded and that he was among them. Since you have a laissez-passer, go to his house. He lives on Rue de Bourgogne."

On Place de la Concorde I was not allowed to cross the bridge. Some cavalrymen were camping there. In their midst were several men dressed in black wearing in their lapel the same ribbon as those I had seen in the captain's office. I went up to them and, addressing the older one, I said, "Monsieur, I would like to go to Rue de Bourgogne."

"Certainly, madame, if you would take my arm, I shall take you there."

I refused, in his interest. What were people going to think seeing a representative of the people with Mogador on his arm? He insisted; I resisted. Another joined him, and, in spite of myself, I was escorted by both of them. All along the quays, on the other side of the bridge, there were National Guards, and among them, M. Charles de la Gui . . . , a friend of Lionel's.

"Oh! This is too much!" he told me laughing out loud. "A man in my outfit was saying as he saw you coming that we should arrest you because you are probably carrying cartridges to the insurgents!"

Once I was Rue de Bourgogne, I stopped at the entrance. The concierge came toward me.

"Who are you looking for, mademoiselle?"

"Monsieur Adolphe, please."

"He lives here, but he is not in. He was wounded in the leg, and he is at his mother's."

"Do you know whether the wound is serious?"

"No, it is practically nothing, fortunately."

I gave him my name and left, reassured.

Lionel was waiting for me at my house. He let out a cry of joy when he saw me. His concern made me feel good. He was looking at me and seemed happy to see me again. Lionel was my own family! I had only him in the world, so what did I care about the rest!

In a tiresome way people were singing these two songs: "To Die for the Motherland" and "The People Are Our Brothers" (for one sentence, it was a show of fist, for some other it was a hand on the heart); they were also singing, "And the Enemies' Tyrants!" I do not know whether Lionel had a political opinion, although he probably did, but he never expressed it, especially not to me. He said that women who were involved in that should be whipped. That was my opinion. We were in agreement on that point. Only, when a singer came to our courtyard, he would pelt him with two sous coins so he would go away.

IS IT THE RIGHT DEPARTURE?

Lionel was waiting for money so he could leave again. I offered him what I had left of my winnings. He refused and waited several days. Paris was in mourning. A lot of people had perished, and confidence was a long way from returning. Lionel had gone to see his business manager. He came back very sad and said, "Still no money! Listen, Céleste, I love you very much, but I am not rich enough to keep you with these expenses. My château has no more furniture in it; if you wish, bring yours, and we shall live happily at my place. If, one day, we separate and I get married, I shall pay you what I owe you."

In a matter of hours I had gone to see the landlord to tell him I was moving out and to ask him to rent my apartment for me, had gone to the horse livery, and had packed my bags.

My furnishings were quite substantial. We could not take everything without incurring great expenses. I rented a little lodging for the furniture of one of the bedrooms; that way we would have a pied-à-terre in Paris if we needed one. I found a small vacant apartment at 42 Rue de Londres for six hundred francs. I had the furniture from a Persian room brought there. In the living room I put the oak furniture from my dining room.

I made Lionel take five hundred francs in gold that I had left. That same day he bought me a piece of jewelry worth more than three thousand francs.

25

Château Life

The Squalid and Unsanitary Berry of Those Days—
On the Heath . . .—The Hunt, Love's Rival

ONCE I WAS at his château I set up my embroidery frame and started ambitious projects. My stay at Lionel's no longer had a transitory quality. I had to create for myself an occupation that would help me pass the long solitary hours. Thus, everyone who passed through the garden to go from one road to the other could see me at my bedroom window working industriously. I began work at eight and did not stop until dark. I had brought Marie, who was preparing a tapestry. I never went out. Some poor little children would come visit me; during those visits I would put my embroidery aside and, with some old linen Persian drapes found in the château's closets, we would improvise a sewing workshop. My little girls would leave with a good dress.

Little by little the household servants became used to me. Célina, the steward's daughter, would come visit me. She was twenty-three years old; she was ugly but kind and considerate. Each day I had a little more freedom. Sometimes I would go horseback riding.

One little girl visited more often than the others. Her name was Solange. Her parents had seven very young children. One day she told me, "Why do you not come visit me, demoiselle? Grandmamma is blind, but she is not deaf, you know. Le Ris, it is not far from here. When are you coming?"

"I do not know. One day."

"Yes, oh, good!" said the little girl jumping up and down. "That day we shall put my grandmother's hair in a bun."

THE SQUALID AND UNSANITARY BERRY OF THOSE DAYS
I had read Madame Sand's books, and I was rejoicing at the idea of visiting the countryside she had described.[1] I was going to see the Devil's

216

Pond. How disappointing! I found a pond full of sludge festooned with lots of ducks. I was becoming disillusioned about the region, which I had imagined as an enchanted province. Everyone was sick with fever. Each one was bony and skinny. The culture is so backwards, you would think you were in some primitive country. The peasants are shabby and live miserable lives in their huts. They do not take care of themselves or their health or the lives of their parents. For example, there was a sick seventy-six-year-old man living near us. His family had not sent for the doctor because that would cost money. I asked the doctor to go check on this poor old man.

He went immediately.

"Always the same story," he told the daughter who was there. "I am sent for when it is too late."

"Oh! *Monsieur le médechin,* too bad I *don'* know this morning!" she said.

"Why?" said the doctor.

"Because I *d'have* bought some bodkins to bury my papa with."

"That is all right," said the old man to his daughter, "you will find some on the mantle in a little canister."

They just let themselves die. They all have a field, a meadow that they rent. The poorest of them have some possessions. They shorten their lives so they can amass more and they let themselves die rather than deplete their money.

The little money Lionel gave me was used for alms. I could not witness this misery without feeling sad. If you did not see them where they live, you were not so shocked. For example, on Sundays when the bagpiper passes, everyone goes out. The girls wear a white headdress and a silk apron. The lads, as they are called, wear a burlap shirt, sometimes a very clean jacket, and a large black felt hat with wide brims. They pair up and follow the music to the town square where everyone dances. Then the bourrées begin. There is no letup from noon until six o'clock, when, finally, all you can see is a cloud of dust.

The next day in the square there is a sunken area where the dancers had been. The men, who deprive themselves all week, drink four liters of wine on Sunday.

Sometimes I paid the player. Lionel allowed dancing in the garden. It was quite a feast. I would dance the bourrée or the boulangère. Even though I had strong legs, the villagers were giving me some competition.

The foreman had three daughters. One was named Justine, a small thirteen-year-old brunette. I showed her how to embroider. In the evening we played with a kite.

The gardener had two daughters. One of them often came with us. She was sixteen. She was as strong as I and my size. Her sister was epileptic. Her family kept an eye on her, and there was always someone with her. One day I went into her room and saw, near the fireplace, seated in a large chair, an adorable creature. I spoke to her, but she did not answer. Her sister ran in from outside.

"Oh! Excuse me, madame, she will not reply; she is an imbecile."

ON THE HEATH . . .

Winter was coming. Lionel relished the thought that soon he would be able to go hunting. Aside from a few little lovers' quarrels, our time together was passing rapidly. His Paris friends would come see him. He went to a great deal of trouble to welcome them and that cost a lot of money.

One day he told us during dinner, "If you wish, tomorrow, we shall hunt hares on the heath. Céleste will come too."

Everyone was delighted. Especially Montji, the painter who had done Lise's portrait and later mine. He did not handle a horse as well as a paintbrush.

At five o'clock everyone was ready. The saddled horses were pawing the ground in the courtyard. Montji, who when he came to the château did not expect to be riding a horse, had not brought anything to wear. Lionel had to lend him some boots, a jacket, and trousers. They were all one size too large. His cap fell over his eyes. He was riding Henriette, a small ticklish mare that, since she had been ridden by the foreman, wanted to stay close to the dogs.

Once we had reached the end of the central alley, which was one league long, we came upon a huge expanse; it was the heath, uncultivated lands that belonged to Lionel. In other regions they are called the *landes*. It was a fantastic hunt. The area seemed flat like a wide road, except for a few little ditches or furrows; in fact, one could see a hare or a fox from a great distance. The foreman let loose twenty dogs that began tracking and sniffing every clump of heather.

Reckless Montji let out a loud cry of joy. Seeing the dogs on a trail, his mare took off like an arrow. Montji was not expecting that. His cap flopped down over his eyes. Fortunately for him, the hare crouched low, the dogs lost the scent and came back over the false trail. Henriette stopped. Montji was pulling himself together when, having fortuitously found the trail again, the dogs darted off once more. Henriette joined the race again with the unfortunate Montji astride her neck, near the ears.

After some great feints the dogs caught their hare stiff from the race. We returned around eleven o'clock. Lunch was cheerful at the expense of Montji who would wince when he sat down.

Hunts through the forest are quite different. I thought I knew how to ride a horse, but I was wrong. In the Châteauroux forest six leagues from the château, the hunt was for boars. The foreman, his dogs, and his post horses left the night before to sleep near the gathering place. The foreman got up at three o'clock and went through the woods with his bloodhound. As for us, we had to get up at four. On those days Lionel would shave, don white velvet trousers, soft leather boots, a buff colored vest, a dark blue frock coat with crimson velvet cuffs and short cape, a gold belt, an ivory handled knife, a black velvet cap, a French horn, and the attire was complete. He looked very handsome in it. The white tie was de rigueur. Once the hunt was underway, he did not have much to do with me. His full attention was devoted to Saint Hubert. The mornings were cold. We would leave either in a landau or on horseback. At nine o'clock we arrived at the Trois-Fouinots, a magnificent junction in the forest where we would meet. The trees there are gigantic. It is a woodland whose timber the government reserves for its navy ships.

At each corner of the crossroads, three dog keepers guarded a relay of twenty dogs each. Four servants held the reins of the saddled horses. They all wore livery emblazoned with Lionel's coat of arms. All the forest wardens were gathered around a fire they had built for us.

Eight roads circled the junction. Lionel often said, "Do you not see anything coming?" To one of his queries a guard replied, "Here comes Pinoteau." He was the first foreman. All the dogs' ears pricked up. Pinoteau arrived being pulled by his bloodhound on a leash.

"Well," asked Lionel, "do you have a good trail to report?"

"M. le Comte knows quite well I do my best. It rained last night and the paths are wet. I found a herd, but my dog lost its scent. I saw the tracks of a young boar. It went in circles all night long, then at dawn it went in the direction of the Saint-Maur woods."

"Fine," said Lionel frowning, "if La Feuille (that was the name of the second foreman) was no more successful than you, I shall not have a hunt."

THE HUNT, LOVE'S RIVAL

La Feuille arrived.

"M. le Comte, I spotted a five-hundred-pound lone boar. I found it at the wallow, behind the guardhouse. My dog was pulling hard enough to cut my hands. It was going toward Ardentes. I circled its territory, and I am certain it is still there."

Lionel jumped on his horse.

"Hark!" he said. "Get the dogs ready! Watch your relays!"

At that moment all the dogs began howling with impatience. They were struck with a few lashes of the whip, and the pain drew a few cries from them, but they continued yapping even louder. Lionel motioned for me to follow him. I followed him. What a crude form of recreation this is! Dashing through the forest, sinking deep into ruts, my horse sunk in up to its breast, being whacked in the chest by limbs. . . .

By evening, the monster had been forced out, but it had confronted the hounds. Four were killed and six wounded.

We returned to the château dead tired. I cried for the dogs. I began to hold hunting and boars in horror because I saw them as rivals.

26

Richard

Stormy and Endangered Love Affair—Flowered Homage:
Returned to Sender—Secrets among the Masters and among
the Servants—The Critic Apologizes—Victorine and
the Bottin Address Almanac

THE EXPEDITIONS into the forest took place three times a week. For a
while I went along so I would not be alone, but they were too strenuous
for a woman, and, because of my health, I had to give them up.

I spent almost all my days and evenings alone in a large living room
where the wind blew through the many openings.

I told Lionel, "My friend, I am bored. Could you not stay with me
more often? I do not like the country; I am used to the bustle of Paris.
To agree to live here, I must love you a lot. If the time you spend here
allows you to save money, I shall be patient, but hunting makes you
incur tremendous expenses."

"Why do you stay? Am I keeping you here against your will? I love
hunting, and I intend to go on hunting for as long as I wish. Those who
are bothered by this are free to go. As for admonitions, I do not tolerate
them from anyone."

I left the living room and went to my room. He had never addressed
me in this fashion.

STORMY AND ENDANGERED LOVE AFFAIR

He followed me and surprised, asked, "But what are you doing?"

"As you can see, I am packing my trunks. I shall leave tomorrow."

"Leave! But why?"

"Because for a remark that was accurate, you threw me out. Well, I
am telling you again, this way of life is ruining you. You will not be able
to continue without adjoining another fortune to yours; that means you

will have to marry. Then you will send me away once I have become accustomed to this life. Bringing me here was a regrettable decision on your part. I do not like the country. It is a grave where my vivaciousness is being buried. What interest could I possibly take in what is around me? What does it mean to me that the poplars are growing and earn twenty sous a year? My interest is dancing and the theater. I want to leave!"

"Your nerves are distraught. I did not understand a word you just said. I did not do anything to hurt you. I let you sleep in my mother's bedroom, you, Céleste, who just a while ago would grow pale when looking at her own past in the mirror! Forgive me this word, but it was a profanation. My family is alarmed since they know you are with me. Not a day goes by that I do not receive letters asking me to send you away. I do not have the courage to do so. You are my weakness. If I have any regrets, I forget them when I am kissing you. Do not make me unhappy; stay near me; no one will love you more than I. You miss Paris. Well in a few days we shall go there. Please, unpack your trunk."

For a few days I was quite gloomy. Marie, the servant I had had for a long time, was being courted by the butler. Lionel asked me to send her away. I did so regretfully. My life was becoming a voluntary constraint.

"Well," Lionel told me, "get ready, we are going to spend a month in Paris. I received some business letters."

On the road, he told me he could not stay at my apartment because he was taking his cook and his butler with him.

"But . . . until you have found . . . ?"

"I wrote ahead, and an apartment was reserved for me at the Cité d'Antin. I shall stay there."

"Now, tell me the truth. You do not know how to lie. Why are you going to Paris?"

"I am going to Paris to bring you back there, Céleste. I do not want to leave you, but I must pretend that I do. I must go out in society as my relatives wish. You shall go to balls on your own. Seeing us apart like this, they will believe we have broken up. You will come over every night, in hiding, and I shall give you one hundred francs every week."

My blood was boiling. It was a separation again.

"Fine! I shall do as you say. There is a ball at the Jardin d'Hiver Saturday; I am going." [1]

I was seeking a maid who also knew how to sew dresses. A woman applied.

"Make me this black crepe dress with five notched flounces, and on each flounce, three little satin ribbons."

I ordered a gold honeysuckle crown set in green leaves.

Lionel had seen me get dressed.

"Here, something is missing from your attire."

He handed me a box containing a magnificent diamond cross.

I took it without joy, even though it was quite beautiful. It was probably a good-bye gift.

"Keep a place for me in your heart once you are back spinning in your pleasure circle."

"Would you like for me not to go?"

"No, go, you must. Did you let your friend know?"

"No, I am going to get her."

"Then I shall take you there."

All the way to Victorine's doorstep, he had not said a word. Obviously he did not love me anymore. It was a polite separation.

He kissed me and left, saying, "See you tomorrow."

FLOWERED HOMAGE: RETURNED TO SENDER

Once inside Victorine's apartment, I began to cry.

"Oh, my!" she said. "You did not think he was going to marry you, did you? Find another."

"I shall never be able to forget him. If you only knew how much I love him!"

"That is why he is leaving you."

"No, his affairs are in difficulty."

"But, I thought he was rich! . . ."

"Yes, he is rich, but he has expensive tastes and enormous expenses."

"He is rich, and he is not keeping you! It means he is more ambitious than in love. Stop caring about him and he will either leave you for good or will come back to you."

We were on our way to the Jardin d'Hiver. The room was resplendent with flowers, lights, and diamonds. I had been out of circulation for a while and everyone took an interest in me. I did not want to dance, yet a tall, thin, blond young man invited me to dance with such persistence that I accepted. My dancer overwhelmed me with his attentiveness. I tolerated it in the hope that the game would continue to entertain him, that he would try to see me again, that Lionel would notice, and that jealousy would bring him back at my feet.

However, not wanting to rely on myself, I consulted Victorine.

"What do you think of him? Do you think he is handsome enough to make Lionel, who is so perfect, jealous?"

"Certainly," she said, "he looks fine."

My dancer asked for permission to send me flowers. I did not categorically say no, which, coming from a woman, I believe, means yes.

During the conversation, talented Victorine found a way to reveal my address to my lover, who was now sure of his success.

Not too soon, in fact, because Victorine's patience was wearing thin.

"What a chore I have taken on for you, my dear! I am bored to death here; I know no one, and I cannot say evil things about people I do not know."

"Do you want to leave?"

"Oh, yes!" she said.

As we were picking up our coats from the cloakroom, many people were coming in.

"Oh," said Victorine, "we are leaving as the best is arriving. Look at those two hairdos: a vegetable garden and an ostrich!"

"But look at these on the other hand, look how lovely they are!"

Mesdames Doche and Plumket were coming in wearing crowns of daisies and charming outfits. Ozy was following them.

"Yes, but a crown does not make up for a nose."

"Oh! You are not saying this for Madame Doche."

"Oh! I have been seeing her for twenty-five years."

Once back home, I began to think about Berry where at first I had been so happy, then so sad later on. "I certainly prefer that memory to the fake pleasures I just saw!" I was telling myself. At noon I received a gorgeous bouquet of Parma violets surrounded by white camellias and a card attached to it. It was from my young man of the night before who was asking for permission to pay me a visit at four o'clock. The reply was yes.

Lionel arrived at two. He walked up to the table, read the card, and said, "Do you know this gentleman? He is the son of a stockbroker. He is very nice, but they say he is dumb, not your type."

A carriage stopped at the door. He took my bouquet, opened the window, and, very casually, let it fall, as if by accident, right on the head of the person coming out of the carriage, who was none other than the young man who had sent it to me. He did not bother picking it up; he got back in his carriage and left.

I was delighted. Lionel still loved me since he was jealous. That night he was the one going to a ball. I gloomily watched him get ready. Among the social set attending this ball, there must be many seductive, young, rich, beautiful, and upstanding individuals!

I waited up for him. At the sound of each carriage passing by, I would go to the window. When he returned, he scolded me for waiting up so late.

SECRETS AMONG THE MASTERS
AND AMONG THE SERVANTS

The maid I had hired had said she was married to a coachman. One day when she was fitting me for a blouse, I noticed her thick waist. I asked her, "Caroline, are you pregnant?"

"No, madame."

I did not bring up the subject again. She was a good, frugal worker, and I was quite pleased with her.

There was something mysterious in all of Lionel's comings and goings. He was writing and receiving a lot of letters that he concealed from me. I was determined to learn his secrets. While he was having lunch, I took and hid the key to his desk, and once I was alone at his apartment, I opened the desk and found letters from a relative. They all mentioned me in dreadful terms:

Are you finally done with this woman? . . . I hope you are not seeing her anymore. . . . Think of your future. . . . Mademoiselle de B—— wishes nothing more than to marry you, only she wants to make absolutely sure that you no longer have unfortunate liaisons.

In a drawer I found an unfinished letter in Lionel's handwriting. It was most probably addressed to one of the relatives of Mademoiselle de B——:

My dear friend,
In asking for the hand of Mademoiselle de B——, I know what I am committing myself to, and I am too forthright a man not to fulfill my duty. As for Mogador, it is possible that I was seen speaking to her in the street. The poor girl has not done me any harm, and I do not know why I would pass by her without looking at her.

Dear friend, you know what the life of a bachelor is like. One must find distractions. I found this one. What do you want me to do? One does not drown the girls one has lived with. As soon as I am married, I shall leave with my wife. Do what you can to get Mademoiselle de B—— to decide.

The letter stopped there. My heavy heart dissolved into tears; then hatred for the world took hold of it. What had I done to all these people? Why were they all scheming to take my Lionel away from me?

I put the letters back, locked the desk, and left. When I was back home, the concierge gave me my key.

"Caroline is out?"

"Yes, madame, she went to the hospital at Faubourg Saint-Honoré to give birth."

"What! So she was pregnant?"

"Did madame not notice?"

"Get me a carriage, I am going to see her."

On the way I tried to figure out what I would do. Write Lionel? It was better to wait until he announced his plans to me.

I found Caroline.

"Are you mad to run away from me like that? Why did you not tell me about your condition; you are married?" Since she was blushing, I continued, "And even if you were not, I am too much in need of tolerance myself not to have any for others."

"How wonderful! Then madame will take me back when I leave the hospital?"

"But of course."

"Oh! How kind you are madame! And if I could ask you. . . ."

"What? Go ahead and ask."

"To be my child's godmother?"

"I gladly accept."

When I left I went to see Victorine.

"Oh," she said, "I get a visit; so the love affair is still not going well?"

"Tomorrow it will be all over. I shall never see his château again; all the needlework I did will be destroyed. He will send me the money for my furniture; he will be free to offer it to another woman. The windows will be opened wide so that the impure breath I left there will fly out. So, that is how it has to be! There is a ball at the Jardin d'Hiver tomorrow, will you go with me?"

"My dear, anything you wish but that. Balls bore me to tears. My little fortune does not allow me to conform to the extravagance of today's foolish women. Believe me, you should spend less on baubles and not go to balls so often."

"Do you think I am going to this one for fun? No, I need distraction so I can forget him. I need to be talked about, to be loved, to have money spent on me. Come with me tomorrow; it will be the last time."

"On that condition, I am willing to. I shall come by for you, and try to have it all over by then."

That evening, I went to Lionel's for dinner. His butler was getting his clothes ready.

"You are going out tonight, Lionel?"

"Yes, I am going out in society."

Not a word was said between us the whole evening. When his carriage left, I began to write a long letter, which I burned. It would be better to tell him all this. . . . I had never had so little courage. I could picture him at the ball, near the person he was going to marry, smiling at her, telling her, "I love you!"

A carriage stopped. It was he!

"Why are you not in bed?"

"I am sick. I have a fever, . . . but what I have, I can relieve it by telling you about it. . . . Mademoiselle de B—— has finally said yes?"

He turned pale but did not reply.

"Go ahead and tell me you love her! Why put on this twisted act with me? Am I not worth the trouble?"

"My poor Céleste, I do not know who is feeding your imagination like this. You are not being reasonable. I am yielding to the wishes of my relatives who resolutely want me to be settled. I had not brought up these new plans because they could not work out and I was delaying the thought of causing you sorrow uselessly."

"Oh! If only one could drown the girls one has lived with, things would be easier!"

"You dared read letters that you were not supposed to look at. . . . Too often you forget who you are, Céleste. Do not make me regret what I have done for you. In the future, keep in mind that letters not addressed to you are sacred. Your furnishings are at my house, and if I marry, I shall pay you for them. I shall give you twenty thousand francs. We shall never see each other again, but I shall remember you fondly."

THE CRITIC APOLOGIZES

To talk about tears so often is tiresome. . . . I was still crying at noon when a package arrived containing the few objects I had left at Lionel's apartment. A two-line letter accompanied it:

As soon as I shall receive some money, I shall send you some. From afar, as well as near, I shall watch over you.
    Lionel

That evening when Victorine came for me, I was not ready. She was the one who dragged me to the ball after mechanically dressing me. I was wearing a white lace dress and a crown of pomegranates. The evening was even more festive than the first time. When I was dancing, my vis-à-vis was my fake sister. . . . When I say dancing, I mean standing,

227

looking at each other because there were so many people we could not move. Victorine was in a very good mood.

By two o'clock the crowd had thinned a little. The dark cloud of sadness that was weighing on my heart had begun to evaporate, and I did not miss a single waltz, polka, or mazurka. There were many actors there. Hyacinthe was making enough noise for four.[2] People were assembled around him, and he was showing off, at no charge, his long nose and his large hands. He was exhibiting his own witticisms, which were just as good as what the playwrights usually had him recite. His producer had not thought about these performances, otherwise he would have banned them in the contract. Everyone surrounded him and jostled to get closer. He was cheerful and was having as much fun as a child pursuing a forty-year-old woman who was alone and dressed in the most grotesque fashion. He was following her, calling her Elvire, and saying, "Dance with me, madame, I love you. Do not be cruel or I shall stab you with my nose."

Grassot, who is always the same, was just as silly and amusing. He would twirl around the women, but stop by the prettiest ones, take them by the arm and, although he did not know them, address them in the familiar form.[3]

A quadrille was about to start when I heard my name called out loud.

"Here is Mogador! How beautiful she is!"

"You think so?" said another voice. "I do not understand why people find this woman beautiful."

I turned slightly to see who was typing me this way. It was a very handsome boy.

"Well anyway," said the first man to have spoken, "it does not prevent her from having beautiful arms, a lovely waist, a nice shape, being tall, having beautiful hair, lovely eyes, and teeth as white as a young dog's."

"Possibly; I did not look at her," said my critic.

I wanted him to look at me, but to no avail; he was not paying any attention to me. He seemed too occupied with a woman who was not at all pretty.

I was vexed and was about to walk away when the shorter one, who was his cousin, stopped me.

"Mademoiselle, you are an exquisite dancer, and, if I were not such a bad dancer, I would invite you to dance."

"Oh! But I accept with pleasure."

I was hoping that his friend would follow him, but not at all. During the quadrille, I told him, "I certainly owed you something for the way you came to my defense. This gentleman over there does not care much for me."

"Oh! You heard? He is tactless! He must apologize."

I wanted to hold him back, but he took off.

By the looks of the pantomime going on, I could tell that the other one was defending himself. But the short one was stubborn and brought him to me.

He was a twenty-two- to twenty-four-year-old young man, tall, slightly heavy, but well built. His blond hair and sideburns framed his face. His complexion was a dull white. His thin mustache emphasized his mouth. His forehead was charming and his eyes were the softest in the world. He was distinguished and elegant, and he had the feet and hands of a Creole.

Victorine, who had not seen nor heard anything, nudged my arm and said, "Look at this handsome young boy!"

"Yes, he is my foe."

"Oh! Too bad! He would have made your Lionel wildly jealous."

He was standing near us and seemed quite embarrassed.

"My goodness, monsieur, do you find me so unattractive that you lost the use of words?"

"Oh! Not at all, mademoiselle. If I spoke of you in these terms, it was because I had not looked at you, and I sincerely ask your forgiveness."

"Watch out, monsieur, you are sitting on my dress; it is made of lace."

"Oh! Excuse me! I am clumsy."

"I overheard your opinion of me; you would not have expressed it had you thought I was listening."

"I want to convince you that my remorse equals my crime. I have had too unfortunate a beginning with you to be very ambitious, but I would be very happy if I could become your friend."

"No, monsieur, no. I would drop even lower in your opinion of me. Character is even more important than physical appearance. . . . Adieu, I am going to dance."

He remained pensive.

VICTORINE AND THE BOTTIN ADDRESS ALMANAC

A half hour later his cousin asked me, "What did you do to Richard? Now he is mad about you. He claims that you have mesmerized him and says he must see you again."

"Oh, really! He must think I was really wounded by his opinion of me to go through so much trouble. Reassure him I have forgotten it."

In the meantime, Richard was talking to Victorine. It was time to leave. He asked my permission to take me home. I thanked him but refused, and we left alone.

"He is charming," said Victorine. "Only, you are letting me have an odious and boring role; I feel like the Bottin address almanac. I do not need to tell you that he asked me for your address."

"You did not give it to him, I hope."

"Done. You need distractions!"

27

Cholera Gives Me a Godchild

Beaujon Hospice, 19 March 1849—"You are all she will have"

I WENT TO SEE Caroline at the hospice. She was in pain, and the doctor handed me such a frail little girl that I said to myself, "She will never live."

The father was present. He asked me to hold the little girl at the baptismal fonts with one of his friends, whom he would be bringing the next day at ten o'clock.

M. Richard kept his word. At four o'clock he was at my house. I teased him about his sudden change.

He urged me, "Agree to come dine tomorrow with your friend and my cousin. It is the only way you can persuade me that you do not hold anything against me."

"I hold nothing against you, but I have too much to do; I am a godmother."

"You will be free at six o'clock and I shall come by for you."

"No, send your cousin, and you will pick up Victorine."

BEAUJON HOSPICE, 19 MARCH 1849

The next day at nine o'clock, I was at the hospice with my little bundle. I dressed my godchild for whom everything was too big. I had to gather her little bonnet. At the church my heart sank. There was a wedding ceremony. I thought about Lionel, and a couple of tears dropped from my eyes down to the little girl's forehead. I showed the spot to the priest, who wiped it with holy oils.

I gave her the name of Solange in memory of Berry, and mine, so she would remember me. On the way out of the church I held her pressed against my heart. I felt like running away with her as if she were mine. I walked toward the hospice and ruefully placed her in her cradle. I

231

took charge of finding a nursemaid. I did not return to see her until the next day.

Caroline looked pale and hollow-eyed.

"Have you found a nursemaid?"

"Yes, she will be here tomorrow."

"Oh! Madame, it is not tomorrow she must come, but today. Death is in this room. Since your last visit, five women and four children have died."

"Do not worry, tomorrow will be here soon."

"But, madame, look across the way."

And she lay back down. I crossed the room and, in fact, I did see something atrocious: a young woman, who must have been about twenty-two years old, was holding a tiny baby in her arms. She was trying to nurse him, but he would not suckle. I stopped an orderly and asked her what that meant. She looked skyward without replying.

"Here," I told her as I slipped five francs into her hand, "take good care of the woman over there."

"Oh! You are her daughter's godmother? Take her away right now."

She walked off to take care of the sick woman.

"Did you see?" Caroline said.

"Certainly, but do not torment yourself. I am taking Solange with me. The nursemaid wagon where I went, on Rue de la Victoire, will be there another three days. I shall keep her at my house. I shall return to see you tomorrow."

In Caroline's absence I had hired a German girl who had previously worked for me by the day.

This was 19 March 1849. That day the Beaujon Hospice was all astir because rooms were being rearranged. Women in labor were moved from the first floor to the third. Everything was scrubbed and impeccably clean. In spite of these precautions, death was reaping a terrible harvest. Since Caroline's admittance, seventeen women and children had suddenly been taken away. Mortality was two-thirds more prevalent among women who had just given birth.

I asked for the intern on duty and requested that he tell me frankly what he knew.

"Well! Mademoiselle, if you care for the life of this poor woman, take her away, even though she has not been here the nine days. There is no longer any doubt, it is cholera."

"Tomorrow her husband will bring her to me. Have her card signed."

The next day a carriage stopped at my door. Caroline was carried in more than led in by her husband. I took a step backward; she seemed so changed. Her eyes were sunken, her cheeks hollow, her lips black. I put her in my bed and sent for my doctor, Lionel's.

The doctor looked at her for a long time and told me, "Send the child away before she sees her. She must not come near her bed."

"Adèle," I told my German girl, "go get me some powdered camphor."

I put some in my little godchild's swaddling clothes, in her bonnet, in her fichu, and I handed her to her mother so she could hold her one last time.

I was nervous, since her mother's breath could poison her.

Once the child was gone I felt more at ease.

I spent the night at Victorine's.

"YOU ARE ALL SHE WILL HAVE"

My doctor came twice a day. On the third day he took me aside and said, "There is no hope for her. Since her husband is at her side, leave and go to your friend's house."

"Oh! My dear doctor, do not worry about me. She has a child. Use all your scientific knowledge, bring in one of your colleagues, but save her."

"I have done all I can, there is no hope."

That evening at six o'clock I left this poor woman to go to Victorine's. All night long I dreamed about Caroline. I got up at seven.

As I was going down Rue Amsterdam, which led to my house, I met a young actress named Virginie Mercier, whom I had known at the Délassements and who was at the Vaudeville. After I asked about her health I told her about my situation.

"Do you want me to go with you?"

"That would please me greatly."

When I walked into my house Caroline was stiff, her eyes were closed. The German girl told me she cried when she was asked if she wanted a confessor.

I took her hand and told her, "Caroline, can you hear me?"

She moved her chin without speaking. There was a roaring fire in the fireplace. I asked for some towels and warmed them, with Virginie's help, and put some on her feet, her hands, her stomach, and her chest. She gradually warmed up, and she was able to speak.

"Kind mistress, I was waiting for you."

"Well! I am here, and I shall stay with you. Why did you refuse to see a priest? I am sending for one now and we shall pray together."

Her husband understood me and went to the church. She motioned for me to come closer and said, "You will take care of my little girl, will you not? You are all she will have."

"Yes, I shall take care of her, and you also. You will be better tonight. Here is your husband."

During the prayer she struggled, and her body almost rolled off the bed; we picked her back up. She experienced a horrible contortion, stiffened, and fell back, mouth and eyes open.

I placed my right hand on her still-warm forehead, my left hand on my heart, and I swore to her that I would raise her daughter and would make an honest woman of her. I knew the father could not do anything. He was married to another woman, and without me the poor little girl would only have the Foundlings Home.

28

Dramatic Follies and Folies-Dramatiques

Richard Is Sacrificed—Finding a Woman and Two Millions—
I Hire, Therefore I Pay—The Sweet and Kind Confidant—
Dressing Rooms and Backstage

I HAD GIVEN UP my apartment, which was too far away, and had
rented a pretty one facing the street on the third floor at number 24 of
Boulevard Poissonnière.

I decided to go back on the stage.

Once I had moved in I inquired about Lionel's activities. He was in
Vendée with a relative.

Sometimes Richard would visit me. He was extremely sweet and always affectionate. One thing pained him: constantly having to hear me
talk about Lionel.

All the furniture I had was one distressed-oak dining room set and
a magnificent bed; the rest had been taken to Berry.

Richard sent me his decorator with instructions to get me whatever I
needed at his own expense. Two days later my apartment was furnished.
For all his kindness, Richard barely got a thank you or a smile in return.

I was sad. My love for Lionel ruled me and it was futile to fight against
it. As hard as I tried to forget, it was useless. Lionel was one of those men
who do everything well. A fine gentleman in the smallest details, kind,
generous, a quick mind, honest. Passion magnifies everything, and yet
those who have known him know that I do not exaggerate.

Richard had great qualities, but in no way did he have anything in
common with Lionel's character, which was so exuberant in ardor and
imagination. Richard was sweet and kind. One evening, not too long
after my getting settled in, he came to take me to dinner. We were at the
alley's entrance when I saw Lionel. He stopped in front of us, looked at
Richard, and said to me, "Could I have a word with you?"

I looked at Richard who, without knowing him, had guessed it was Lionel. He was pale with irritation and anger. I looked at him imploringly and said, "Would you be kind enough to go on ahead and wait for me at the Maison-d'Or?"

Their eyes met and flashed menacingly.

"Go," I told him, pushing him a little.

As he walked away, he looked back. Lionel, arms crossed, was watching him, then said to me, "I am sorry to have disturbed you, my dear. I needed to talk business with you. I should have known that when one has left a woman like you for just a few hours, it is necessary to write ahead to avoid running into others."

"You had the right to leave me, and I had the right to replace you. I have no fortune. I would rather die than ask you for anything."

"So, you do not love this man?"

"No, unfortunately."

"Well, then, stay with me. Do not have dinner with this man, you owe me that much. I have broken off everything. I cannot live without you, but if you go out with him, I am leaving and shall never see you again."

"I still love you, Lionel. What you have just said makes me very happy, yet I cannot accept the price you are demanding. It would be base boorishness to abandon M. Richard like that. I was quite glad to find him; I am not an ingrate, so I am going to go meet him. After dinner I shall go home and write to him that I cannot see him anymore."

"Go," he said, "I shall wait for you."

I arrived at the Maison-d'Or. Richard let out a cry of joy when he saw me.

"Oh! I was afraid you would not come! How did your encounter go?"

"Well. I am going to see Lionel in a little while; we have business to talk over."

"What? You are going to see him after dinner?"

"Yes, my friend."

"All right, Céleste, do not lie to me. You are sacrificing me, is that right? You are leaving me? I cannot compete against him; you love him. I must resign myself to that fact, and wait." He held my hands, kissed them, saying, "Leave—your presence hurts me—but do not forget me."

I had just sacrificed a lot for Lionel. He was waiting for me and greeted me coldly. He was looking at each new thing in my apartment with a sneer. I stood up for what had been given to me. He became very piqued and came up with a folly; he gave me a set of emerald and diamond jewelry worthy of a queen.

"I shall never have the occasion to wear such beautiful things, and besides, they must be very expensive!"

He replied that it was none of my concern.

These jewels, which consisted of a bracelet, a brooch, earrings, and rings, purchased from a principled merchant, would be worth twenty thousand francs. They must have cost Lionel double that amount from his Palais-Royal jeweler.

Lionel took advantage of my enchantment to tell me, "Pack your trunks, I am taking you with me."

Forgive me for so often taking you down the roads leading to Berry, but it is not my fault that my life was some twenty times entangled in this same brushwood.

FINDING A WOMAN AND TWO MILLIONS

I had not been in Berry more than two weeks when the same old scenes started again.

"Really, Lionel, you are making me unhappy, and you are not happy. You have regrets and I am the cause. Do you want me to leave?"

He was going hunting more often than ever, and his affairs were becoming more and more muddled. I was more aware of that than he, who seemed to feel quite secure. One day he did not get his boar, and I was the one paying for the defeat.

"Oh, but my dear, you came back to me of your own free will. I tried to make up for what you sacrificed for me; if you think it is not enough, name your price."

The tone in which all this was said hurt me deeply. I thought of sweet Richard.

I replied, "You gave me some beautiful jewelry. I have the right and the pleasure to be able to show it off in the sun so it can glitter. This château is bad luck. Your gardener just lost his two daughters in less than a month. Solange just lost her mother. All I hear are howls all night; there is rabies in your kennels. Each day one or two of those beautiful dogs I practically raised must be hanged. You spend money madly, and this household is ruining you. You made me an accomplice in your follies by giving me these magnificent jewels. While we are on the subject, I shall tell you what I needed to be happy near you: to see you curtail your expenses. My love for you and the thought of encouraging you in straightening out your fortune would have made me stay cooped up here for as long as you wished."

Several days after this explanation, he was absorbed in his thoughts.

"What is the matter, Lionel? A new project worrying you? Does my presence bother you?"

"No, Céleste, but I have just lost an important amount on the stock market. I am preoccupied."

I always tried to get to the bottom of his thoughts. When you are jealous, you look for the truth until you find it, and then you are ten times more miserable.

"Since you care so much for this château and for these lands, go ahead, accept a marriage that will make you twice a millionaire."

He held his hands out to me saying, "You are right. I am mad. I have been offered a marvelous proposition. I turned it down because of you, and you are so bored here and would be happier in Paris among the people who love you and surround you. I am giving you back your freedom. You can leave whenever you wish."

"Have me taken into town tomorrow."

I returned to my room resigned, but as I was getting my things ready, a great storm was raging in my heart.

"He should not have accepted and should have dropped everything to come live with me if he really loved me."

I would not come down for dinner, and the next day, at ten o'clock, I asked for him.

"How are you this morning," he said to me in a calm tone, which he might have been faking.

"I am ready. Try to make this separation the last one. With each of these separations, my love cracks and eventually it will be reduced to dust. See to it that yours, if you have any, wanes with mine, because a lack of education left me with a untamed tendency toward evil. The day I shall stop loving you, you could be killing yourself at my door, and I would walk over your body to step outside."

He did not detain me. He said adieu with a determination never to see me again, I think.

I HIRE, THEREFORE I PAY

I returned to Paris in despair, as always; and yet, I had to make a decision. I had to take care of myself, of my future, and that of my godchild, Solange. I received news about her; she was doing fine.

I decided to get work in the theater. I made several futile attempts. I had been told to go ask M. Mouriez, director of the Folies-Dramatiques, but he had a reputation for being fierce, and I was afraid to face him. I decided to write to him. He let me know through his stage manager that he would see me the next day. Everyone knows that he is one of the best theater administrators in Paris. He made his fortune by paying his actors well, the opposite of many others. His advice, although a little blunt, is always good. All his former performers speak well of him.

So I went to his office. He looked at me sideways, because he was writing, and said, "You have never acted?"

"Yes, monsieur, I have, but very little and not well. I was in a play at Beaumarchais and one at Délassements."

"And so you would like to be here? I must warn you that you will have to work and be on time."

"If you want to try me out, you do not have to pay to start."

He jumped in his chair and replied dryly, "Mademoiselle, I do not hire for nothing. I pay the people who serve me. Someone brought me a parody of *The Wandering Jew;* you will debut in it. There is a part for a Bacchanalian queen. Will that do?"

THE SWEET AND KIND CONFIDANT

I left elated. I wanted to shout to the passersby: "I have been hired at the Folies! I shall be paid and I was told they would furnish the costumes!"

At that moment I was on Boulevard Saint-Denis where Richard lived. I could not think of anyone more interested in me, and I went up after inquiring whether he was in. Although his apartment was very attractive, it was on the sixth floor, and when I reached the fifth I was overtaken by the fear that he would refuse to see me. I went back down to the second, but I felt my precious contract in my pocket, and the strong desire to show it off returned, so I went back up the stairs without even breathing. Richard opened the door.

I began to talk like a magpie. I had so many things to tell him that I went on for twenty minutes without his understanding a word. He looked at me with a surprised look.

"I thank you for thinking enough of me as your friend to come tell me what might have happened to make you so happy."

He seemed quite cold. I remained ill at ease.

"But tell me how is it that you are free?"

"It is not difficult to guess. Lionel sent me away with orders to leave Berry within twenty-four hours, and the ten hours for the train ride were included. Now that I have an engagement, I shall be able to hold out more firmly. I shall never leave Paris again."

"You!" said Richard sorrowfully. "All he will need to do is give you a signal and you will go back."

"It looks like this is hurting you, and yet you do not love me anymore, right?"

"I thought that was so; I did everything to make it so. You were wrong to go into the theater; you will end up spending more than you will earn."

"You knew quite well, Richard, that there had been one fateful day in my life. I am forced to drag my chain without being able to sever it."

"Oh! If I had use of my fortune, I would quickly erase this sorrow. But stay with me, be patient, and soon. . . ."

DRESSING ROOMS AND BACKSTAGE

I rehearsed at the Folies with Lassagne, an actor beloved by the public.[1] He was talented but he was too sure of himself. He talked of opening a school to give lessons to Bouffé, to Arnal, to Odry.[2]

He took advantage of my self-consciousness on the stage to play tricks on me. He would add to his part. I would miss my cue and not know what to do. Just for effect, he would have had his best friend booed. M. Mouriez would speak to him harshly. Mme Odry asked him many times to stop what she called his "stunts," or she would have him fined.

Among the women was Angélina Legros. She had been there fifteen or sixteen years and had become too worn to play her role well. In each novice she saw a rival. It so happened I debuted playing one of her parts. I needed to make female friends in the theater, and I had been naïve enough to count on her. I quickly gave up that illusion.

I knocked on other doors. I went to see Dinah, a pretty, rather silly little brunette. She had all the minor defects of childhood. I moved on to Duplessis. That one was hopeless. That left Frenex, an extraordinary creature, small, skinny, reddish blond hair, a nose like there are not many, teeth like it is easy to get with money, a large mouth, and albino eyebrows and eyelashes. The whole, painted black, white, and red, was tolerable. She was witty, she was cute, elegant, a good actress, capricious, and coquettish.

For her, a new friend was a conquest. So she gave me a very good reception. That lasted a few days.

She was unlucky in affections, and I felt the brunt of her bad mood. Saddened by this break, I moved on down the hall to Léontine's dressing room.

It is unfortunate that she can barely see. And for that reason she is forgiven a little foolishness. She cannot see herself well anymore, and so she gets angry that she is not given ingenue roles.

There are no foyers for the actors at the Folies, and backstage is so small that we wait for our stage entrance in our dressing rooms. These dressing rooms are as roomy and bright as the interior of a closed trunk. I had gone to visit all these ladies, but to approach them was not so easy. They had all exclaimed when they learned I was hired and I was going to debut at the Folies, "It is disgraceful to give us a Mogador as colleague! What kind of respect will there be for the Folies actresses now?"

Only one of my colleagues gave me advice and was very kind to me: Mme Odry.

As for the men—Hensey, Coutard, Boisselot, Hoster—they were all very charming with me, and fought over the pleasure of giving me the advice I so desperately needed.

29

 Proud Women, Passionate Men

RICHARD HAD diligently courted Mlle Ozy, then he suddenly stopped.[1] She had inquired into the reason for such an abrupt cooling. She hated me without knowing me.

One day Richard and one of his friends, the Count de B——, were dining at my house.

"By the way," said the Count, "I hope you are going to the ball at Ozy's tomorrow because I am afraid I shall not know anyone otherwise."

"I would go," said Richard, "if Céleste had been invited."

"Is that all?" said his friend, relieved. "I shall get an invitation for her; I just have to go next door."

And sure enough, he was not gone more than a quarter hour. I went into my room, intending to listen in.

"So," said Richard.

"Well! Dear friend, you did not tell me that you were intimate with her. She told me, 'I do not mind if he comes, but I do not want to see Mlle Mogador. Horrors! This girl will never set foot in my house.'"

"Do not say anything," said Richard. "Céleste must never know."

I came back into the room pretending not to know. I promised myself that the proud Ozy would receive me within a week. Victorine knew her. I went to see her.

THE WORLD OF GOSSIP

"My dear, yesterday I received a grievous affront. Someone requested for me an invitation to Mlle Ozy's house, and the woman refused in terms that wounded me. I want to know her and I want to be seen with her. Can you help me?"

"No, I do not see her anymore. But I am surprised by her scorn; her talent is like yours. As for the name of Mogador, you could do like her: change it. Alice Ozy is a nice name, but it is not her name. I believe she could receive you on an equal footing. In fact, right now she is associated with Rose Pompon. You must know Rose Pompon!"

I went to see Rose Pompon, who proceeded to tell me all sorts of things. At her house was a woman who was her piano teacher; she sent her to convey her compliments to Mlle Ozy. I understood that this piano teacher could be useful to me. I asked her to come see me. She came the next day. She was about forty years old. She began to malign Ozy in spite of the fact that she was dressed from head to foot in clothes she got through Ozy's generosity.

I said, "You see, madame, I have an extreme desire to make the acquaintance of Mlle Ozy. They say her apartment is quite sumptuous."

"And you would like to see it," she said with a slight air of superiority.

"I must admit, that is why I went to see Pompon, but not being sure of her influence, I did not ask her anything."

"Oh! You were right! Mlle Alice is sick and tired of this Pompon. She is a liar—constantly makes promises and breaks them. I am going to tell Ozy that you are always talking about her and of her affluence. Send her some flowers and within two days she will invite you to come visit her."

And so, Ozy sent word through the piano teacher that I was being extravagant, that she had received from me a gorgeous basket, and that she would like for me to come over to see how beautiful it looks in her living room.

I did not wait for a second invitation, and I did not regret it. She was charming. The next day she sent word asking if I wanted to dine with her by the fireplace. My reply arrived with a superb bouquet. She gave me a complete course in philosophy. She talked to me about the Bible, the greatness and the decadence of the Romans, and their simple and modest tastes.

A GOOD REPUTATION IS WORTH
MORE THAN EMERALDS

I received an invitation to her ball. What a great occasion to wear my emeralds! I was the first to arrive. Her apartment was flooded with lights and flowers.

Two women came in. She went to greet them. When she came back, I asked her their names.

"Mesdemoiselles Ber——"

"They are sisters?"

"No, they are mother and daughter."

The daughter was skinny and lanky as a beanpole. She was dressed like a child with a wide ribbon belt. She picked up a book and went to pout in the little living room saying that if she had known she would run into such bad company, she would not have come. I was the bad company.

Among the women who were in this living room, there was one in particular I liked. She was pretty and seemed quite pleasant. She was young Page.[2] I did not dare speak to her. Ozy would not introduce her to me.

LIONEL IN PARIS

Richard came to see me; he was very pale.

"What is the matter my dear friend?"

"All right," he said, "do not lie to me. You saw him, did you not?"

"My goodness, but whom are you talking about?"

"Whom? Your friend Lionel of course, whom I saw this morning. He is in Paris."

I could not reply; my legs gave way. Richard grabbed my arm and declared angrily, "You see, you do still love him, you are shaking."

"I never told you that I did not love him anymore. I told you that I would never go to his house again."

He slumped back on a chair and burst into tears.

"Now, really," I said, "do not be a child; you know that I shall never take a step toward him. Why did you tell me you had seen him?"

"But I told you, Céleste, because he was coming in this direction, and I thought he had just left your house. I think he turned back and saw me come in here."

Kind, devoted Richard; I was looking at him with fury. I wanted him out of my sight.

"All right, Richard, go home. I shall go see you tomorrow."

"You are sending me away."

"No, my friend, I just want to be alone, I do not feel well."

He spouted all sorts of reproaches. I ordered him to leave. He seemed crestfallen, but I did not pay attention. I was as miserable as he.

LOVE RESEMBLES HATRED

My maid brought me a letter; it was from Lionel and it read:

I am spending a few days in Paris. If your work at the theater permits it, come shake my hand. I live on Rue Royale, and I am inviting you to dinner. I need to talk to you.

I took a cab and went to see him.

His apartment was on the mezzanine floor. I saw his face behind a curtain; he was waiting for me.

"What," he said, "a woman as elegant as you takes cabs? Your lover is not very generous. You had it better when you were with me."

"You wrote me to tell me this; it was not necessary. Maybe I am not given much, but I am not asking you for anything."

I walked toward the door. He called me back and said, "Fine; you are in a bad mood right now. Forgive me and let us make peace. I love you enough not to lose sight of what interests you. I know you went back on the stage. That is a pedestal. How are your finances? Oh! Do not get angry, I want to help you. A girl like you cannot go out on foot, the police could arrest you. I am going to give you a carriage."

He walked toward me. His eyes were fiery, his lips white. He was scaring me.

He continued, "You see, I did have something to tell you. I want to tell you that I feel only loathing for you. An honest man cannot love a creature like you. I was mad to have taken you to the château of my ancestors. Because of you I have lost esteem in society. What did you give me in exchange? A wilted body and a vile soul. That is what I wanted to say to you. You can repeat it to M. Richard."

He pulled the curtain back to let me out.

Blood had rushed to my head and was blinding me. Anger overcame me.

"So, you had me come here so you could insult me. And by what right, if you please? You should be ashamed of how you just reproached me, because I have not hidden from you the fact that I am on the register, but I can look straight into your eyes with a clear conscience. You have taken me, left me, then taken me again and left me again. You did not want me anymore, and another man has loved me. Is that a crime? You throw me out and another man has the temerity to take me in!"

I ran out, unable to breathe. In the carriage I burst into tears. I rushed to Richard to tell him everything that had occurred. He sympathized and gently faulted me for going.

I went home hot with fever. Lionel sent for me, probably regretting the pain he had caused me. I refused to see him. Soon after, he showed up. He closed the living room door and sat next to me. I got up and opened my armoire. I took out all the jewelry he had given me, and lifting the box over my head, I threw it across the room with all my might.

The box opened; the diamonds, the emeralds, the pearls went flying all around.

"You are mad!" he said kicking the box.

"That is correct! Yes, I am mad with rage; I hate you. I no longer have anything of yours, so get out."

Thank goodness I had just sat in a chair. He rang and had a glass of water brought to me.

"My presence should not irritate you, Céleste. Yesterday I was on my way to see you, since I made this trip to Paris for the sole purpose of being near you; then I met M. Richard. He was coming here, and I lost my head. When you came over I was still in that mood."

He tried to take my hand, I pulled it back. Excited by anger, I shouted, "Oh, God! Make me die now! Oh! I would kill myself to be rid of you and a world that is making me pay too dearly for my disgrace. Go away, and leave me alone. I am cursed."

Lionel got on his knees and tried, with kind words, to calm the sort of delirium that had swept over me.

"Forgive me. I swear to you I shall never do this again."

MOGADOR SHOT IN EFFIGY

I spent all of the next day in bed. He never left my side.

I received a letter from Richard:

I waited for you all day. Obviously you do not know what it is like to wait when you love as much as I love you. Céleste, I have loved you because I thought you had a kind heart. Have pity on me. If I cannot see you tomorrow, I will do something drastic. I am well aware that you do not love me as you love him, but I have a right to your friendship. You cannot reduce me to despair; I would give my life to spare you a tear.
Richard

His entreaty was so sweet that I could not possibly ignore it. Yet I hated lying. The stratagems I would have to use made me hesitate, and I told Lionel, "My friend, I am going to the theater where I am expected."

Once on the boulevard, I turned around to look at my window. He was there and watched me until I was out of sight.

When I arrived at his apartment, Richard had a large box near him. He had written several letters and was still writing.

"Oh! It is you!" he said standing up; he was so pale I felt sorry for him.

"Thank you for coming. What pained me the most was dying without seeing you again. As you can see, I spent the night writing."

He showed me the letters, then he opened the box, took out one of the pistols it contained.

"I fear only one thing, that I would miss."

I ran over to him.

"Put this pistol back in its box, Richard!"

"I am madly in love with you; you cannot love me. So, as you can see, I have to die. Who will miss me? My father was poisoned in Mauritius when I was twelve. My mother died when I was fifteen. No one will shed a tear for me. I am leaving you everything I have. No one will ever love you the way I love you."

As he was speaking he was handling his pistol. I heard a sound; he had just loaded it. I threw myself on him. He pushed me back, the pistol went off to the side, and the bullet hit and broke my portrait.

Alarmed, his butler entered.

"Oh! Monsieur, forgive the intrusion, but this discharge. . . ."

"It is nothing," said Richard. "I was playing with my pistol and the shot went off by mistake."

When he was gone, Richard looked at my portrait. The bullet had torn the forehead.

"I swear, Richard, that I am your most devoted friend. If I had met you sooner, oh, how I would have loved you! All this will change. Perhaps we can leave together. . . . But do not drive me to despair. I shall come see you."

I went home moved by this incident.

A few days went by like this. Lionel knew me too well not to notice the change occurring in me. One morning he said, "I am leaving tonight. That should make you happy, since your freedom is so dear to you! I wanted to give you something before leaving, but it is not ready. You will probably receive it tomorrow."

"But, my dear friend, I do not need anything. You should not have spent your money."

"Oh, yes, my child. Your theater is far away, so you need a carriage."

THE CARRIAGE OFFERED BY LIONEL
DOES NOT DAZZLE RICHARD

This double life weighed on me so much that for the first time I greeted the news of his departure without regret. And besides, at the word "carriage" my imagination was aroused. Lionel left that evening. I spent the next day looking out the window. At four o'clock I saw an adorable little surrey stop at my door. A man jumped from the seat, a piece of paper in his hand. I had a caller. The carriage was for me. It was drawn by a pretty bay horse. The harness bore my number. On the door panel there was a small garland that went around my initials with this motto: Forget me not.[3] The surrey was painted bright blue and the interior was lined in silk of the same color. I walked around it ten times. I climbed in it on one side and got out on the other; I touched the ivory ornaments; I opened and closed the windows; I looked at the passersby with pride.

Lionel had rented a stall at a stable on Rue Rougemont. The coachman, dressed in English style, had received orders to arrive at four o'clock, the customary time for carriage rides. I quickly went upstairs to dress. I was so thrilled, I put on a green dress, a red shawl, and a yellow hat. I must have looked like a parrot. The two-hour ride through the Bois de Boulogne seemed very short to me. Everyone would let out "oh" and "ooh" when they saw me.

Once I had exhausted the gaze of all the passersby, I went home. At the corner of Rue de la Madeleine, I saw Richard. Oh, dreadful flightiness! My first reaction was one of vanity. I nodded to him and signaled for him to come closer. But my carriage did not seem to please him as much as it pleased me. He walked away gloomily.

Once back home I dressed in a less showy way and decided to go, *on foot,* to pay Richard a visit.

Instead of complimenting me on the beauty of my carriage, he coldly said, "How much income have you been provided with to support this kind of life?"

30

London

Between Two Love Affairs—My Name and
Forty Thousand Francs—I Did Not Want to Get
Married!—Exchange of Diplomatic Notes
between Two Agonizing Hearts

I WENT TO SEE the nursemaid unannounced. I entered the house and found, alone in a cradle, a poor little creature so pale, so weak that she seemed on the verge of death. I recognized her clothes as the ones I had bought for my godchild. The nursemaid was in the fields. She came back a half hour later.

"Are you mad leaving this child alone? I certainly pay you more than I owe you."

This woman gave me the worst of explanations. The husband had come in a few minutes after his wife and seemed at least as embarrassed as she. The baby began to cry; the nursemaid rocked her.

"But," I said, "she must be hungry."

"Oh! My goodness, madame," said the husband, "we did not dare tell you, but the child has been weaned because my wife is with child."

"You poor wretch!" I angrily exclaimed, standing up. "You are going to poison her with your bad milk, and rather than lose the money I am sending you, you are finishing her off. Go get a doctor."

The doctor arrived a few minutes later.

"They are all the same; they wean them when they are three or four months old, and they feed them cabbage soup and potatoes like their pigs. They all end up with stones after a couple of weeks. This one has them, but you might be able to save her with proper care."

I took my dear little girl away, and I returned to Paris by train, a bundle on one side, a bottle of milk on the other, and my godchild on my lap. I kept her with me three days, and after having found a good place for her, I occupied myself with my beautiful carriage.

249

Lionel came to Paris. My life of deception was going to start again and it was frightening me so that I made a decision.

I went to see Richard and told him, "My dear friend, I have come to ask you for proof of your affection. Lionel is here. I would not be able to see you without fear. You told me that you had business in Belgium. Then, go to Brussels. If Lionel leaves me, which should be soon, I shall go meet you."

After a thousand objections, he promised to leave the next day.

Lionel had returned to his apartment on Rue Royale. His moods were exceptionally erratic. One day he would shower me with tenderness, another he would chase me away, then he would ask my forgiveness only to insult me once more. Each reconciliation was accompanied by lavish gifts. He gave me a lovely barouche lined in deep blue that belonged to him but that he had inscribed with my name. He also gave me two beautiful black horses that I had seen harnessed to his phaeton.

I owned one of the most beautiful equipage on the Champs-Elysées; I was covered in jewels, cashmere, and lace. Yet I shed many a bitter tear under my veil. Lionel was as incapable of parting from me as he was of making me happy. He would become raging mad when he realized that he could not evict my image from his heart. When Richard was in Paris, his presence infuriated him. When Richard was away, he was calmer, but he was less restrained and that was not any better for me. Fortunately there came an occasion for us to see each other less and I grabbed it eagerly.

I was called to the theater for a new play called *The Martyrs of Carnival.* The theater annoyed him because I had to dance in all the plays. The poor walk-ons who earned twenty-five francs a month were happier than I.

Richard's absence only endeared him more to me. It was not love but tenderness. My memory of him benefited from each sorrow caused by Lionel's offenses. And then, Richard would write me such tender and affectionate letters!

At the same time that we were rehearsing *The Martyrs of Carnival* we were also rehearsing *Blanche and Blanchette.* In the role of the lover a dark, thin, handsome young man of extreme pallor was making his debut. His name was Alexis Didier.

Didier is that very sleepwalker that M. Dumas studied for so long. He would stay close to me and we would talk together. . . . When the chatting would go on for more than ten minutes, I would get tired and numb!

"Please, leave me, Didier. People are going to say you are courting me!"

"Let them!"

I would leave. When I had strolled around a bit, I would return to him. He would then laugh and say, "You see; you are the one seeking me out! . . ." I would reply yes and not budge. Of course, people must have thought I was in love with Didier, yet that did not enter my mind.

MY NAME AND FORTY THOUSAND FRANCS

One night at the theater I received a note; it was from Richard:

I must see you tomorrow. . . . Come to my house, or I shall go to yours!

I went to see him. He seemed tired. He asked me to sit down and told me, "Céleste, you will see how my love for you is part of my life! I have thought about it long, and this is what I am offering you: a happy, honorable future that will help you forget a past I shall never again mention! I shall give you forty thousand francs! . . . We shall immediately leave for England where I shall marry you without difficulty since I am English and have no parents!"

I hid my face in my hands to weep.

"But it is impossible! . . ."

He stood up like a madman. I drew him to me and said, "I had no idea you were going to say something like this to me and I am dizzy. . . . And besides, are you sure that can be done in London? Go there for two or three days and come back to get me once I have written to you."

"You are deceiving me, Céleste. You will not write to me!"

"I swear I shall write."

I wrote to him, but to make him give up on this mad idea.

A few days later I had dinner with Lionel at his apartment on Rue Royale with one of his friends. Midway through the meal he tried to start a quarrel, as usual, for no reason.

"Once and for all," I said to him, "for what do you reproach me?"

"I reproach you for having poisoned my heart. I hate you because . . . I hate you, finally, because I love you."

He left me with his friend, who said to me, "He is mad!"

"Yes, and it is a mean madness. It would be better to part than to live like this."

And I told him what Richard had offered me.

"If it is true," he told me skeptically, "you should not have refused, because Lionel is ruining himself! He absolutely must marry."

"You know quite well that he has tried hundreds of times and that it never panned out. . . ."

"Because he knew you were there!"

Lionel came back. He was sorry for his bad mood and did his best to make me forget it.

I received a letter from Richard. In spite of what I had written, he repeated his offer.

Acting was boring me! . . . To be an actor, one needs a stable life. It is difficult to be cheerful on the stage, to sing, to dance, to make others laugh when one's heart is sad.

To prevail on my skepticism, Didier continued to exercise a magnetic influence over me, which was tiresome!

One day that Lionel had Montji to dinner, he started a quarrel with me again. The scene became so terrible that I blurted out my secret.

"After all, my dear friend, do you think that I need you? Do you think that outside your door I shall not find a friend who will extend his hand to me? Well . . . I was asked in marriage and offered forty thousand francs if I would leave you. I wish I did not have to tell you, but this life is hell! It would be better to leave you for good. . . ."

"Bravo!" he said, bursting out laughing. "What great acting, what imaginative blackmail. Oh! So someone wants to marry you? You are telling me how much you have been offered so I shall keep you at the same price! Well! I urge you to accept."

I left exasperated, swearing that I would never see him again, and determined to go away. I went to the theater and begged M. Mouriez to grant me a short leave. He gave it to me.

I went home. I was handed this letter from Lionel:

When one loves a woman unworthy of oneself and one feels too weak to leave her, one becomes deaf and blind, as I should have been. The heart of a girl like you is like a disreputable inn. The honest wayfarer who inadvertently enters endures the sneers of the regular guests. You say that I have not loved you, but the love I have had for you is my only excuse. Your fake love, however, began with a caress and ended with a price. I am not rich enough. You are free.

    Lionel

I picked up a pen and wrote Richard. My maid announced his arrival. I asked him, "When are we leaving?"

"Tomorrow night, if you wish. You will need your mother's consent, and I would like for you to deposit this money before your departure."

On my toiletry bag, he set a wallet, which I returned to him.

"No; I do not want this money."

"I want you to deposit it before we leave Paris. It will help you rear your little girl. Whatever happens, these forty thousand francs are yours."

I DID NOT WANT TO GET MARRIED!

I almost fainted when the train took me away. My rebellious heart was bleeding at the thought that it was leaving Lionel.

During my first stroll I hated London. The fog blocked the daylight and parted only to release a black snow that stained my white hat and flecked my face. I went back inside, furious. I wanted to wash with soap and water; I looked like a chimney sweep. It had spread. I managed to clean my face with cold cream. After that I went out only by carriage. I visited all the monuments. One thing surprised me: one had to pay at all entrances and exits and give I do not know how many shillings to see a few jewels in a glass case. I was sad and bored. Richard did not know what to invent to distract me.

He had prepared everything for our wedding. The moment was approaching, not without giving me great fright because I doubted myself and my determination. It was worse after I went to the post office and found a letter from Lionel. He had contacted my maid, and in spite of my orders she told him where I was and how he could write to me. This is what he wrote me:

If you receive another letter from me, do not believe that I hope for a reconciliation between us. There is now a barrier I shall never cross. With you, Céleste, I have had nothing but suffering! I have suffered for the past, I have suffered for the present, I shall suffer all my life. For you to marry this man is sheer madness! . . . Once the whim has passed, all you will have left are regrets and bitterness.

You have reproached me for letters and words induced by anger; they hurt you because you did not know how to find in them what they held of passion and despair. The woman who loves would like to be the last one in the whole world, to owe everything to the one she loves and to be proud of it. You were like that when you loved me. . . .

Forgive me for disturbing you amid your joys and pleasures.

Adieu.

Lionel

After reading this, I cried. Yet I was happy; this letter proved to me that he still loved me.

The forms to fill out for our wedding were done. Richard told me, "Céleste, today you will be my wife, and I can give you no greater proof of my love for you."

In London he had ordered a complete outfit for me. . . . Mechanically, I got dressed. . . . I was afraid to say anything. . . . I did not want to get married!

I had a pearl gray brocade dress, a black lace shawl, and a white hat. "This outfit," I told him, "is terribly gloomy!"

On my hat he placed a veil that had been made for the queen and that he had bought the day before.

I let myself be led away, but when the carriage stopped I regained vitality and vigor.

"No, no," I told the coachman, "do not stop, keep going! . . . Richard, tell him to go past this door, I must speak to you."

I sat back in the carriage and held on to the cushion as if I were being forced to get out.

He gave orders to return to the hotel. Once back in our apartment, he showed me to a chair, sat down, and asked, "Now, Céleste, what do you have to say to me?"

He was saying this so sweetly and was looking at me with such kind eyes, that I did not know what to reply. I was shaking and my teeth were chattering.

"You were just frightened by what you were going to promise me. . . . You do not love me and you do not have the courage to give me your whole life. You do not love me and you will never love me. I shall destroy my love or it will destroy me!"

He hid his face in his hands to cry. I threw myself on my knees.

"Richard, you should have nothing but contempt for me; I am not worthy of a love like yours. . . . Send me away; I am a wretch!"

He remained silent for a few moments, then, looking at me with anger, he said, "How you love this man!"

The rest of the time was spent in silence. We left the next day with much different feelings in our hearts.

Once back in Paris, he went to a hotel, Cité Bergère, because he had had his apartment sold during our absence.

I received another letter from Lionel:

EXCHANGE OF DIPLOMATIC NOTES BETWEEN
TWO AGONIZING HEARTS

I forgive you all the pain you have caused me. What! . . . When I tell you that I love you, that I am suffering, you do not find in your heart the echo of a memory! Céleste, it is evil to be ungrateful. You cannot forgive me a moment of wrath. If you only knew, however, how much love, tenderness, passion were in my kisses! How these kisses originated deep inside my heart! So it is over, I shall never see you again. . . . I am going to leave, to go far away! . . . Come see me, at least to say adieu; I have never hurt you. Do not abandon me thus; I love you. . . . Come back, and you will have more than you could have dreamed of! I cannot live without you. . . . Come, come, my heart is calling out to you. I am sick in bed. . . . Would you refuse a bit of pity to a man whose only crime is to have loved you too much?

The next day, there were races at the Champ-de-Mars. . . . I had my barouche harnessed. On my way down I found my carriage filled with roses. . . . I thought it was a gallant gesture from Richard, and I left carrying a short note I wanted to personally bring to Lionel's house, in which I said:

You love me today, because I belong to another; if he were not around anymore, you would not bend over to pick me off the floor. I warned you! You know that I love you, and you teased me and taunted me. I left. . . . I made three people unhappy. I shall be admired. . . . I am on the same level as these women I used to despise. Horses, carriages—with all that, there is no need for a heart. . . .

All the reproaches you level at me I throw back at you. . . . Is my heart not a disreputable inn? . . . I throw you out of it to spare your being in such bad company.

I gave this letter to a delivery boy. . . . I could not rely on my courage to hand it over myself.

31

Unfortunate Encounter

The Little House in the Forest—Maria, the
Polka Dancer, Clara Fontaine, and Other Celebrities—
The Lace War Starts Up Again

THE NEXT DAY, at ten o'clock, the doctor who had taken care of me
when I lived at Place de la Madeleine, and whom Lionel still saw, asked
to speak to me.

After coldly greeting me, he said, "Strange as my endeavor might
seem, rest assured, mademoiselle, that this visit is of my own choice.
I just came from the house of M. le Comte de C———. I have been to
see him four times since yesterday at six o'clock. I have bled him twice;
blood is choking him and he is delirious. His personal valet told me that
last night twenty times he asked that you be brought to him. No one
dared do it. I have come to plead with you to go see him, even for just
one hour."

When I arrived at his house on Rue Royale, the servants were running right and left. He had just suffered a terrible seizure. I went to his
bedside. He looked at me for two or three minutes, then grabbing my
wrist, he said, "Oh! It is you. Come nearer so I can see what a woman
who can cause so much pain looks like. What magic did you use to
seduce me, daughter of Satan?"

He let go and placed his hands on his forehead. His shirt became
stained with black blood. I rang and the doctor rebandaged his arm
after bleeding him again.

As a result, Lionel seemed calmer. He told me, "So, there you are! I
am glad you came. Where were you? It seems like I have not seen you
in a long time."

He spoke of this and that, then fell asleep. The doctor told me as he
was leaving, "Do not leave him. I shall return tomorrow early."

When I was alone with the silence and my patient, I sat at a table where there was writing material and I began a letter to Richard:

My friend, I am not worthy of your love! It is with my head bowed that I ask your forgiveness for the pain I am going to cause you again. Forget me, I am an ingrate, unworthy of you. Louise, my maid, will hand you this money, which I cannot keep. Do not try to see me. Lionel is in critical condition; I am at his bedside, and I shall not leave his room until he is out of danger. Adieu! A bit of courage will spare you a life of regrets. Forgive me!

I spent a week without leaving Lionel. Illness had not changed his personality. He would become furious with me for no reason, sometimes ringing his servant so he would not have to ask me to hand him the herbal tea that was right next to me. He would say that my presence distressed him. When I cried without replying, he would fervently ask my forgiveness, kissing my hands and saying, "I love you more than my life. If I could not see you anymore, I would go mad!"

After a few days he recovered. He let me go home where I found four letters from Richard, all sweet and full of regrets.

My mother came to see me. After I made her promise she would not see Vincent anymore, I told her that I would buy her a tobacco shop or a lodging house. Three days later I got her settled on Rue de Cléry at the hôtel of that same name.

Three months went by. Lionel was terribly sad. He was kind, but he could not get my trip to London out of his mind. A simple handkerchief or a mere word would serve as reminders. Richard was still away with relatives. I dreaded his return. My only quarrel with Lionel was over the gifts he kept giving me.

One day one of Lionel's relatives came to see me. He was a fat, jolly man. Even though he made a great display of his interest in Lionel, he would not have given him twenty-five louis. But he was generous . . . with advice.

"Now," he told me, "you love Lionel and you are letting him go broke like an idiot! Tell him he should get married! What will you do with him when he has not a single farthing left?"

That evening I spoke to Lionel about his future. I told him, "I fear for you. If you wished to marry, I would not be angry with you. If my presence were an inconvenience for you, I would leave Paris. We would go from this great love to friendship that always endures."

"Yes," he replied, "but I want to see you, to have you near me in the future. We shall leave for Berry and we shall buy a little house where you will put everything that belongs to you and is now at my house in the country."

We agreed, and we left a few days later. We found a darling little house whose yard is adjacent to the forest. Lionel took it upon himself to arrange everything at my retreat, and I returned to Paris.

Once there, I went to see my mother. Her brightest idea had been to rent the first floor apartment to M. Vincent. I became so angry that I threw them both out. I resold the house almost immediately.

I wrote to Lionel, who was terribly lonesome in Berry, but who remained there to prove to the world that he was not seeing me anymore.

One day, at four o'clock, M. Richard was announced. I would have preferred not to see him. He held his hand out to me but made no reprimands.

"My dear Céleste, I have just arrived. Be assured that I made inquiries and was told that M. Lionel is at his estate, so here I am. I ask for nothing more than permission to come see you sometimes."

"But of course, as often as you wish."

Now that was very reckless. I was still writing to Lionel, but I did not see the necessity to inform him of Richard's return. I do not know who did. . . .

MARIA, THE POLKA DANCER, CLARA FONTAINE, AND OTHER CELEBRITIES

One day I invited Maria to dinner.

Maria is a tall woman with a pretty figure, but she has a harsh appearance and is extremely skinny. I met her in the days when I was going to Versailles. I ran into her again at a masked ball at the Odéon, a ball given by M. Lireux,[1] stage manager of the theater in those days, and Louis Monrose had hired me to dine with the other actors.[2] On my right was a fat girl with wide nostrils and large prominent eyes. Her name was Clara Fontaine. She was enviously eyeing Maria's costume.

The dinner was magnificent; we put away cases of *pâté de foie gras* and truffles, and the champagne flowed freely. Maria ate carefully because she had kept her gloves on. Clara asked her in her pretty, high-pitched voice, "Why in the world are you eating with your gloves on, do you have the mange?"

I thought her remark so mean that I asked Clara, "Are you hoping you gave it to her?"

"Me!" she said, placing her two large hands on the table.

"Please, hide this," I told her. "This is not proper in front of people."

Maria came to thank me. Lireux, Monrose, and Bernard-Latte took my side, and Maria became my friend.

Across from me was the actor M. Milon. He looked very smug and planned each of his gestures. He would examine himself and seemed so pleased with his person that I left my seat to give him a view of the mirror behind me.

I asked Maria, "Do you want to dance?" She was wearing a man's costume, so she took the lead. And just as I was performing some step, I do not recall which, I stepped on the foot of a woman wearing a domino. She shoved me, first calling me stupid, then, horrid woman!

I turned around and yanked on the bottom of her mask. What I saw was a monkey face. I began to laugh and said, "Look, does Madame have the kind of face that allows her to call me a horror!"

Oh! My goodness! What had I done? There was one, only one upstanding woman at the ball, and she was the one who had called me stupid and whom I had unmasked.

I was advised to flee. I did not and I should have, because someone came to tell me to go to the police station. Thank goodness for me, Louis Monrose, as kindhearted as he is a good actor, proved to the commissioner that if this lady had not put her foot under mine, I would not have stepped on it. He obtained my pardon and took me upstairs.

Lireux had a good laugh over this story. We often went to see him because he kept large crates of oranges in his office. I always went away with six of them.

So that is how I met Maria; then I lost sight of her until the day she was named Maria the Polka Dancer and I became Céleste Mogador. She is the daughter of a manual laborer. She had become very elegant and would walk along the Champs-Elysées wearing velvet dresses with trains. And when by chance I would run into her on my way out of the Hippodrome, she would look down her nose at me and would not greet me. She took the name Mme de Saint-Pase.

Long after placing herself under the protection of this new saint of her own invention, she took on airs and told me her father was a great lord, that he threatened to have her locked up if she continued to wear his name, Saint-Pase. I told her quite frankly that, whatever she did, people would always say when seeing her, "Here is Maria the Polka Dancer."

She almost had a fit.

A month later I inquired about her of the concierge who replied, "Don't know!"

I walked away irritated. Fortunately she looked out the window and called me back.

"But why are you leaving?"

"Well, I was told they do not know you."

"Oh! I understand. Today my name is Mme la Comtesse de Bussy."

She was taking her name seriously. Everything in her home had a crown on it. I told her, "You look like you got your furniture and your clothes at a secondhand shop. When things are really ours, they seem beautiful, but if we dress up in those we have no right to, they make us look ridiculous."

Obviously my opinion was dim-witted, because she came to my house for dinner in a carriage marked with *three crowns* as big as the moon.

THE LACE WAR STARTS UP AGAIN

It was five o'clock and the table was set for two when Richard came to visit.

Right after that, the doorbell rang. I thought it was my guest arriving and asked Richard to open the door. It was Lionel!

"Fine!" said Lionel looking at the two place settings on the table. "I know what I wanted to know."

Then addressing Richard, he told him, "You wanted to marry this girl; you can have her. She is yours now."

I joined my hands together and looked at Richard. He probably understood, because he replied in the most natural way, "I thank you for the advice, monsieur. You have known her for four years. Well! Four years from now, I shall give you an answer."

Lionel left, casting a look full of loathing in my direction. I asked Richard to leave me alone.

Maria arrived. She tried her best to console me. She had her qualities. She came over several times to try to chase away my sad thoughts.

To salvage his self-respect, Lionel found, at a *table d'hôte,* a girl from the provinces a man had brought to Paris for the sum of ———. He offered her double what the other one had promised. She knew he had a mistress he loved. She accepted the position and fulfilled it with boldness.

And of course, my resentment settled on Richard. I reproached him for everything I was suffering. He would ask forgiveness for the anguish he had not caused.

I received a note from Lionel. He had bought a magnificent apartment. He wrote:

Come see me, I need to talk to you about your interests.

Richard arrived as I was reading this note.

"Your Lionel is spouting all sorts of things about you. Yesterday, he told one of his friends that you would go to his house anytime he wanted."

Furious, I crumpled up the letter.

Once Richard had left, I replied to it:

What would I be doing at your house? Looking for scorn! I know what you think of me and what you are saying about me. Adieu!

An hour later, he wrote again:

I wanted to see you briefly at my house, not in the hopes of asking for your sympathy, but so I can wallow in the misery of hatred you have left me in. I want to end up between the bottle that supplies the drunkenness it promises, and a pistol that will grant me forgetfulness. One day the letters that I have taken back from you will be returned to you. They have been the essence of my heart and my life. Enjoy your life of pleasure, but be careful; old age creeps up, and it is dreadful to find nothing but reproaches, hate, and spite among one's memories.

As if on purpose, not once was I alone that day. I was in need of distraction, but everyone exasperated me.

I told myself as I hid my letter, "I shall go see Lionel tomorrow."

32

The Girl from the Provinces

A Lot of venom, a Little Blood—After the Storm—
Richard Cannot Live "Without" Either—Stroke
of Luck, No Cartridges—How the Favorite
Dismisses a Rival

"LET US GO to the Cirque," Richard suggested. "It will distract you. There is a beautiful benefit performance."

The room was resplendent with lights and costumes. Sadly . . . it all seemed dreary to me. Suddenly the room lit up . . . my eyes were dazzled, my head began to swim, and I felt faint.

Richard looked at me, then, taking my arm impatiently and angrily, he squeezed it and said, "How pale you look!"

I looked up and found myself facing Lionel. Standing on my right, he began talking with this woman I had been told about and who began to gesture extravagantly to attract my attention. . . . Ten times I thought I could see her kissing him! I asked Richard to take me home. "No," he said, "he would notice your agitation. I beg you to remain calm until the end of the show. Spare my pride; you know I have never given it much thought, but today, in front of these people who are observing us, make the effort, only for one hour!"

I let myself be taken home like a child. Once at my door, Richard said, "Céleste, I thank you again. I am expected by friends at the Maison-d'Or. I would have invited you, but you need rest."

A LOT OF VENOM, A LITTLE BLOOD

I went to bed hoping to calm down, but in vain. As if a voice were summoning me outside, I got up and got dressed.

"Louise," I said to my maid, "come with me; let us go after him or this is the end."

262

And picking up Lionel's letter, which bore his new address, I ran along the boulevards. Once on Rue Joubert, I rang at the porte cochere. It was almost one in the morning. I was let in and I went upstairs without asking anything, leaving Louise under the covered way.

Once on the second floor, I rang powerfully enough to make the house shake. I heard a door opening and a voice, Lionel's, asking, "Who can that be?" Then, appearing on the landing and lighting my face with a candle, he continued, "You, here! What do you want from me now?"

"What do I want?" I said, shaking all over and showing him his letter. "I am here because you wrote to me yesterday!"

"Oh," he said, laughing, "so I did, after lunch! If that is all, then you can go back home; there is no danger, I am very happy! How is it that M. Richard lets you go out so late at night? . . . It is unsafe. I shall let him know tomorrow."

The snide way he had said all this gradually made my violent temperament return. He saw the flashes in my eyes.

"Come in," he told me uncovering the door. "I do not love you anymore, but I am too polite not to invite you to rest a few minutes."

The room he had let me in was a dining room with carved walls and ceilings.

"It seems," he said, "that this visit on your part is without objective, my dear Céleste; you did not choose your timing well, because I am not alone. I have been in love with you; today I do not love you anymore. Go back to your Richard."

"Now really, Lionel, do not blame me! . . . How could I know that this letter contained nothing but lies and trifles? You mentioned killing yourself. . . ."

"No," he replied, "no, you did not come here out of concern for me! . . . You came because you saw me with another woman. She is here, this woman, behind this door. She can hear everything I am saying to you. . . . I love her! She is beautiful, as beautiful as you are ugly!"

"Lionel," I stood up and said, beside myself with anger, "what you are doing now is craven! You insult me in your house; you should respect yourself by not insulting your past weaknesses. Why did you write to me in London? . . . Without your letter, I would be married, I would be in Scotland, and I would not be annoying you."

I turned to leave. He stood in my way.

"No," he told me, "you are too agitated, do not go yet. . . . Anger becomes you! I despise you, you miserable wretch whom I picked up out of the mud, and in gratitude, you have defiled me! You used me as a ladder. You placed yourself on the auction block and sold yourself to the highest bidder."

I looked around me. I saw a knife on the sideboard. I picked it up, and holding it tight, I yelled, "Not another word! Leave me alone, or I shall kill you!"

"Finally," he said, laughing, "I see you suffering a little! Put this knife down, you are going to cut your fingers."

"Oh," I said, "do as I tell you, or I am going to kill you! Banish this woman who has heard everything you said to me!"

He shrugged his shoulders and did not budge. So twice I plunged the knife into my chest. He did not see any blood and probably thought I had been pretending. He walked up to me to take my knife away . . . and I stabbed him in the right arm. Blood flowed. . . . At the sight, I regained my wayward sanity and asked his forgiveness. I took a few steps and brought my hand up to my chest. . . . My head began to spin and I collapsed.

AFTER THE STORM

When I came to, I was in a large bedroom draped in garnet velvet with gold braids. I was lying on a François I-style bed trimmed in white satin with four gilded posts. My chest felt cold. A large sponge dipped in water and vinegar had been placed on me. Voices were coming from the next room.

"Forgive me, my dear friend," Lionel was saying, "for such a terrible night. . . . As soon as daylight appears I shall send for a carriage. Her wound is not serious."

I remembered everything and I burst into tears. He drew near my bed and said, "You are feeling better? . . . My word, you are insane; you knew what you were doing when you left me; I want to be free."

I looked at the door, which had remained open; this woman was listening.

"Close this door; I am leaving. Louise, come help me get dressed."

I wanted to get up, but I could not stand. Louise shouted, "Madame is fainting! . . ."

"Again!" Lionel replied. He came to help her support me.

The woman I had seen at the Cirque came in and spoke to Lionel. She had a pronounced provincial accent. Her hair was short and curled in the ancient Roman style. I simply asked her to leave the room so I could get ready to leave. . . . She did so, laughing, and I heard her kiss Lionel.

He did not shake my hand. The window was open; after watching me leave, he closed it.

The streets were empty. I dragged myself up to my apartment, my body broken. On my chest was a huge scar.

"Now," said Louise, "you must go to bed, madame; I am going to fetch the doctor."

"No," I said, "there is something I must do; I have to warn Richard. Go to his house . . . and tell him to come over."

RICHARD CANNOT LIVE "WITHOUT" EITHER

When Louise returned, she told me, "Oh! Madame, M. Richard's concierge would not let me go up; he said, 'There is no one home . . . M. Richard just went out with Madame.'

" 'But,' I replied, 'Madame is at home. . . . She is the one who sent me!'

"He remained speechless for a moment then said, 'Good gracious! I just did something dumb; she is not the one who was upstairs!' "

I went to bed and cried profusely. When I ran out of tears, I reviewed the events.

"Nothing!" I told myself, "I have nothing left. Lionel was pitiless with me. And Richard is withdrawing his friendship."

Louise came into my room and said, "Madame, the nursemaid is here with your godchild."

I said, "Oh! Have her come in; she is in time to remind me that maybe no one loves me, but she has no one but me in this world."

My little girl was brought to me. She seemed as delicate as a flower. Yet the woman taking care of her said she was in good health. The poor angel responded to my caresses with caresses.

Louise came in to ask if I wanted to receive M. Richard.

I sat in the shadows so he would not see my face.

"Well! Your dinner at the Maison-d'Or went on quite late?"

"No," he said, "I came home at midnight. You know that wherever you are not, I am bored."

"All right," I said, "enough acting and pretense; tell me the name of the one who consoled you during this long and sad night?"

"Oh! Céleste," he said dropping to his knees before me, "forgive a moment of infatuation; during this dinner, I lost my mind, and you had hurt me so much! . . . Oh! this woman. . . . She is the one who enticed me."

"I asked you her name."

"Oh! Céleste, Céleste, you are without pity, you have no heart. Her name is Adèle Célier."

I said, "Oh! I have seen her twice. She is a pretty woman, tall, blond, right?"

"I shall kill myself if you do not forgive me."

"Now, I have already asked you not to say such stupid things to me. Leave, and on your way down order my carriage. Come back for me at nine o'clock; I want to go to the Ranelagh."

I dressed in my most beautiful clothes; I put on rouge to conceal my pallor. I rode in a barouche so splendidly decorated that everyone would say as I passed by, "How happy this woman is!"

When I arrived on the Champs-Elysées, many people seemed surprised. All my acquaintances knew what had happened the night before, and everyone wanted to see the woman who drove Mogador to stab herself, and Lionel was making many jokes at Richard's expense.

STROKE OF LUCK, NO CARTRIDGES

One morning Lionel showed up.

"I have come to see how you are doing."

"I am fine. So you are not afraid of me anymore that you are coming back?"

"No," he replied. "Do you want to offer me lunch? The table is set."

"I am sorry, but I am expecting someone."

"Well! You will see him another time."

"And what will you do in return?"

"I shall dismiss my roomer."

At those words, my heart jumped.

"Fine! We have a deal."

Richard rang, I went to the door, and I asked him not to come in.

"Go," I told him, "find your Mlle Adèle. Lionel is here. Today—I can tell you the truth—I am not giving in to my heart, but to my pride."

"Adieu. You shall never see me again."

Lionel tried to justify himself.

"Yes," he said, "I still love you a little, but I am the only one to do so. I do not know what you have done to the women, but they all hate you. Judith wrote to me, she cannot stand you."

"My dear friend, I do not know what Mlle Judith bases her comments on. I know her only by sight."

Lunch was served. Lionel was so cheerful, I was hurt.

"All right, I am going to give this woman some money, rent an apartment for her, and I shall come pick you up at six for dinner."

He left. A few minutes later, I was handed a letter from Richard:

I told you, Céleste, that I shall never see you again. One of my friends is going to California and I am leaving with him. I deceived you about my

position: I am ruined. I have barely enough money left to pay for my trip.
Losing you is the only thing that makes me unhappy. Adieu, I love you. I
have never loved nor shall I ever love anyone but you. . . .

This news terrified me. I would have been indifferent to his departure, but his ruin frightened me. I wrote to him to offer him what I had.
My maid was told that he had left his house that morning. Remorse ate
at my heart. Lionel was as much the cause of this distress as I was.

My head on fire, I waited until six o'clock. It finally arrived and Lionel
did not show up.

Seven o'clock!

"Louise, a coat, a hat."

Once on Rue Joubert, I found the valet.

"Where is your master?" I asked him.

"He went out, madame; he is entertaining. He told me he would be
back at eight."

"Fine; and was this woman with him?"

"Yes, madame."

"Where are her things?"

"There, in the dressing room."

I went into this room where I found a large trunk and dresses scat-
tered about. I had everything put in the trunk, and I ordered the valet
to take that to the Hôtel des Princes. He obeyed.

"Now," I said, "it is the three of us. But first the two of us."

Then I opened his pistol case with the firm intention that, if he did
not do what I was going to demand, I would blow his brains out and
then kill myself. Luckily for him I could not find the cartridges, because
when his carriage stopped I went to the window and saw him come out
of an open phaeton and take this woman in his arms to help her out.
Oh! I am certain that I would have killed him, and that he would not
have made it upstairs. I was particularly skillful for a woman; I could
score nineteen bull's-eyes out of twenty when I shot. My hand was cold,
but it was not shaking.

I was waiting for them in the living room, which was all lit up for the
evening. The walls were covered with embossed white and gold leather
and the furniture was upholstered in green brocatelle. This apartment
had been decorated for Mlle Rachel.

HOW THE FAVORITE DISMISSES A RIVAL

He came in and looked stunned. No one had dared tell him I was there.

"Well! Does my presence surprise you? Had you forgotten me?"

His companion entered. I addressed her, "Did he not tell you that he had gone to see me this morning and was supposed to pick me up for dinner?"

"It is true," said Lionel, "but then I thought that I could not dismiss Madame in one day, that it would take time to find her lodgings."

"Oh," I replied, "well, well! But it seems that you found her at the Hôtel des Princes, and it does not take very long to go back there. I just had her trunks brought there!"

Lionel was completely nonplussed.

"Now really, Céleste, I promise you that Madame will leave tomorrow. I am expecting guests."

"Oh! So you are expecting guests, well! I am going to provide them with a real party."

The girl from the provinces said to me, "But if Monsieur does not love you anymore and if he loves me. . . ."

"I do not know you, mademoiselle."

"I am madame."

"Too bad for you!"

She began to cry.

"All right," I told him, "I do not wish to put Madame outside at this late hour; follow me."

He gave her a few kind words of consolation, excused himself for his weakness, and ordered his servant to tell all his friends that the party was postponed for a week.

On the way back to my house we were silent.

The next day this woman wrote to him at my home asking him for money. He sent her some to get rid of her.

I went with him to make sure she was really gone. The apartment was empty, and, as a souvenir, she had taken an enormous *pâté de foie gras*.

Later on the girl from the provinces found so many consolers that soon she became, like me, one of those sad celebrities, one of those women who devour fortunes and futures.

33

Death Throes of a Fortune

Mlle Page — A Dangerous Woman — Another
Missed Marriage — The Theatrical Demoiselle and
the Indigent Aristocrat — Lionel's Prose Is
Better Than Murger's Verses

A WEEK LATER Lionel was entertaining. The stakes were high; he was losing. Although he was a good sport about it, I noticed little beads of perspiration on his forehead.

By the end of the party, he had lost eighteen thousand francs. His possessions were mortgaged, and all he could find were usurers who charged twenty-five percent.

"You know," I told him, "my grandfather is rich; he ran a hotel for fifty-five years. His property was just expropriated by the government, so he has some cash. If you wish, I can have him lend you twenty thousand francs."

He accepted. I got him twenty thousand francs in income coupons from Spain. But he gambled again and lost part of the money he wanted to return to me! Every day it was dinners and parties. I no longer opposed his extravagances; I shared in them, and sometimes I even encouraged them. Adorned with his gifts, radiant in my conceit, I wore his ruin like a trophy.

MLLE PAGE

He gave a masked ball. It was splendid and pleased me greatly because it gave me the opportunity to become friends with young Page with the dark languorous eyes. I was also delighted to get to see up close such famous and prominent persons of the stage as Mesdames Octave, Nathalie, etc. Nathalie had come looking for distraction after the end of a love affair; she sprinkled her tears over the ball. Up until now I had only seen Mme Octave on the stage; it was during the days of her great success in *Property is Theft*.[1]

I watched these women attentively. I noticed in particular a charming girl from Bretagne. She was the young Durand, a pretty girl with a nice figure. During a quadrille, I was the vis-à-vis of a tall and beautiful person. I was told, "That is C——, an actress from the Variétés."

The dance ended at the other end of the living room. Lionel ordered a window opened. Mlle Page had just fainted. The heat had made her sick. I took care of her. She told me as she left, "I would appreciate it if you would come see me."

"Poor Page!" said a short woman I had not noticed. "She wears her clothes too tight."

These parties Lionel gave were very expensive. He had ordered an eight-spring surrey and he gave it to me.

I went to see Page and made her my friend. Time went by, and Lionel was not returning the money I had lent him. I was beginning to worry, but I accompanied him on the road to ruination.

A DANGEROUS WOMAN

Lionel had some business in Berry and was away for two days.

I was engaged at a women's dinner given by a rather famous actress. The dinner was catered by Potel et Chabot. There were eight of us. We all exchanged polite remarks; we put on airs like grand ladies to make up for having eaten potatoes in our youths. I had eaten as many as they had, but I did not know how to pick up a pince-nez to look in my plate; I did not at the slightest opportunity drape my arm like a garland or position my hands as if catching a butterfly.

During the whole dinner the topic of conversation was means and stratagems for snaring money from men who become blinded by passion.

Once back home I fell asleep, dizzy from all I had heard. My soul was not sufficiently polished to prevent bad advice from quickly sprouting there.

"Oh!" I told myself, "I have also been around. Deligny is in Africa, Richard in California, and Lionel is ruining himself. She who bears the name 'kept woman' is a heart's leech, a soul's usurer."

It so happens that, since the day I tried to kill myself at Lionel's, the devil had captured my heart. I had become mean and ungrateful; I had an excuse for everything. Finally I acquired the unfortunate reputation of being a dangerous woman. I was faulted less for that than for dancing and being called Mogador. If a young man courted me or spoke to me, his parents would make him leave. I was proud to inspire such terror.

ANOTHER MISSED MARRIAGE

I went to see Lionel. He was back. He had not been able to procure any money and was trying to sell his lands because he was in debt for almost three hundred thousand francs. Although they were worth eight hundred thousand, the interest was eating up the revenues. He had been offered six hundred thousand francs, but he turned that down. I asked him to reimburse me the money I lent him for his gambling debts. He could not.

"But I would like to have what you owe me, or a security, in case something happens to you!"

"I cannot give it back to you right away; I would have to sell."

His attempts had been in vain. He was deeply depressed.

After dinner I asked him if he wanted to go out.

"No," he replied, "we must talk. You are right to think about the future, but I am a wretch for taking this money. I am going to try to get married, otherwise I would have barely enough left to live after the sale of my lands. I cannot give you a mortgage because my lawyer and my family would soon find out, and they would think it was a gift. Here is what I propose. I am going to give you bills of exchange and as soon as I can, I shall pay them back. I have to go to Lyon in a few days, and I cannot keep this apartment. Tomorrow we shall go see the landlord and I shall ask him to keep you on as tenant in my place. You will come live here."

"What about mine?" I asked. "What am going to do with it?" (To be closer to him, I had rented a little cottage on Rue Joubert.)

"Well," he said, "you can rent it."

Two days later the lease was put in my name. I handed my valuables over to my mother with strict orders not to give them back to me for any reason. They were my little adopted daughter's fortune.

It was with a heavy heart that I sold my beautiful tapestries that reminded me of my stay in Berry. Mlle Amanda wanted to buy my furniture. Lionel strongly urged me to accept; it had all come from Richard and that bothered him. I sold my little cottage for twenty thousand francs. It was charmingly furnished, had beautiful clocks, carpets in every room, oak and rosewood furniture, a piano, an organ, and drapes. It was to be paid off in three years.

Lionel left. He was leaving me to get married. Perhaps I would never see him again.

One of my new acquaintances, whom I had brought to my house, saw my godchild.

"Oh, look!" she said. "How pretty she is; she will be a dancer."

"No," I said, "she will be rich, but if I had to give her a situation, it would not be that one."

I went to Place de la Madeleine and went up to see Mlle Page. She was unhappy in every way. Her little girl was dying of a wasting disease. Page's own health was delicate.

To spend more time near her, I asked her to get me hired on at the Variétés.

She introduced me to M. C——, the manager. He promised to hire me. I wrote to him. He had me come back to his office and gave me a contract to sign that stated I would get twelve hundred francs in salary, with a twenty thousand franc penalty clause.

These demoiselles fussed a lot about my being hired.

I was given two roles in the *The 1851 Revue;* I was rehearsing when Lionel arrived from Lyon.

He told me, "Well, I shall never be able to get married; I was bluntly turned down because of you. I am going to sell my horses, my hounds, get rid of three quarters of my staff, and we shall stay together."

"But my dear friend, thinking you were never coming back, I got work on the stage and there is a penalty clause; I am now in rehearsal. Sell the barouche, the big surrey, and the little carriage."

He seemed quite annoyed about my engagement, but he sold his horses, his carriages, and stayed in Paris only briefly. Amanda asked me if I wanted to sell some of my jewelry.

I consulted Lionel who replied, "That is your business; it seems to me it would be a good idea." I was twenty-five years old and I wanted my little girl to be rich. I agreed. I sold for a little less than what it cost. I gave three years credit without interest. Page approved my decision.

THE THEATRICAL DEMOISELLE AND
THE INDIGENT ARISTOCRAT

One night Lionel told me, "I ran into a young man I know. He is distressed because they are going to arrest him. I might be able to prevent that since it is my jeweler pursuing him."

"Be careful," I told him. "Do not get mixed up in a troublesome affair. You know what I think of your jeweler."

Alas! A few days later, it was all done. Lionel was answerable for twenty thousand francs for a man who was broke.

He left and went to the country. I asked him to check on my little house. I wanted to build a cottage next to the rented property. Because of the location so near the forest, he advised me to build a hunting lodge, which I could rent out until the day I would live in it. I told him to take care of that for me.

He left and I debuted. I still could not act. I was as frightened as at the Folies. Page encouraged me. The newspapers jeered me! If you do not subscribe, they tear you apart. Poor actors do not make enough money to buy a subscription to three or four bad newspapers that all say the same thing. The newspaper *Le Corsaire*, the savage dog of literature, was sucking my blood.

I was going to be in another play, *Paris Asleep*. M. C—— told me, "You absolutely have to go see M. J——; he is not happy with you."

That day I went to see Amanda, who knew him. Alas! I forgot that she was in my debt, and from that day, she began to hate me.

My heart unhinged from climbing the five flights of stairs, I met with M. J——. He received me while talking to his parrot.

"Monsieur, I know that my past damns me in your opinion; yet I would really like to do serious work on the stage. I have come to beg you not to speak ill of me."

"Oh," he replied, "I am sorry, but my article is finished, and anyway I cannot pass up that line in your part: 'You must have style to pinch them.'"

"But monsieur, I am not the one who wrote the play."

He probably thought I was ridiculous, but he did make some changes to his article.

Victorine came to see me the next day.

"Oh! My dear," she said, "you have set foot in hell. Once you begin keeping company with journalists, authors, actors, you might as well camp at *Combat's* tollgate, billeted in the doghouse. You would not get as chewed up or as mangled."

Since my return to the stage, Lionel had come to Paris several times. Each time he came to take me back with him, but in vain.

Seeing that I did not want to go back with him, he lost interest in his lands and put them up for sale. He wrote me letters that were at times tender and kind, other times mean and harsh.

I am no longer rich, you do not want to see me anymore. Fine! You will not hear from me again.

Six hours later I would get another letter.

M. Philoxène, an actor, sent me an invitation to a ball he was giving on Christmas eve. I put on a low-cut dress and the jewelry I had left.

When I walked into the living room, there was only one place for me to sit, and on this same sofa was a lady wearing a red dress. I did not look at her face, and I sat next to her, but she got up, jumping as if I had burned her. I recognized Mlle Judith![2]

All the gentlemen rushed toward me to avenge me of this offense. That provided me with the pleasant opportunity to meet M. Henri Murger.[3]

Toward the end of the evening, M. Murger wrote an extemporaneous poem on each of the guests still present. He set his verses to a melody by Quidant:

> To that poor actress's chagrin
> Whose jewelry is fake,
> Céleste, who her name did take
> From distant Morocco, can be seen
> Behind a garden bright with flowers,
> Proudly strolling like a queen.
> At the house of Philoxene
> We were eighty merry rhymesters.
>
> Her shoulders did Golkonda array[4]
> With sparkling diamonds, and Visapour
> Spangled her hands with lights so pure,
> She glistens like the Milky Way.
> When she sees such starlit splendors,
> Judith will reject Holophernes.
> At the house of Philoxene
> We were eighty merry rhymesters.

I was about to start in a new play when I received this letter from Lionel:

Céleste, I cannot live this way. I relied too much on my strength; I cannot live without you. Do you know what it is like to love as I love you? It is madness! I am insane: I am offering you my fortune, I am offering you my life, my name, my honor. I am going to liquidate what I own. In a few days I am selling my lands; we can be happy far from here. Do not refuse me; answer me.

I could not believe my eyes. I read this letter twenty times. My pride was shouting: "Accept!" My heart dictated the following letter:

My dear Lionel, I am returning this letter, of which I am not worthy and which cannot be addressed to a woman like me. Your crown of nobility would be my crown of thorns. I would not be able to look at these poor outcasts I have lived with, and I would never have the right to look at an honest woman. There are two paths: yours and mine. Let me be Mogador, you continue being Lionel de C——. Get out of this frame of mind. I shall always be your friend.

34

To the Antipodes

Only Page's Misfortune Is without Remedy—Ruin, Separation,
Exile—London, 12 May 1852—Southampton, 15 May 1852—Wednesday,
19 May 1852—Friday, 21 May 1852—Saturday, 22 May 1852—Sunday Evening,
30 May 1852—Sunday, 6 June 1852—Sunday, 13 June 1852—Sunday, 20 June
1852—Friday, 25 June 1852—On Board the *Chusan*, 20 July 1852—
Tuesday, 27 July 1852—Thursday, 29 July 1852 at Ten P.M.—
Sydney, Monday, 20 September 1852.

SIX DAYS LATER I received another letter from Lionel. It gave me a
shock from which I did not recover for a long time:

*Your prediction will come true: we will not be square until my last sou. I
just learned I am ruined. . . . A businessman to whom I had given blank
power to sell an estate during my absence, abusing my trust, just sold my
land for half of its value. All I have left is a life of poverty and isolation,
which I shall escape. My brain will be splattered on your stage dress and
your pleasure bed. When I sold my possessions, I had my papers and my
family portraits sent to your house. I am going away leaving everything
there, even my personal things. Sell them, because any reminder of me
would cause you remorse. I shall not go to Paris; on the 10th I am leaving
for Africa.*

*The way I feel for you is an enigma to everyone, even to me. To love,
there must be respect, and I despise you. This child you are rearing will
despise you also. Do not write me anymore!*

ONLY PAGE'S MISFORTUNE IS WITHOUT REMEDY

I shall never be able to express the amount of pain reading this letter
caused me. I had to make a great effort to reply:

*Two days ago your letters were sad, but good. Today you heap abuse on
me for no reason. The first day I met you, I told you how I was. I find your*

276

accusations so exaggerated that I feel somewhat exonerated in thinking that I never lied to you. I went on the stage because I did not want people to rejoice at our separation. If I had my little fortune, I would leave this comfort that conceals so much sorrow. I have loved you; I still love you. You have been and you will always be my only, my last love.

Believe me, although my body is degraded, there is a chaste part of it where I shall keep the offer you made me. . . . All I have is yours; take it when you wish. It is impossible that you could take such a desperate measure. . . . Oh! Answer me. . . . I love you.

I was looking for a refuge from my despair. I went to see Page, and we cried together because she had just lost her little Marie. I reluctantly went home. To help me become more resigned, this is what Lionel wrote me:

Everything you have said has been lies. Your heart, like your boudoir, was offered to the highest bidder. You had only one thing to offer me in exchange for my love, and that was your body. You sold it, to some for money, to others for pleasure. But I was giving you my life and you soiled it.

I shall no longer be in the running for a love I cannot afford anymore. On the 10th I am leaving for Algiers; your money will be returned to you. The lie must stop here.

We were even, and, in turn, I was thinking more about vengeance than justification:

I am now rebelling, and I am tired of getting this undeserved bad treatment. I am returning your letter, which nauseates me. I cannot bear a correspondence that drives me to despair. I am tired of crying.

RUIN, SEPARATION, EXILE

I would have killed myself if it had not been for the letter I received from the people taking care of my adoptive daughter. The woman had just fallen ill, and I was told that they could no longer keep her. It was barely dawn when I left. The poor little angel was beginning to talk. She called me mother. I took her home.

Two days later three men came to my house to seize the some of forty-six thousand francs that Lionel owed his jeweler.

I wanted to write to Lionel, but I threw my pen down furiously.

"No," I said, "I shall be more generous than he."

I put on a veil and went to the theater. I danced and sang with a heavy heart, but I was used to this ritual.

277

I had finished my play (*The Queens of the Ball*) at nine o'clock. On my way out I saw a man in the alleyway. Like a shadow he was slinking along the walls.

It was Lionel, pale and disheveled. His eyes, usually so ardent, were veiled with sadness, but his scornful lips had not lost their irony.

"Oh, no," I told him, "you will not avoid me; you owe me an explanation."

Tears choked my voice. He told me to get in the carriage and he took me home

"I was afraid of what is happening," he said, "and that is what brought me back to Paris. My possessions have been sold for half their value. I am not only ruined, but I am also in debt."

"Yes, well, I am being pursued because supposedly what I have belongs to you."

"Show up their lies, Céleste, defend yourself with all your energy and intelligence! There are judges. I would carry too many regrets with me if I knew you were miserable. I wanted to join the army, but I am too old. I am thirty-three. I am leaving for Australia."

He stayed at my house. We paid for our bygone joys with long, tearful nights.

A letter from Berry pulled us out of our despondency. My house and my furniture had just been seized. The mortgage he had given me in payment was going to be challenged.

"Well," I told him, "you had nothing but insults and disdain for me; you wished misery, hospitalization, or prison for me. You can leave satisfied. Now we are even. Go away, leave me to my despair."

He left slowly, accepting my words like an order of exile.

I went to see a solicitor who gave me the address of a lawyer, and I did what I needed to do to face the storm. A hundred times beaten down, I got up again with uncommon efforts. I was dragged through courthouses.

I left my apartment on Rue Joubert for the duration of this trial, because, in case the judges were misled by false appearances, I did not want to be thrown out of my own home. On Avenue Saint-Cloud, I rented a little house with a yard for my daughter, who needed some fresh air.

All the women I had known were dancing around my ruin like witches. I did not want to let them have this joy. I tried to deceive them and to deceive myself, and so, with fear in my heart, I led a life of luxury and pleasure.

Lionel had left. He had fought until the last moment; defeated, he faced his ruin, and, fearing his weak will, he put five thousand leagues between himself and the dust raised by this calamity of lost happiness.

Here are excerpts from his travel diary which, from the start, were his correspondence.[1]

LONDON, 12 MAY 1852

I do not want to leave Europe without writing you one last time. This morning I could still see the coast of France and did not take my eyes off it until it had disappeared. Adieu dreams, joys, happiness!

Here in London I am waiting for a clipper leaving on the 9th. My passage is booked. Oh! I feel that I shall never return, but remember, Céleste, all those people you sacrificed me for will have nothing but disdain for you. It will be your turn to be alone, and you will not have one friend left. You can be such a beautiful courtesan when you want to! One who knows how to devour, shred, trample a destiny like mine. Mogador, for whom this poor Lionel sacrificed everything! . . . Well, she must be quite a beauty! Lionel, who overcame his prejudices, who escorted her before all of Paris!

Since I met you, I have not had a single thought for another woman. I will think of nothing else for five months of crossing.

Adieu! I am worn out, I cannot see clearly anymore, I am going to throw myself on my bed, my poor, miserable bed in a tiny dark room. But I shall leave it only just before our departure.

I am sailing off with a group of emigrants, almost all Irish. Not even the captain can speak a word of French.

I had your portrait put in a box frame. When I get to Sydney, I shall write you, if God has granted me life. If en route I can manage to send you a few words by way of another clipper, I shall do it. Once more, adieu; I forgive you. One day it will be your turn to be alone, all alone, without friends, and I shall not be there anymore. May this moment come as late as possible for you.

Adieu, adieu. Accept all my thoughts, as well as all my pain.

PS — Tomorrow I shall write again to your attorney, Monsieur Picard, to request that he take good care of your interests.

Drop me a note in the mail on Tuesday or Wednesday — send it to the dead letter office — to tell me what the courts have decided about your affairs. Do not tell me about anything else.

SOUTHAMPTON, 15 MAY 1852

I am writing while on board the clipper that in one hour will be taking me away from you forever. I am leaving without illusions or hopes. In London

I had a ring made for you that I am giving to Monsieur Godot, the only human being who has expressed any interest in me.

You were beautiful and splendid at the Champ-de-Mars races. You will see on the ring I am sending you from London the date 15 May, from Southampton. That is the day everything ended for me. I am dying of sorrow; I am dying without leaving any memories behind me. I am leaving heartbroken and dry-eyed, without a single pound sterling to live on. I paid for my passage. I am going even much farther than Sydney. I shall stay there only a week; then I shall set sail for much more remote islands. I am intent on obliterating my mental pain with physical suffering. This ring that I am sending you, as well as my portrait, will allow you to increase your value and demand a higher price for your personal assets. Hurry because your life is ticking away, and my only vengeance, which time will grant me, will seem hideous and terrible to you. Today as I am leaving, I realize it was not you, Mogador, I loved, but a dream.

I forgive you, but God will damn you, you are such a heartless and soulless woman.

No one will know where I am. I hope the motto on your carriage, Forget me not, will not be a subject of jokes about a man who had a fortune, a name, a future, and who is making a living with his hands.

WEDNESDAY, 19 MAY 1852

I am off the coast of Africa. I have been spending all my time on the bridge seated in a corner, day and night, thinking about the past that each gust of wind takes farther away from me.

Why did I have to place all that my heart contained into some kind of scourge whose life breathed only destruction and ruin? All who will love you will be destroyed by you; all that is beautiful you hate. Evil is your essence; the more there is of it, the more you smile.

Sunday, you must have gone to Chantilly. For me, the future holds this: work in Sydney with Europe's refuse, amid the mire of English citizenry and galley slaves!

My only companion on board is a young Pole some twenty years old who can say a few words in French, and who, exiled because of the Hungarian wars, is going to try to make a living over there.

The rest appear to be an assemblage of dreadful riffraff fleeing England to escape the law. The ship is very drab; it is its maiden voyage. They say that first class is more comfortable, but in second, the food is disgraceful. With the sailors we eat the leftovers from first class. In first class there is a Frenchman, a merchant from Rouen who is running away because he is bankrupt.

To the Antipodes

We shall reach the Cape of Good Hope around June 20th. I shall be almost halfway there. Until then, sky and sea.

If the winds are favorable and if there are no accidents as we cross the Indian Ocean, I shall arrive in Sydney between the 1st and the 15th of August.

I drank a lot the last days I was in London, not to give me energy, but to drown my sorrows, to forget.

Since I am insane, I cannot get it out of my head that upon leaving Southampton I saw you on the pier! It is mad, but when I close my eyes I see you. I saw a woman crying as she watched the clipper depart. Of course, I must be mad; she could not have been you. Besides, does anyone love me?

Adieu until tomorrow.

FRIDAY, 21 MAY 1852

I have just spent a horrible night and day. The sea is calmer this morning. This past night, which I spent on the bridge, did not seem too long. The sky was clear; there was only a burning wind blowing from Africa.

Oh! My poor château! Poor Poinçonnet! You have roses, and I, who took care of you with such pleasure, I, who wanted to turn you into my little paradise. . . .

If the weather does not improve, it will take us four months to get there, and we have been at sea only one week. Four months at sea!

How I would love to see a flower! When I reach Sydney, it will be winter. When it will be midnight in Sydney, it will be noon in Paris; and the month of August is the middle of winter. So it will be a long time before I see greenery and flowers.

SATURDAY, 22 MAY 1852

A week has gone by. I spent the major part of the night on the bridge; the wind was quite calm and the sky magnificent. I sang those beautiful lines from Musset, which I put to music and sent you from Poinçonnet: 'If you do not love me, tell me, silly girl.'

I have made a good friend on board: a little terrier, a dog belonging to the captain. He has taken a liking to me and I call him Finoche in remembrance of your little dog, which now nuzzles the lucky man of the day.

We are off the coast of Madeira Island.

Sometimes the captain visits second class and I can see that he wishes he could speak French to find out why I am here. He must think I am either a very unhappy man or a very poor one. I am learning English; that is my occupation during the day. The food is disgusting, and most of the time I eat only sea biscuits.

For four days now we have been ashore at Sao Vincent, a Cape Verde island, a desolate country, a cursed land! To punish me, God is showing me wretchedness and suffering worse than mine. Here the soil is dry, the countryside is a desert. Death is at every door. When the people here go from house to house, it is customary to say adieu as if going on a long journey. Out of the city's twelve hundred inhabitants, seven hundred have died of yellow fever.

I went to see Lady C——, a great lady, a sainted woman spoken of here only with admiration and respect. She lives amid this disaster seeking out and helping the miserable creatures around her.

After squandering a considerable fortune in England, her husband had to leave. His wife followed him after she had used everything she possessed to pay her husband's debts. Her two sons live near her; each works independently.

Yesterday I had your name tattooed on my arm; it cannot be removed. If ever my heart forgets you, God willing, this name will always be there to remind me how mean and cruel you were to me.

We are not even a quarter of the way there, and I am already very tired; second class is very uncomfortable, and we have barely enough water to drink. The captain let me know yesterday that if I wanted to pay a few louis more, I could get a reduction for first class, and he would be happy to help me. I thanked him as best I could, and I told him that since I had started out this way, I would finish the same way, not wanting to offend anyone. The real reason is that I have two francs left, which will have to last me until the day I arrive at the mines.

Listen, Céleste, and remember well what I am going to tell you: if you suffer, if you are miserable, if you finally decide to run away and leave this life that cannot last, send word to Sydney. It takes three months for a letter to arrive. Only one thing can bring me back to Europe and that is to come for you; but this is madness. How could you need me? What can I do for you?

If by chance the things I left with you at Poinçonnet were not sold, I would like to have my clothes and my suits because I have absolutely nothing. Would you be kind enough to crate all my personal effects as well as my father's portrait?

My cabin neighbors are an Irish couple. I can overhear what they say to each other in anger; I try to let them know I can hear by dragging my chair or coughing, but they continue.

The man must be about twenty-eight. He is tall with broad shoulders; his naturally curly hair is combed back and looks like a lion's mane. The young woman with him, and who passes for his wife, is blond and delicate like a child. Her eyes are such a soft blue, they seem to have dropped from the heavens some lovely spring day.

Yesterday, after spending part of the night gambling, he came back drunk. She was waiting for him and she must have made a remark because he lost his temper; she softly rebutted each reproach.

I heard her cry a good part of the night. I promised myself that the next day I would offer her my services and protection to help her get free of a man whom I regarded as her tormentor, but when I saw her on the bridge, she was leaning on her lover's arm, smiling at him, and looking at him with great tenderness.

How she loves this man unworthy of her affection! Well! My heavens! I love you, Céleste!

SUNDAY, 13 JUNE 1852

I found a Frenchman among the crew and we became friends. His name is Jocelyn Moulin. He is barely twenty years old but he looks thirty. He has a sad and worried look. I should write he had, because he is dead as I write these lines.

Yesterday the second-class passengers were complaining that every night someone was robbed. One, it was his tobacco; another, his brandy. The captain did not listen to them. A young Englishman, who was among those passengers, told them, pointing to Jocelyn who was walking at the front of the ship, "Do not trust this young man and watch him; he stole some money from his master who threw him out. I know, I was taking art lessons from him."

Jocelyn heard him, and grabbing the Englishman's throat, he yelled: "You are lying; I am going to strangle you!"

Before we could separate them, Jocelyn was perfidiously stabbed twice in the chest.

"You do not have the right to call me a thief anymore," cried Jocelyn as he fell, "you are a murderer!"

An English sailor who saw the incident was, like us, stunned by such despicable cowardice. He snatched the knife from the murderer and threw it overboard, telling him, "You are a bad Englishman and I am going to break your jaw!"

It was as if the signal had been given for a party on board. Jocelyn's former mate could neither back up nor escape. The circle closing around him looked like a human chain ready to tighten and choke him at his first move. His antagonist had very wide shoulders and the sailor was hitting so hard against the painter's chest that we could hear a sound like that of a blacksmith striking his anvil. Each blow would draw a roar, a cry, a moan; he fell on the deck, writhed at our feet for a moment, then lay still like a dead man. Blood was oozing out of his mouth, his nose, and his eyes. I am a man, and I almost fainted while some women were clapping, congratulating the winner. The loser was just brought to his cabin. It is believed that all his teeth are broken and several of his ribs smashed. Several of the stolen items were found in his cabin.

I have just given a bottle of brandy to the sailor who defended Jocelyn so well, because the poor boy will not be able to thank him himself. All is over! He was the only human I could talk to during the long nights. Now he is dead!

I would like to give you an idea of what a burial at sea is like. Four sailors, heads bare, were carrying a sack on a stretcher. A fifth one lifted one of the panels in the ship and put the sack there. After a few quiet words it was time to throw it, but the panel did not close up fast enough to throw Jocelyn's body out far enough, so he rolled down along the side of the vessel, and the steel ball placed next to the dead man to make him sink was hitting the boards.

I watch the long wake the ship leaves behind. Sometimes the tunes you used to sing come back to me. Then I fall into some sort of trance; my heart returns to Berry, to each corner, each place where I have left a memory.

SUNDAY, 20 JUNE 1852

I am ill as a result of this wound I got in Spain. For two days I have been consulting the doctor on board. I have to have surgery, but I am going to wait until we get to the Cape of Good Hope where I shall go to the military hospital to consult the chief medical officer; I shall make my decision then. When I say a decision, I mean, I shall kill myself.

Do not reprove me for my harsh letters. Look carefully, and in the end you will always find a love that you will never encounter anywhere else.

FRIDAY, 25 JUNE 1852

I arrived at nine in the morning and I must depart tomorrow. Therefore I cannot possibly get medical care until Sydney. As for everything else, since my arrival I have been feeling an inexplicable happiness. The loveli-

est camellias and the most beautiful geraniums grow along the edges of the fields.

I am sending you a heliotrope blossom that I just picked for you.

ON BOARD THE *CHUSAN*, 20 JULY 1852

I barely had time to seal my letter at the Cape of Good Hope; I wanted to send it by a ship setting sail on 28 June.

We just had fifteen days of awful weather; everything is damaged, masts and sails. Finally this morning the weather is calmer. The second-class passengers, made up of the lowest class in England, were spending their nights drinking gin or brandy. There were fights and horrible screams among these inebriated people sleeping helter-skelter in every corner of the ship. This is the middle of winter. All I have to eat is salted pork that smells bad, some moldy biscuits, and one liter of water a day to drink and wash with.

Two weeks from now I shall be in Sydney. There I plan to sell the few pieces of jewelry I have. I shall buy all the tools I need for the mines and I shall proceed, since the provinces where the gold can be found are about one hundred leagues from Sydney.

TUESDAY, 27 JULY 1852

In two days we shall be in the first port of Australia, called Port Phillip. It is near there that the most important mines are located, and almost all the passengers are planning to disembark.

In Sydney I hope to find a man who will be my associate in the mines. The difficult part will be finding someone who is not a thief or a murderer.

The mines where I plan to go are located near a village called Bathurst, one hundred leagues from Sydney, in the interior.

Yesterday I found among my belongings a little box you gave me two years ago. My whole fortune is made up of your portrait, my horseshoe pin, this box, and four letters from you. Those are the only things I cherish. Even though your letters are nothing but lies, I reread them every day.

THURSDAY, 29 JULY 1852 AT TEN *P.M.*

What a terrible day I just had! I had just finished my letter to you yesterday, Wednesday, and I had been in bed two hours when we went up on the bridge; the ship was being battered on all sides by a horrible storm. A cry of despair rose from all of us; a sailor fell from the top of a tall mast, passed right before my eyes, and rolled into the sea; two shipboard officers, followed by four sailors, used an ax to cut the cords tying a little lifeboat and they rushed off, in spite of the captain, in search of the poor man. The vessel was making fourteen knots. The skiff got left behind. We lost sight of it for two hours. The passengers were yelling and losing hope; they wanted to stop the ship and wait for the poor men. I had words with the captain because he was hesitating. He gave an order and the ship turned around. Finally we glimpsed the skiff, which was bobbing freely on the waves because the men in it were worn out with fatigue. Their search had been in vain; the sailor was lost. Lieutenant Bencraf and the sailors who had gone with him dropped on the ship's deck and passed out.

We can see the Australian coast. The first thing that comes into view is a ship wrecked on a rock.

SYDNEY, MONDAY, 20 SEPTEMBER 1852

In one hour I shall be on horseback.

I used the last of my resources. After selling everything to buy a horse, I am leaving for the mines.

I am going to the interior of the territory, two hundred leagues from here. It will take me from eleven to fifteen days to get there.

Céleste, I do not want to begin my journey without sending you my last adieus, you who have been the only love of my life and whose memory will leave my thoughts only when my life ends. It seems that my love for you has increased in proportion to the pain you have caused me.

I love you as I have always loved you.

35

My Law Lesson

Courtesan, Actress, and Litigant—Hôtel de la Promenade:
Sanctuary for Integrity—Return from San Francisco

TODAY, AFTER REREADING Lionel's letters, I am happy and proud
to have inspired in this kind and brave man such a tender and devoted
passion. But in those days my heart was too confused to know what it
could love or hate.

When, like Lionel, one has held a lofty social position, been a rich
noble, it is possible to face ruin without despair. To fall from high causes
vertigo, but there is always the hope of rising again.

But when a poor creature like me, without the protection of a family
and with a past like mine, is ruined, it is forever. I had no illusions about
a courtesan's future. Aware of the disdainful way my kind is spoken of,
I had promised myself that I would not undergo the humiliations of old
age. I had always told myself that if by age thirty I had not found a way
to be independent, I would seek refuge in suicide.

Therefore I had to either fight or die. But to fight, I needed courage
and experience I did not have then.

COURTESAN, ACTRESS, AND LITIGANT

As I expected, my apartment on Rue Joubert, my carriages on Rue de
la Chaussée-d'Antin, and my house in Berry were seized, and there was
opposition to the mortgage Lionel had left in payment for the money I
had lent him. All his possessions were divided up, and I was being sued
everywhere.

Lionel's departure and the fanfare of my liaison with him had made
a lot of noise around my life. Bad reputations are like good ones: they
are acquired slowly, but past a certain amount of time they take on a
life of their own.

The world was seeking me out, and out of necessity I climbed a few more rungs up this ladder of elegant corruption, when in fact I no longer possessed the heart my character required.

My life depended on a double lie: a financial lie and a moral lie. It was thought I was rich, and the ground under my feet was mined. It was thought that I was more wicked than ever, and my soul was worth more than my life.

So I had four proceedings to deal with. My future and that of my little daughter depended on justice.

My attorney in Paris, M. Picard, gave me some excellent advice. He sent me to see M. Desmarest, who was willing to plead my case, or rather my cases. In Châteauroux my attorney was M. Berton-Pourriat.

I asked that my rights be explained to me; I researched the code of laws, I listened, I asked questions. Somewhat defiant by nature, I asked people for clarifications to be sure that the moneymen were not taking advantage of me, because one of them, having shown too much zeal for my adversaries, was about to go before a judge.

I spent my life in bailiff offices, in attorney offices, in magistrate offices. Over a period of six months I became acquainted with every room of the courthouse.

When all my proceedings finally came to court and I could rest a little from my quibbling activities, I occupied myself seriously with acting.

Acclaim no longer went to my head. I knew that this life was not going to last. Courtesan, actress, and litigant—more than enough to fill a lifetime. I was running from the Bois to a waiting room, from a waiting room to the Variétés.

It was then that I got some very sad news. A woman told me that Deligny had been killed in a duel.

I won my proceeding on the Rue Joubert furniture. This victory gave me some confidence.

HÔTEL DE LA PROMENADE: SANCTUARY FOR INTEGRITY

The proceedings on the Poinçonnet property would be pleaded in August in a Châteauroux courthouse. I had to travel to Poinçonnet. It was a painful trip because of all the memories flooding back with each turn of the wheels.

I ran into some difficulties when I tried to go inside. A guard had been assigned to it upon its seizure. I had to wait in the courtyard an hour before I was allowed to enter my own house.

A few days later my adversaries came to search the house. They poured over Lionel's most secret papers. They hoped to find proof that I was not his proxy.

These incredible stratagems ended up confounding my adversaries. They also outraged the judge and swayed him in my favor. I was defended by M. Desmarest, who had come to Châteauroux to plead for me.

The people of Berry remembered Lionel fondly, and when the affront was flung at him in front of the whole audience, the judges and the spectators protested.

I stayed at the Hôtel de la Promenade, anxiously waiting for the verdict like someone awaiting a death sentence. Mme Edouard Suard, the owner of the hotel, did everything she could to reassure me during two gloomy days. It was not the first time I was able to appreciate her generosity.

When I came to this region for the first time, we stayed at this hotel, and Lionel brought me here again when he was on a hunt in the forest. Without this kind and indulgent woman I would have stayed alone, cooped up in my room for days on end. She would come to my room to spend a few minutes, or she would make me come downstairs to be near her in her private living room, a little sanctuary full of flowers, handmade crafts, and precious heirlooms that were evidence of a life of order, work, and faith.

In the company of an honest woman, my heart would relax, and my soul would be lifted. With a few good words and a little perseverance, I could easily have altered my character, but there is always one half of the world that prevents the other half from doing good.

I learned the result of this proceeding only three months later. The trial had taken place on 31 August, but the judgment was not rendered until after summer vacation. In spite of the long wait, I was extremely happy. Alas! My problems were not over. I had won only one round; my adversaries appealed to the imperial court in Bourges.

Still these two early and significant victories allowed me to hope. As calm returned to my heart, my past appeared less bitter; I was becoming less demanding of happiness. I felt more indulgent toward others, less strict toward myself.

RETURN FROM SAN FRANCISCO

To get to the little house I was living in on Avenue Saint-Cloud, it was necessary to go through an enclosed garden. The living room was on the first floor.

It was starting to get cold. I had a fire lit. I was seated in front of the fireplace and was absentmindedly looking in the mirror when I saw the gate open—but no one had rung the bell.

It was Richard. . . .

I recognized him immediately, although he seemed horribly changed!

When my maid asked if I wanted to see him, I remained glued to my chair, unable to find an answer.

"Do you not want to kiss me, Céleste?"

"Oh! Yes. But I dare not; you must hate me so!"

"I! I have never stopped loving you. I always had the hope I would see you again. I was sick almost the whole time. A fever never left me. However, I had almost rebuilt my fortune. One of my friends and I had a house together. It was destroyed by fire. From time to time I had news of you from Frenchmen coming to California. I learned about M. Lionel's misfortune. I feel bad for him and I forgive him. Time allays pain and abates hate. Only my love for you is untouched by it. I built another house in San Francisco. I rented it to a banker and here I am. How good it is to see you!"

"And I am so happy to know that you do not hate me! . . ."

"I hate you so little," he said, "that if you wanted to accept my offer of two years ago, I would make the same offer again."

"My dear Richard, you have a heart of gold. I am being punished for the pain I have caused you, and I am no happier than you."

"If you have enemies, you know you can always count on me."

I looked at my clock in horror. The excitement and the pleasure caused by this visit had made me forget that I was due at the theater.

We were rehearsing a play called *Taconnet* for Frédérick Lemaître's debut. We had to be on time; the great actor was not patient. Richard escorted me and did not leave me until we had reached the entrance of the Variétés.

36

The Variétés Theater

Rachel—Malicious Gossip Thwarted—Why Cats?—
A Star—Tonight, Passage des Panoramas

I WORKED DILIGENTLY at my craft of acting, but managers and actors insisted on casting me as a soubrette, a grisette, or a dancer. I did not have the voice, the height, or the look for these roles.

I was not pleased at all with the role that I had been assigned in the play just released. I had to play the queen of the Maenads. That was not what I had been promised, and I advised the manager that if he was not going to give me a challenging role, I would leave the theater. The authors were consulted, and in the end, when another actress turned it down, I was given a role in *The 1852 Revue,* at the Palais de Cristal.

A new dance had just arrived, *l'impériale.* I was asked to dance it with Page. I accepted, although I had long been wanting to put an end to this dancing I was repeatedly asked to perform.

RACHEL

I like everything that has to do with talent.

It goes without saying that I was a fanatic of Rachel's, a magnificent, sublime, undeniable talent, who nevertheless had her detractors among the mean blowhards whose sole conviction is small-mindedness. They would criticize her either for her appearance or her mind.

After attending a performance of *Phaedra* I went home excited. This concentrated power, this smile full of hate and disdain, this gaze full of ire or love—it was all new to me and seemed magical.

So, as I was saying, like all great people, Rachel was criticized, and I rebelled when she was found imperfect.

"She is proud, impertinent, and arrogant," a pretty little Jewish girl said about her one day. "I knew her when she was poor; I even lent her

291

some of my dresses when she was singing in the streets, and today she will not even say hello to me."

I thought this lack of gratitude was not consistent with Rachel's personality. I knew she was generous to a fault and carefree about the greatness wrought by her genius. So I contradicted my dear companion. She vehemently swore that she was telling the truth. I believed her less than ever, and I decided to clear up the matter.

Mlle Rachel did not receive people just any time of the day, if she even consented to see you, otherwise the curious and the meddlers would have invaded her little house on Rue Trudon. I had been warned about that, but I went to her house after the theater anyway.

The concierge, who was in a pretty little alcove on the right, motioned for me to sit in a beautiful Voltaire-style armchair and invited me to look at paintings and knickknacks while he went to see if Mlle Rachel was receiving. I regretted coming. What was I going to say? How was I going to present myself?

I was deep in thought when a liveried servant entered. He told me, "Madame is in her study; she is not receiving today; come back Thursday at two. Madame will see you then. If what you have to say to her is urgent, write her a note."

That evening I was having dinner with someone whose house had a beautiful garden. I was permitted to pick some flowers for a bouquet. I thought it was so beautiful because of the rare specimens it contained that I sent it to Mlle Rachel with a letter in which I thanked her.

I shall never have a royal audience, but, if I ever had one, I would not be more intimidated than I was when the servant told me, "This way, mademoiselle. Madame is ill, but she will see you anyway."

When we were on the third floor, I was announced.

The room I had just been brought to was simply furnished. The drapes were Persian, and the carpet was from Smyrna.

Rachel was reclining on a bed, which faced the door. Her torso was partly visible. On top of a peignoir of exquisite batiste, she wore a green velvet jacket trimmed in gold; its sleeves were Greek-style. Her head was intricately wrapped in a brightly colored Algerian scarf. On each side of this sort of Jewish turban, fringes hung down to her shoulders. Her black and naturally curly hair stuck out here and there in little silky curls.

Immediately I thought of these Israelite beauties described in the holy book so nicely illustrated by Horace Vernet. I had always been told that I looked like Rachel. For the moment the resemblance seemed impossible, even insulting to her.

"Sit down," she said. "What can I do for you?"

"Oh, my goodness, madame, I have come here, under pretext, out of a huge desire to express my gratitude for the wonderful emotions your talents have stirred in me. What could possibly seem like curiosity, actually comes from the heart."

"I must speak low and little because I have a cold and my throat hurts. You are completely forgiven. I am always happy to hear that someone is fond of me."

Then her sister came in with a roll of paper in her hand.

"Leave us," Mlle Rachel told her as she kissed her forehead. "Come back in half an hour."

She left, glancing in my direction. Obviously she was looking for the famous resemblance.

After the door was closed, Mlle Rachel asked me with a smile, "And may we inquire about your pretext?"

"Theater tickets for the benefit of a nice young man who asked me to place some tickets for him."

"You were right to give a different reason for your visit. From morning until evening, and sometimes from evening until morning, I am besieged with requests. How many tickets do you want to give me?"

"One, since you are willing to grant my wish."

"Send me another one for my mother."

"I would prefer to bring them to you myself if you will let me."

MALICIOUS GOSSIP THWARTED

I returned on Saturday. She was in her living room, on the first floor. On the left, by the entrance, was a trellis covered with ivy; all around the living room was a damask print Persian sofa; on the right was a glass door credenza filled with thousands of knickknacks. Mlle Rachel was seated in a large armchair with her back to the daylight. Above her head, in an oval frame, was a portrait of her oldest son.

Her attire that day was dark. She was wearing a black dress of antique moire with wide pleats from the waist down; over it, a black cloth jacket trimmed with little black braids; a solid-color collar and smooth cuffs imprisoned her neck and wrists; her hair was in flat bands, and a little ringlet on her forehead was the only evidence of straightened waves.

"Forgive me, I am eaten up with worry. I have just turned down a part. They will force me to play it, but I shall leave the theater. Oh! Here, for your friend's loges."

The performance was held five days later. Beautiful as a star, she came to the Variétés.

293

"Come see me," she told me.

I thanked her with a look, but I did not want to abuse her generosity, and I did not go back to Rue Trudon until two weeks later. That is when I talked to her about this woman who said she knew her well. Mlle Rachel assured me she had never seen her. I teased my good friend about it so much that she left the Variétés.

WHY CATS?

Most of my day was spent in rehearsal. I rarely saw Richard. One evening I got some very sad news.

"I have come to bid you adieu," he told me. "I misled you about my fate; the fire in San Francisco left me with nothing."

"And what are you going to do?"

"It is not a matter of what is to be done; it is done. I enlisted as a mere private in the foreign legion, and I am going to join my regiment in Africa."

My proceedings were still pending; things were moving distressingly slow.

I was invited to dinners and balls everywhere. I went. I invited people to my home, but less from a desire to have fun than from a desire to escape.

I worked five hours a day at the theater. I had already acted in a play created by the authors of the revue, both handsome young men. One, a real scatterbrain, could mimic Paris's best actors; he could woo you in the voice of that bewitching Pelletier, the actor from the Funambules, and could continue sounding just like Laurent from l'Ambigu. The other one was very reserved with actresses, but since I was the only exception to that inclination, I was grateful for the friendship he showed me. This kind of support was doubly needed because the women waged a dogged war against me under the guise of lots of caresses and embraces.

Ozy, with her sweet voice and pretty mouth, was not even nice to her close friends. One day M. C——, the manager, asked her where she was going.

"Well! I am going where you condemned me to go, to see Mlle Mogador, since you made me her partner."

"But," he said, "I did not make the obligation to see her part of your engagement!"

M. C——'s cashier was an Armenian Jew whose administrative strategy consisted of paying no one. When we asked for money or for costumes, he would reply in German. If we insisted, he would speak Hebrew. One day the theater concierge handed him a bill.

"Thirty sous for lung meat," said the cashier. "What is that for?"

"Monsieur, it is to feed the cats." ·

"Why cats?"

"But, monsieur, to eat the mice, who otherwise would eat the scenery."

"Well," replied the Armenian, "if the cats eat the mice, they do not need lung meat, and if they do not eat them, then there is no need for cats."

I wore three different costumes in the revue, and I had to pay for all three.

A STAR

My entrance at the Variétés gave me the opportunity to meet Mme Ugalde, one of the stars shining over Paris, and one of its quintessential ornaments.[1] She neither needed Camille dresses nor Laura hats. Her only adornment was the voice of a nightingale, and she might not dazzle the eyes, but she enchanted the ears. She left the Opéra-Comique[2] and came to the Variétés to play the part of Roxelane in *The Three Sultanas*.

Since I was the bad actress, I always went on right after the curtain rise. I had just finished playing in *The Queens of the Ball*, when Boullé came to tell me, "Before you leave, you must meet Mme Ugalde; I shall take you to her dressing room."

Boullé was the stage manager; he stammered, was excitable, and was prone to anger. His son, who acts under the name of Nanteuil, is not better treated than anyone else.

So I went downstairs, since I changed on the second floor, and called on the first floor siren. Boullé announced me, and Mme Ugalde came toward me, a smile on her lips, probably to show off her white teeth.

Not in the habit of formulating my sentences ahead of time and, wishing to make an exception this time so I could properly address the great soprano, I was totally at a loss for words like a child who has forgotten a compliment. She continued putting on her makeup as if I were not there.

Gradually, under the layers of white, red, and black skillfully applied, I could see reappear the beautiful Opéra-Comique enchantress with the roses. That gave me back my voice, and when she let out a practice roulade, my admiration came back.

That day we were opening *The Three Sultanas*, and the theater was packed. She asked me to go hear her so I could tell her what I thought of her. At first I thought she was joking, but she insisted, so I went.

The declamations and the arias were applauded and encores, requested. The performance lasted twice as long as usual.

When I returned to Mme Ugalde's dressing room, she was dressing for the last act, and I heard a discussion between her and her hairdresser.

She was supposed to go on stage in a slave costume wearing her hair down. Her hair was almost five feet long and draped over her like a coat. But she had made up her mind that she had a hollow spot on the back of her head, and she absolutely insisted that the space, which everyone more or less has, be filled.

Charles (the hairdresser's name) was at his wits' end. He could not find anything to fill the supposed cavity, when Mme Ugalde handed him a fistful of stuffing she had pulled out of a chair. Everyone protested, she stomped her feet, and the hair artist categorically refused to cram part of this mop into the soprano's gorgeous hair!

TONIGHT, PASSAGE DES PANORAMAS

One night when I was working I was handed a little piece of paper folded like a notice. I walked over to the oil lamp and read:

Madame, I must speak to you tonight at ten thirty; meet me at the Galerie Vivienne, Passage des Panoramas.

At first I thought it was a presumptuous admirer, then when I looked again, I recognized a woman's handwriting.

I left at exactly ten thirty, and I carefully looked everywhere as I went across the *passage*. I did not glimpse the shadow of a woman, but I saw a short young man who seemed to be walking toward me. I was about to get into a carriage on Rue Vivienne, when he told me as he gracefully removed his hat, "I am the one who wrote you; I did not take the time to remove my costume."

His hair was a beautiful shade of black, abundant but curly, slicked down in a way I always dislike in a man.

When he mentioned the costume, I looked at him more attentively. He told me with a smile, "You do not recognize Adèle, the little florist who worked on Rue du Temple, the walk-on at the Belleville Theater?"

37

 A Dead Woman and a Ghost

A Familiar Story—Baptized near Her Dying Mother—
The Good Mother Was Burning the Letters—This Poor Médème

THIS YOUNG MAN was a woman, and I do not understand how I could have been fooled even for one minute. I asked her if she wanted to get in my carriage so we could be comfortable to talk. She accepted after telling me that she was coming to take me to a woman who wanted to see me before dying. I asked her the name of the sick woman, and she replied, "To rue d'Angoulême, on the corner of the boulevard." [1]

And my coachman took off.

Now I asked her to tell me more clearly who she was.

"I am your age," she said. "I was born the same day as you, and we apprenticed in the same house, on Rue du Temple. My mother died on Rue de Bondy, and for a long time the street vendor who is on the boulevard, at the entrance of the Ambigu-Comique, every evening would give me some stale rye bread or some overripe cherries she had not been able to sell during the day.

"I was a walk-on at Belleville when you came to play the part of a grisette in *Canal Saint-Martin.* For several months I have been living at a hotel on Rue d'Angoulême. Two months ago a young woman moved in the room next to mine. Well, one morning I heard moans and I went in. A doctor was immediately sent for. The poor woman remained in pain until two in the morning. She barely heard, 'It is a girl.' She sank into some sort of lethargy.

"I entrusted the little girl to the care of a neighborhood woman. The drawers were empty, and I paid the first month for a nursemaid. Since that time, the poor woman has been getting worse. She told me, after she had written two letters that remained without answers, 'I had a friend some time back; however, if the one I loved so much has abandoned me at a time like this, then why would she remember me? But go see her anyway, you will find her at the Variétés Theater.' "

A FAMILIAR STORY

We had reached Rue d'Angoulême. I sent my coachman away and followed her. The house was not elegant, the stairs were straight up and narrow, and on each landing were eight or ten doors with numbers. The apartments looked like snuff boxes.

Adèle cautiously opened a door. I saw a small room in disarray. I could not make out the sick woman's features. A candle was burning on a night stand.

"Thank you for coming," said a voice that startled me.

I was already near the bed cradling Denise's head in my arms. It was my friend from reformatory. The first woman, perhaps the only one, who ever had a real affection for me. She led me into a life of sin without realizing what she was doing.

Adèle put a cup of herbal tea on the night stand. Denise left her hands in mine for a long time. Gradually I could feel them getting warmer.

I went to see the hotel manager, and I asked him to heat up a little bit of sweetened Bordeaux wine. I had Denise drink a few spoonfuls of this wine. It revived her strength and her memory.

"I am all right," she said, rising a little. "I feel better, but I have so many things to tell you that I do not know where to begin. Eight years ago, in Rouen, I met a young man named Edouard who worked in a shop. His mother lived in the country, and I lived with him and took his name, even though we both knew where we stood. He wanted to marry me as soon as his mother could be convinced that I loved him enough to make him happy. Several times he suggested we do it in spite of her, but I refused. A year ago Edouard changed suddenly; he became pensive and preoccupied. His boss was leaving the business and was thinking of putting him at the head of his establishment, but there was one obstacle: me.

"One day I could not contain my joy, and I announced to him that I was going to be a mother. Instead of smiling at me when he heard the news, Edouard turned pale.

" 'My mother has obtained some information about your past,' he told me, 'and she learned. . . . A marriage between us is now impossible.'

"He began picking fights with me, and I endured them for the sake of my child, but one day he faulted me for a past I had admitted to him.

"I ran away, taking with me what I had on. I went to a hotel, and he sent me my things and fifty francs for the move.

"When I learned that he was going to marry the daughter of a merchant from Elbeuf, I realized it was hopeless, and I came back to Paris, determined to work to feed my child. I wrote letter after letter to Rouen, not asking anything for myself, but for my child. There were no replies."

She motioned for me to give her something to drink, then she continued. "I do not want you or any woman to take care of my daughter. Oh! I know that you would not entice her into a life of sin, but we do not always do what we want. Among the lost women I have met, I have never known one who was raised at the Orphan Home. Being there is better than knowing one's mother when one must despise her."

BAPTIZED NEAR HER DYING MOTHER

The Orphan Home seemed like the saddest and most dismal place to live, but I had to respect the dying mother's last wishes.

Yet, I decided to try one more time with the father. I wrote a long letter to one of my friends who lived in Rouen. I attached to it a few lines for M. Edouard.

At daybreak I sent for a doctor. He declared that the sick woman could not be transported to my house, that her condition was hopeless.

I had the little girl brought to me. She was sweet and sparkling clean. Adèle had bought her a pretty baby outfit.

I returned to see Denise the same day. She was worse. That night it looked like it was all over and I was sent for at midnight. Adèle was rubbing her temples with vinegar.

"Her daughter has not been baptized yet," Adèle told me softly.

I asked the hotel servant to go to Sainte-Elisabeth for a priest and to send me the child's nursemaid. To avoid frightening Denise, I told her that I was going to have her daughter baptized until the regular christening ceremony could be arranged.

At seven o'clock the priest arrived. We left him alone with them.

The child received the first sacrament in the room where her mother had just received the last sacrament.

THE GOOD MOTHER WAS BURNING THE LETTERS

At nine o'clock my maid brought me a letter from Rouen; it was from my friend and here is approximately what it said:

My dear Céleste, I went to see M. Edouard. His mother was the one who received me after making me wait for almost an hour. She told me her son is gravely ill, and that complications from a serious illness would sent him to his grave.

The poor woman burst into tears, and I had to wait for her to compose herself so I could read her your letter. Her tears redoubled. I was not surprised because I, myself, had cried reading it.

"Oh! Monsieur," she exclaimed joining her hands together, "you will drive me insane. My poor Edouard is not mean; he has not even seen the latest letters from this woman because I am the one who received them, and recognizing the handwriting, I burned them without reading them. If I had known that she was so miserable, I would have gone to Paris myself. Where does she live? I want to write to her and beg her to give me his child. But she must not come herself; my Edouard is married. I just wish that she would entrust her child to you."

I read this letter to Denise several times.

She pressed my hand with the little bit of strength she had left, then she whispered, "He is ailing. . . . I feel better knowing that he did not receive my letters. My daughter must leave right away."

I had the nursemaid come. Denise gave her daughter a last long kiss; her lips remained parted, her gaze transfixed, and she died!

The nursemaid left at noon. As she saw the child leave, Adèle cried; she was already thinking of her as her own.

The day after next I received a letter from Rouen that totally reassured me on the child's fate. Her arrival had been celebrated by Edouard's mother, but the joy did not last long. Edouard had been seized by fever and delirium; he could not recognize his mother or his wife, and he died in their arms twenty-four hours after Denise.

THIS POOR MÉDÈME

It is about this time that I received the first letters that Lionel had written me at sea.

I had a terrible reaction. I became ill, so ill that, after the eighteenth performance, I had to interrupt my work on the stage for a while.

In fact the dramatic road I was on was so arid that I had often felt like putting an end to it. If it had not been for Page, I would have abandoned the theater. Unfortunately, she also fell ill and left the Variétés.

I was looking for distractions from my own worries. Disparaging attacks against Lionel gave me back all my energy. It was being said that, foreseeing his own ruin, he had made me his proxy.

The trials started again; for three months newspapers were preoccupied with nothing but this affair and thus publicly linked an honorable name to mine.

A few letters written by me to Lionel and seized at my house were brought up at the trials. They were printed in *Le Droit* and contested. Supposedly they had been dictated to me, written for me, who knows?

I did not sleep anymore, ate very little, but I had one goal: to prove that what I had in my possession was mine, that Lionel might have been flighty, but that he was incapable of even thinking of the odious calculations he was accused of.

A friend had talked me into making a confession that could enlighten the judges. So I wrote down my whole life hoping to make my defense easier.

Studying during the day and writing at night, nothing daunted me. I got to work, and I was delighted and surprised to discover a new interest. I had written several letters to Richard, and these letters remained unanswered.

One day my maid announced that there was military man in the living room who wanted to speak to me.

I was surprised to see Deligny! Deligny in the uniform of an officer!

"Well," he said, "do you not recognize me? Must I give you my card?"

"Yes, of course I recognize you, but I had been told you were dead."

"Me!" he said laughing. "I would have sent you a notice, but thank God I am in good health. I have been in Paris for two days barracked at the Ecole Militaire. I am wearing my plain uniform today," he added twirling around. "The dress uniform is quite beautiful. I shall wear it the next time I come see you, if you will allow me."

"Are you still quarrelsome?"

"Nothing has changed," he said taking my hands, "and my affection for you less than the rest. And you, are you happy, Céleste?"

"Yes, my friend, very happy to see you."

"Really," he said, kissing my hands, "well, good! By the way, I would really like to see you act. Oh, and you know that this poor Médème is dead; he was killed in a duel. Everyone thought it was me."

"Poor boy, he was so sweet!"

"Oh, well! We must not think about it. Good-by, my dear Céleste, we shall dine together one of these days. I shall introduce you to my friends."

As Deligny was leaving I was handed a pack of letters from Australia.

38

A Miner's Diary

A Party of Gold Diggers—Céleste, What Have You Driven Me To?—
The Most Honest Are the Aborigines, Who Disdain Property—
He Sends His Four Crumbs of Gold to the One for Whom
He Ruined Himself

I LEFT SYDNEY *at eight in the morning with a Frenchman, M. Malfi-lâtre, who, like me, is going to the mines.*

The road to Paramatta is charming.

Lunch in Paramatta at an inn full of drunken natives.

We start off again and after ten miles of road we arrive at the Peurith ferry.

The road climbs and goes along extremely deep canyons. We enter a forest of gigantic trees unlike any I have ever seen in Europe.

Each time my imagination soars, my heart and my thoughts return to Céleste.

I picked a little twig of sweet heather along the way and promised myself I would send it to her with my first letter.

At six in the evening rain and nightfall took us by surprise.

Over the four and a half hours we met a landau pulled by four horses on its way back from Bathurst.

It was escorted; it is the one containing the gold.

We also met some miners returning on horseback, and we ran across a large number of them camping out with huge fires all around their carriages and their horses.

A PARTY OF GOLD DIGGERS

In a secluded canyon, by a little creek, five miners were gathered.

They had just had tea.

The appearance and the clothes of these individuals were most extraor-

dinary. Never did Schiller dream up more tawny faces, more hairy beards, and more unkempt hair for his bandits.

Each one wore a complete arsenal—pistols, revolvers, knives, daggers —all there on their belts. If they had appeared on the stage of a theater on the boulevards decked out in this way, they would have looked utterly grotesque. In an Australian forest, they were terrifying.

Their conversation was loud and their gestures rapid and jerky. A bottle of brandy made the rounds from one hand to the next, from one mouth to the next. Each time a bottle was empty it was refilled from a keg located on a small knoll fifty feet away.

Once their drunkenness reached its peak, they continued chanting, yelling, and gesturing until, exhausted, they all fell down.

The miners' laughter was still echoing when suddenly a shrill and nasal voice was heard, and a tall, skinny, and lanky man of about fifty years of age appeared and stood near the fire.

"Per Bacco! We are having fun here; buona sera, signori, do not let me disturb you."

A kind of grunt was the only reply he got. The newcomer scanned his surroundings with the look of an investigator.

"Hum!" he said. "A party, and there is gold."

This man's features were angular. From a sack he was carrying he pulled out a worn violin whose lacquer was peeling off and whose strings had been restrung and were full of knots.

"Oh, what a wreck! Hey, there, old man, your squeaky fiddle has seen a few wars!"

"No, can you not see that it is yawning because it is bored in his company!"

"Pazienza!" said the stranger as he was applying rosin to his frayed bow. "Pazienza, figli miei," and he began to tune it.

Without replying to the questions, the stranger started to play a sort of rondo; he was terrific. It was almost impossible to follow the movement of his bow; under his steel fingers the instrument laughed, cried, squeaked, whistled.

The energetic rondo sounded clear and precise amid all these modulations.

The miners were shrieking, shouting obscene songs, and the frenzied violin speeded up.

All of a sudden their shrieks stopped, their legs gave way, and our three companions fell into a motionless heap.[1] The stranger put his violin back in his green broadcloth sack, looked around, took a swallow of brandy, and quietly examined the sleeping men.

We left, thinking there was nothing more to see, but we had barely taken a few steps when he started to pile pine branches on the fire to revive it.

The next day, just when we were about to depart, we learned that some miners had burned to death by accident.

They had fallen asleep near a fire that ignited a brandy keg. The burning alcohol had them surrounded before they could wake up.

I wanted to see for myself, and I became convinced that a crime had been committed.

The Italian had disappeared, the miners' gold had been stolen, and the metal rings clearly indicated that the keg had purposely been rolled among the sleeping men.

CÉLESTE, WHAT HAVE YOU DRIVEN ME TO?

We are now on paths that defy reason.

On the way we did encounter three or four houses or bark huts, but, hoping to find at least a decent inn, we pressed our horses on a little farther. At nightfall we reached a rather rapid river. M. Malfilâtre waded in the waters up to his knees to gauge the depth, and I spurred my horse and went into the river, which was only three or four feet deep. Soon we found the road on the other side.

Finally at nine o'clock we saw a light and ran up on an inn.

We were told it was full and were turned away. After some dickering we were let in.

I shall not mention the beds, which were worse than filthy. I spread my cloak on mine, placed my satchel under my head, and slept with my clothes on.

We had traveled forty miles that day. Our horses were worn out, and in addition, my horse's back was peeling.

I would like to see the face of an intrepid French gendarme if he were here in the bush; deceived by appearances, he would probably want to arrest everyone.

I think we were mistaken for police officers because of our mustaches; how else can I explain the more worried than angry looks we were getting.

After a most terrible night, we left at ten in the morning.

The stagecoach from Sydney to Bathurst had come through at nine.

The roads are so muddy that a light carriage with four horses can barely make more than two miles an hour; the carriages sink up to their boards.

The rain and the bad weather continue.

There is no way to leave Bathurst.

We are stopped by a torrent called the Macquarie that has become impassable, even if we were to swim; we are told that it will be a week before we can cross it.

At twelve thirty I make up my mind; I crossed the Macquarie in a little boat.

I attached a long rope to my horse and dragged him to the other side. He had difficulty swimming because the current is so swift. Finally, after much effort, he crossed.

Once across the Macquarie, we reached the road to Sofala, the mining headquarters for the Turon River; it is no more than an assortment of tents and sheds.

Just on that site, there must be between fifteen hundred and two thousand miners and merchants of all types.

It looks exactly like a fairground.

The Turon is a wide, swift torrent full of broad and consecutive bends. Each spot is occupied by "diggers" who have their "claims."[2] These spots are more or less close to each other but usually not more than a mile apart.

Therefore it is very difficult to find sites, or they must be paid for, and they are very expensive.

It is, in fact, very strange to see all these people rinsing their clumps of dirt on the shores of the Turon, dirt that they dig up far away and bring back either in wheelbarrows or buckets. The wells are up to fifty feet deep.

I can no longer go on without doing something. My money is dwindling and my horse costs twelve francs a day to feed and shelter.

Oh! Céleste! Céleste! Céleste, what have you driven me to?

THE MOST HONEST ARE THE ABORIGINES, WHO DISDAIN PROPERTY

The mine population is the strangest one imaginable. You can see the dregs of the world, vile people, prison escapees, next to well-mannered men who have lived in elegance and luxury and who like me have squandered everything.

Even under his red wool shirt and his bad straw hat, you can recognize a gentleman.

I had found nothing. I was coming back sad and discouraged when I ran into a nice looking young man.

He addresses me in very good French and tells me that he has three claims on the shores of the Turon he wants to sell. He wants twenty-five pounds sterling each.

In spite of my fatigue and stifling heat, I went back with him to visit them.

A Miner's Diary

All these property rights to claims are very arbitrary. Legally I could take up any spot abandoned for more than twenty-four hours by paying thirty shillings a month for a license. Some sort of commerce has been tolerated. The first one to come upon a spot marks it and plants a stick. Only a show of strength and some violence could put an end to this kind of abuse.

On the shores of the Turon there are people who work ten, fifteen, twenty claims even.

I would like to have the three claims I am being offered, but I do not have the money to buy them.

Now I know who this young man is who wants to sell them. His name is M. Black. He is a former captain in the queen's army who lost his fortune gambling.

I decide to deal with him for the three claims by paying twenty-five pounds at five pounds a month.

We bought the materials and the clothes necessary for our work as diggers.

Except for the meat, everything here is exorbitantly expensive. Bread is a shilling a pound; butter and tea cost a fortune; tobacco is eight shillings a pound. Everything is fifty percent more than in Sydney, and in Sydney one hundred percent more than in London. A sturdy pair of cleat shoes costs a pound in Sofala.

During our shopping trip in Sofala to buy our equipment we met two women, natives from the interior.

They are misshapen and ugly, built like monkeys, especially their legs. Their only garment is a wool blanket that they wrap themselves in.

The way they carry their suckling children is odd. The child is coiled like a snake around their lower back, its head under the mother's arm. In fact, exactly the way monkeys carry their little ones.

The natives in the known provinces of Australia are sweet but lazy. They eat everything they can find: dogs, roots, and even large white worms that live in tree bark. They are quite indifferent to gold.

The famous hundred-and-six-pound nugget was found near Bathurst by a native who showed it to his master; the latter gave him a splendid herd.

The master made more than one hundred thousand francs, and the native ate and sold his sheep. Today he is no richer than before, and he begs for a little tobacco or meat.

They are intelligent, and they can be given errands some five or six hundred miles away into the forest; it is certain they will always make it.

I hope that tomorrow we shall be able to sleep in the middle of the forest in our calico tent.

Captain Black defrauded us most disgracefully. He sold us what we had a right to take for nothing.

Oh! Céleste, Céleste, what have you driven me to? And yet, all I think about is you!

I am kissing your portrait.

HE SENDS HIS FOUR CRUMBS OF GOLD
TO THE ONE FOR WHOM HE RUINED HIMSELF

I have just finished my first day of work and I am exhausted.

Today I rinsed some twenty buckets of dirt and collected no more than twenty sous' worth of gold. Gold is not where we are looking for it; it is at the bottom of the Turon, but it will be months before we can work it because of the current.

I am going to dig a well in the mountain and keep going until I reach rock.

I do not know how long I can continue this work. My arms are worn out.

All day long I carry dirt by the buckets to the river to rinse it; it yields very little gold.

M. Malfilâtre does not do anything and lets me do the hard work. I hope he will become disgusted with this life, otherwise I shall be the victim of this association.

We are on our last twenty shillings and no letters from France.

No letters from France! Everyone has abandoned me.

We are penniless; I cannot work because of the water. M. Malfilâtre really wants to leave.

I sell my horse in Sofala for ten pounds sterling and I give him seven so he will leave tomorrow.

M. Malfilâtre leaves at nine in the morning. Once he has left I sell my saddle and bridle for four pounds fifteen shillings, and I go into my tent, alone this time.

I organize all my tools and things and go to the middle of the river to rinse a few buckets of dirt that I took from the river bed. They yield a few grains of gold.

I go to bed very tired, but a storm arrives dropping torrential rain that penetrates the tent on all sides.

At noon the weather improves a little. I sit on a bucket and write a long letter to Céleste enclosing the summary of this diary.

A Miner's Diary

I send her the little bit of gold I collected along with some heather I picked for her in the forest during the trip from Sydney to Bathurst.

My memory of her and her face never leave me, even in sleep.

God, have pity on me! Let me forget or give me the courage to commit suicide. No! I am a coward; I hope to see her again.

Lionel de C——.

39

Let My Destiny Be Done!

Couture's Portrait by Mogador (and Vice Versa) —
Victorine Has Not Changed — His Hands Full of Wounds
and Gifts — The Joy of Depriving Herself for Him — Genuine
Reconciliation — The Memoirs' First Readers

MY POOR LIONEL, *I just received such a sad letter from you that right now I feel so downhearted, so guilty, it is impossible to find the words to express my sorrow, my pain, my remorse.*

You repeatedly accuse me of being ungrateful, and yet I live only for you and through my memories of you!

You may be far away, but my soul belongs to you; my thoughts and my love embrace you.

Believe me I have suffered much, but I shall not seek comfort or consolation anymore; I shall live through my tears as a punishment for doubting you.

I feel that my soul will be lost until it is reunited with yours.

I have told you, I believe in you and I have hope in God; only He could have given you the strength to endure this misery.

I am sending you some heather from France.

I love you with the purest part of my heart; reserve another tear, another kiss for me.

Two things stirred my heart: my memories of Lionel and thoughts of my little girl — her tenderness, her games, her chatter, which allowed me to forget. I would catch myself playing with her as if I were her age.

I was given a part in a play titled *The Daughter of Mme Grégoire*. It kept me busy. The nights were so long for me that I spent them working.

Three months had gone by since I received Lionel's letter.

One night in the greenroom at the Variétés I saw a short gentleman wearing an odd, shapeless cardigan. He was very short and rather stout. He was chatting and laughing with a group of people.

I asked one of my friends his name.

"That is Couture, the painter, the one who did the *Romans of the Decadence.*"[1]

I drew nearer so I could hear better.

"Let me tell you," he was saying, "a few days ago I was standing on the doorstep of my studio in casual dress, smoking a cigarette, when a carriage stopped a few feet away. Getting out of it was a very pretty lady loaded down with packages and cartons, who yelled, 'Hey! There!' and motioned for me to come over.

" 'Here,' she said, 'take all that upstairs to my apartment, sixth floor on the left.'

"I looked at her, a little startled; but I took the boxes and I followed her. Once upstairs, I was out of breath. She had me put the packages inside, looked in her pocketbook, and gave me ten sous.

"She had mistaken me for a servant.

"The next day I sent her my card and her fifty centimes telling her that I had been only too happy to be of help and that, if she liked art, she could pay me back by visiting my studio."

Then turning toward me, he said to me, "If you have any errands that need to be done, I am at your service."

"At the same rate, of course?" I asked him.

"Oh! I take whatever I am offered!"

"Well! I am offering you a cup of tea."

He promised he would come and was true to his word. He offered to do a drawing of me, similar to the one he had done of Mme George Sand and of Béranger.[2] Because it is signed by a great artist, this drawing is probably the only thing of me that will endure!

A few days later I won a proceeding that, although of little significance, was going to be important for the profits of others.

To make sure no one would overlook this victory over my adversaries, I gave a party. My portrait was a great success and Couture received many compliments.

Of the people who were at my home that evening, the one I remember most is Alexandre Dumas *fils.* He was distant and had a skeptical, discerning mind that could sometimes be mean, but if he paid you a compliment, you could believe it because he never gave them readily.

He had been in attendance for the premiere of *The 1852 Revue,* and had told several people in reference to me, "She sang, played, and recited divinely; if she is willing to really work, she will have a true talent."

I would have loved to move amidst such superior minds, but of course I had no right to so signal an honor. It is only in passing that I had the opportunity to appreciate Dumas *père,* Méry, Augier, Murger, Théophile Gautier, Camille Doucet, M. de Girardin, and Nestor Roqueplan.[3]

VICTORINE HAS NOT CHANGED

On Rue de la Chaussée-d'Antin one day I saw some darling little bonnets in a store display, and I went in to buy one for my godchild.

When I saw the saleswoman, I let out an "Oh!" of surprise. In the lovely person who was showing me some lingerie I had just recognized the little beggar who had been my companion at the house of correction.

I waited for her to recognize me, but she barely looked at me; my stare seemed to make her uncomfortable.

I took her hand and pressed it. She looked at me in astonishment. I stopped short; a voice inside was saying, "Why remind this poor girl of an encounter as sad for her as for you?"

I bought everything she was showing me. Once I had left, I wanted to cry as I remembered her offering me half her bread.

I went home. A carriage was stopped at my door; Victorine had been waiting for me for an hour.

"What is this?" she said pointing to my adopted daughter. "How could an imaginative woman like you imitate her friends?"

"What are you trying to tell me?"

"What! You are in the theater with her and you do not know the story of the little boy? Your friend does nothing for glory and all for self-promotion: she reads in a newspaper that a woman has just died leaving a little orphan. She does not go to the magistrate in person offering herself as mother to the child; instead she writes to a newspaper, which publishes her letter. The child is given to her; she has to show him off to everyone; she dresses him up in Scottish clothes. She has him memorize a scene from a tragedy. When people are around she asks him, 'How was your mother murdered?' The child makes stabbing motions?"

"I do not understand what you are telling me or what you want to tell me my dear Victorine. I need friends who mitigate my violent tendencies, who polish my mind, and that is not your way, on the contrary."

"In other words you do not want to see me anymore."

"As little as possible!"

311

She left without my noticing.

One of my friends came to invite me to dinner with Maria.

"No, I am not going out today. Come dine here tomorrow if you wish; I am having a few people over."

HIS HANDS FULL OF WOUNDS AND GIFTS

At six o'clock the next day my guests arrived. Since I kept watching the door, I was asked if I expected one more person.

"No, but I am so distracted, I do not know what I am doing."

It was about nine o'clock when my maid entered looking shaken. My concierge was right behind her.

"Madame! . . . If you knew . . . M. le Comte. . . ."

"What?" I asked abruptly.

"Well! Madame, he is in Paris. Since he was told you had guests, he did not want to come up. He is in the Passage du Havre."

There was champagne bubbling in glasses, lights were reflected in the silver platters he had given me, and he was at my door like a beggar.

He had let his beard grow; his face was thin and darker, his eyes were lifeless, his brow was pale. Pain was written all over him.

I wanted to kiss him, but he stopped me with a look.

"You are entertaining; I have disturbed you."

"I invited a few friends to dinner."

"I have no right to ask you who is at your house. Do you want to come to my hotel? We need to talk business."

I followed him, not daring to utter a word, but he could see that my soul was at his feet.

Once we were at his hotel he uncovered cages full of darling little birds of all colors.

"For four months," he said, "I have been taking care of them so I could offer them to you. At night I endured the cold so I could protect them from the wind with my blanket."

I started to cry because he had not kissed me. His hand bore the traces of long scars barely healed. He rolled up his sleeve and showed me my name and the date of his departure tattooed in blue ink on his right arm.

"It is not possible to work a mine alone. Like the others I had a partner, a miner named Faubare, a former sailor who had deserted his ship. He had heard me addressed as *M. le Comte* by this captain of industry who had sold me my claim, and he would say to me, 'Hey there, Lecomte, hand me my pickax!'

"Since my worst aggravation was lacking clean clothes, I would do my wash in the river.

"Often it was necessary to wade in up to the waist. This water is a sort of corrosive sludge that burns your skin. I had sores up to my elbows, my legs were peeling, and all our efforts were in vain.

"When Faubare saw me in this condition, he refused to let me continue.

"I would have died there with just the charity of this nice boy if a young man I had met in London had not come to my help. He said to me, 'I am going to lend you enough to make the trip; go back to France and come back with materials.'

"At first I would not leave, but it was not very difficult to convince me that this trip was essential to my interests. When I left, I gave Faubare everything I owned: my tent, my tools, my pistol, and the title to the claims.

"Nothing will match his complete surprise when I signed the transfer over to him.

"'Comte de C——! What? You are . . . but I thought your name was Lecomte. And I was raised on one of your grandfather's estates!'

"I cried and kissed Faubare, then I went back to Sydney.

"I should have stayed, I should have died over there, but I was thinking of you. You said you were being sued, and I wanted to arrive in time to be useful to you. No one has the right to take back what I gave you when I was rich."

THE JOY OF DEPRIVING HERSELF FOR HIM

He would not come live with me in the apartment that had partially been his.

I understood the feeling that made him act this way. He was too poor to pay his rent, and I had too much heart to splatter him as I passed in the streets with the carriages he had given me.

Without telling him, I sent everything to be sold off.

Someone who was interested in my apartment was accepted by the owner, so I was released from my lease.

For one thousand francs a year, I rented a ground-floor apartment on Rue de Navarin where I had a little yard for my godchild.

I sold most of what I had left in cashmere shawls and jewelry so I could live near him without being supported by him during his stay in France.

Lionel rented a little room in a hotel on Rue Lafitte, but he spent his days with me. My work in the theater bothered him.

I had bought back everything that Lionel's creditors had put up for sale: paintings, belongings, pistols.

A judgment was going to be rendered on the proceedings on appeal at the imperial court of Bourges.

I still could not dispose of my house at Poinçonnet, the pretty little cottage to which the townspeople had given the pretentious name of château, a name that my adversaries insisted on to make trouble.

The Châteauroux magistrates knew better, but in Bourges? I summarized these Memoirs for the court. Lionel wrote a note, but he stayed in Paris.

As I entered the lobby of this large palace built by Jacques Coeur,[4] the cold from the vaults enveloped me like a shroud.

Hidden behind a pillar, I overheard myself spoken of with such disdain that I lost my head and dropped to my knees in tears.

The deliberations, which lasted three days and caused more stir than if the case had been that of a notorious criminal, were closed, and judgment was due in two weeks. I went back to Paris.

A week after the proceedings in Bourges, my lawsuit at the commercial court in Paris was under way.

It concerned forty thousand francs that Lionel owed me and for which he had written me bills of exchange. The court at Place de la Bourse declared these bills of exchange nothing more than bills of kindness and so could not be regarded seriously.

Then the court in Bourges ruled in my favor.

That was a great day for me and created much confusion among my adversaries.

I was going to appeal the Paris judgment when things took a turn I had not counted on. During my absence my residence was invaded by five persons who were all in league with one another; they took what they wanted among my papers and Lionel's.

I complained to the public prosecutor; the Châteauroux court sentenced the bailiff who accompanied them in this unfair search to one month suspension and expenses. In his defense all he could say was, "I was only obeying the orders of the Paris attorney!"

That was enough to frighten these gentlemen. They returned mortified and embarrassed to ask me to withdraw my complaint; they sent some of their friends to plead with me to stop.

Not only did I get free of the responsibility I was required to bear, but in addition I insisted that the jeweler annul the debt of the young man for whom Lionel had vouched.

Then, asking them how much he owed them personally, I paid them the whole sum in his name. It amounted to twenty thousand francs.

GENUINE RECONCILIATION

Lionel did all he could to find that sum so he could reimburse me.

No one helped him pay back what he thought he must call his gratitude toward me. And yet he did not owe me anything since part of those debts must have been incurred for me without my knowledge.

Everywhere Lionel faced mistrust and disbelief. He looked for a position to fill upon his return to Australia, and he was turned down. He looked for supplies to take back with him, and he was taken for a captain of industry.

Finally, after much research and perseverance, he found a prominent merchant, M. Bertrand, who was willing to help him. When Lionel had been assured of work, he proposed taking me back to Australia with him.

I admit that I had never entertained the thought of such a trip without fear. If he took me with him, that would cast even more disapproval on him; his family would be aghast and would persist in letting him live in this rejection that had been so painful to him.

But he was determined.

"I have only you in the world," he said. "If you refuse to follow me, I shall not leave. My courage is you! My country will be where you will be. What do I care for the opinion of my relatives? I am glad of this rejection because it sets me free."

I imposed only one condition, that my adoptive daughter would follow me everywhere. I did not want to entrust her to anyone. His reply was two big kisses on the child's cheeks.

THE MEMOIRS' FIRST READERS

However, I had not dared confess to the existence of these memoirs. Not knowing whether he would come back, I had put them to use. During the worst of my trials, one of my friends, M. A———, asked me to lend them to him. He passed them around without my knowledge.

When he returned my six volumes, they had been read by ten people.

The first one was M. Camille Doucet.[5] His kind and delicate temperament was alarmed by these brutal revelations, but he did not condemn them.

Mme Emile de Girardin, that great lady so compassionate for those who suffer, spent the night reading these pages that had streamed from my hand like tears from my eyes.

"It does not matter who cried," said the author of *Marguerite or the Two Loves.* "We must listen to the lamentations of all who suffer."

M. Dumas read them also and mentioned these memoirs to everyone. He even included a few lines liable to pique the curiosity and interest of his numerous friends in his paper *Le Mousquetaire.*

In those days I had the opportunity to meet a woman whose reputation had made a big stir and of whom a witty man, her friend of twenty-five years, said, "She is either a witch or a fairy."

This same friend, whom we had in common, got in touch with an editor.

When Lionel came back, it was too late for me to stop what was in motion already.

I began preparations for our departure.

My furniture and all that I owned had been sent to Le Havre when Lionel received his nomination to a post he had sought.[6]

He wanted to turn it down because of me. I refused to leave if he did not accept it. For him it was a matter of his future; mine, I did not worry much about.

I am very afraid of going so far away from my country, my beauty, my youth. Soon they will all be just a memory. Only virtue and goodness can be loved for a long time. To love a woman who grows old, she must be respected, she must be the mother of your children.

What if Lionel would once more become violent and hot tempered as in the past!

Perhaps I will die abandoned over there, under the burning sun that devours plants and men.

In this as in all things, may God's will be done! May my destiny be fulfilled!

If my memoirs appear after my departure, Lionel will not know about it since we shall be at sea for four months.

In the course of this long crossing, I am going to tempt the mercy of the one who judges us all. Only God condemns on the ocean!

Notes

The following currencies are mentioned throughout the memoirs:

centime: coin equal to one hundredth of a franc
sou: former coin equal to one twentieth of a franc
franc: the basic unit of money in France since the French Revolution
pound: former coin
louis: gold coin bearing the image of the king; in the nineteenth century it was worth 24 pounds

Editor's notes are translated from the 1968 Les Amis de L'Histoire edition.

1. MY STEPFATHER

1. Today rue Aubriot (3rd arrondissement, then 7th arrondissement). Ed.
2. An acute, infectious disease affecting the skin or mucous membranes. Trans.
3. Plain outside of Lyon, site of a 1793 revolutionary battle. Trans.

2. THE HUNTER AND THE HUNTED

1. A glassworks district of Lyon. Trans.
2. Name for the silk weavers in Lyon. Trans.
3. Archaic: a small room. Trans.

4. M. VINCENT

1. Lace made by hand in the town of Mechlin, Belgium. Trans.
2. Any of various silver and gold coins. Trans.
3. Faubourg du Temple was then the center of the theatrical world. Trans.
4. Today, at this location, the canal is covered by Boulevard Richard-Lenoir. The Ménilmontant bridge was at the present intersection of that boulevard and Rue Oberkampf. Ed.
5. The former Rue Neuve today is an extension Rue des Francs-Bourgeois, which then did not go beyond Rue Payenne. Rue Culture-Sainte-Catherine has become Rue de Sévigné. Ed.

5. THÉRÈSE

1. M. Vincent. Trans.
2. Insane asylum south of Paris. Trans.

3. A women's house of correction and a former convent built by St. Vincent de Paul in the seventeenth century. Trans.

6. DENISE

1. A little room with a boarded-up window where no visitors are allowed, not even the guard. Ed.
2. The young accused. Trans.
3. Women arrested for fighting. Ed.
4. Women waiting to be judged. Ed.
5. Preferential treatment in a prison (which, originally, was obtained against payment of one *pistole,* an old monetary unit); name of the prison where such treatment was available. Trans.

7. THE FALL

1. Located on Boulevard d'Enfer, a sort of amusement park frequented by the young. Trans.
2. That man was the celebrated French poet Alfred de Musset. Trans.
3. On the rue Montorgueil, it is one of the most famous restaurants catering to an international clientele. Trans.
4. Today Place Gustave-Toudouze, in the 9th arrondissement. Ed.

9. THE BAL MABILLE

1. The Turkish sultana, wife of Suleyman the Magnificent. Trans.
2. A sheer fabric of silk and cotton. Trans.
3. Aimata (1813–77), Tahitian queen of the Pomaré dynasty who upon the death of her brother the king, reigned as Pomaré IV. Trans.
4. According to Pierre Larousse, it was on Thursday, 26 September 1844 at 9:00 P.M. that Céleste Vénard received the nickname Mogador. That year the Moroccan city of Mogador had been bombed by the French fleet. Ed.

10. A "QUEEN'S" DESTINY

1. Situated at the present Place de l'Etoile, at the entrance of Avenue Kléber, this circus is one in a series of open air arenas that enjoyed great popularity in Paris between 1845 and 1907. Trans.
2. Member of the family that had founded the Cirque Olympique, the Cirque d'été, and the Cirque d'hiver. Trans.

11. THE HIPPODROME

1. Romieux (Mogador's note). In reality, Romieu (Auguste), alias Coco Romieu (1800–1855). Ed.
2. The Duke of Ossuna, a rich young Italian. This kind of liaison now established Mogador as a courtesan. Trans.

12. LISE'S YELLOW DRESS

1. Alphonse Royer, playwright. Trans.
2. Hermann Cohen. Trans.
3. Lines from an opera *Charles VI,* by Germain Lavigne, performed in the summer of 1844. Trans.
4. A card game introduced in France by Landsknechts, German mercenaries who served in France during the sixteenth and seventeenth centuries. Trans.
5. Musset, who had met her in the brothel. Trans.
6. The Italian tenor, Bettini. Trans.
7. An opera by Meyerbeer, first performed in Paris in 1831. Trans.
8. The opera *Lucia di Lammermoor* by Gaetano Donizetti, first performed in 1835. Trans.
9. Adjective designating people from the far provinces. Trans.

15. ACTS OF DESPERATION

1. Of course it is not the servant Marie mentioned above, but Fair Marie, Denise's friend (ch. 6). Ed.

16. LISE'S RETURN

1. A fashionable restaurant of the day. Trans.

17. DINNER AT THE CAFÉ ANGLAIS

1. The Count Lionel de Chabrillan is named by Pierre Larousse in the article on Céleste Mogador, "CHABRILLAN (Céleste Vénard, Lade Lionel de Moreton, Countess of)." Ed.

18. LIONEL

1. Actually the count's father was sixty-six years old. Ed.
2. A popular club for the dandies of the day. Trans.

19. IN THE COUNTRY

1. The year was 1847. The tracks reached Issoudun 1 November 1848. Ed.

25. CHÂTEAU LIFE

1. George Sand (1804–76), famous for her romantic pastoral novels, was from the Berry region. Trans.

26. RICHARD

1. Located on the Champs-Elysées, it was a fashionable and glitzy place for young people to meet and dance. Trans.
2. Louis-Hyacinthe Duflost (1814–87), comic actor who played at the Varié-

tés and at the Palais-Royal, among others. His nose was extraordinarily long. Ed.

3. Paul Grassot, actor (1804–60). Ed.

28. DRAMATIC FOLLIES AND FOLIES-DRAMATIQUES

1. Alphonse Lassagne, born in 1819, the son of an engraver, died in 1863, mad. Mainly acted at the Folies-Dramatiques and at the Variétés. Ed.

2. Jacques Odry (1781–1853), actor at the Variétés, the Gaîté, the Folies-Dramatiques. Ed.

29. PROUD WOMEN, PASSIONATE MEN

1. One of the lionesses of the times; she had been celebrated by Théophile Gautier, and made famous in stone by the sculptor Auguste Préault. She later became notorious for her liaison with Charles Hugo, the son of the celebrated poet. Trans.

2. Adèle Page became known as one of the best Parisian actresses of the period 1849 to 1853. Trans.

3. In English in the original text. Trans.

31. UNFORTUNATE ENCOUNTER

1. Auguste Lireux, writer and journalist, born in Rouen in 1810, died in Bougival in 1870. Ed.

2. Antoine-Louis Barizain, alias Louis Monrose, actor born in 1809, son of Claude Monrose. Ed.

33. DEATH THROES OF A FORTUNE

1. Socialist *folie* [vaudevillian musical] in three acts and seven scenes by Clairville and Cordier; Vaudeville, 28 November 1848. Ed.

2. An actress at the Théâtre Français, she hated Mogador. She never forgave her for having been her rival in the heart of Prince Napoleon. In addition she accused Céleste of liking women as much as men. Trans.

3. Born in 1822, died in 1861, the author of *Les Scènes de la vie de bohème* (1848), which later inspired Puccini to compose his famous opera *La Bohème*. Trans.

4. Ancient city of India famous for its diamonds. Trans.

34. TO THE ANTIPODES

1. In the 1858 edition, "London, 12 May 1852" erroneously reads "London, 22 May 1852"; "Sunday evening, 30 May 1852" erroneously reads "Sunday, 29 May 1852"; and "Sunday, 6 June 1852" erroneously reads "Sunday, 6 June 1857." Ed.

36. THE VARIÉTÉS THEATER

1. Delphine Beaucée, Lady Ugalde, soprano born in Paris 3 December 1829. Ed.
2. A case of laryngitis made her cancel her engagement. Ed.

37. A DEAD WOMAN AND A GHOST

1. It is now called Rue Jean-Pierre-Timbaud in the part located between Boulevard du Temple and Boulevard Richard-Lenoir. There was another Rue d'Angoulême near the Champs-Elysées, today called Rue La Boétie. Ed.

38. A MINER'S DIARY

1. The 1968 Les Amis de L'Histoire edition shows only three miners at this point.
2. "Diggers" and "claims" appear in English in the original. Trans.

39. LET MY DESTINY BE DONE!

1. Thomas Couture (1815–79), famous painter of the period who later became Manet's teacher, made a plaster cast of Mogador's hand and used her as model for his painting, *Roman Orgy*. The painting in question is now at the Musée d'Orsay. Trans.
2. Pierre Jean de Béranger (1780–1857) was a famous poet and writer of popular and patriotic songs. Trans.
3. Famous writers or journalists of the period. Trans.
4. Wealthy French financier (1395–1456). Trans.
5. Author of *Millionnaire* (The millionaire), *Fruit défendu* (The forbidden fruit), etc. (1812–85). Ed.
6. That of Consul in Melbourne, Pierre Larousse tells us. Ed.

Works by Céleste de Chabrillan

MEMOIRS

Adieux au monde, mémoires de Céleste Mogador. 5 vols. Paris: Locard-Davi et de Vresse, 1854.

Mémoires de Céleste Mogador. 2nd ed. 4 vols. Paris: Librairie Nouvelle, 1858.

Mémoires de Céleste Mogador. 3rd ed. 2 vols. Paris: Librairie Nouvelle, 1876.

Mémoires de Céleste Mogador, 1852–1854. Paris: Les Amis de l'Histoire, 1968.

Un Deuil au bout du monde, suite des mémoires de Céleste Mogador. Paris: Librairie Nouvelle, 1877. Trans. Patricia Clancy and Jeanne Allen, *The French Consul's Wife: Memoirs of Céleste de Chabrillan in Gold-Rush Australia.* Melbourne: Miegunyah Press, 1997.

NOVELS

Les Voleurs d'or. Paris: Michel Lévy, 1857. Trans. Lucy and Caroline Moorehead, *The Gold Robbers.* Melbourne: Sun Books, 1970.

La Sapho. Paris: Michel Lévy, 1858.

Miss Pewel. Paris: A. Bourdilliat, 1859.

Est-il fou? Paris: A. Bourdilliat, 1860.

Un miracle à Vichy. Vichy: Bougarel fils, 1861.

Mémoires d'une honnête fille. Paris: A. Faure, 1865.

Les Deux soeurs émigrantes et déportées. Paris: C. Lévy, 1876.

Une méchante femme. Paris: C. Lévy, 1877.

La Duchesse des mers. Paris: C. Lévy, 1881.

Les Forçats de l'amour. Paris: C. Lévy, 1881.

Marie Baude. Paris: C. Lévy, 1883.

Un Drame sur le Tage. Paris: C. Lévy, 1885.

PLAYS

Bonjour au vaincu. 1 act. Th. des Champs-Elysées, 19 April 1862. Paris: Cosson, 1862.

En Australie. 1 act vaudeville. Th. des Champs-Elysées, 19 July 1862. Paris: Cosson, 1862.

Querelle d'Allemand. 1 act. Th. des Champs-Elysées, 28 Oct. 1863. Paris: Librarie des Deux Mondes, 1864.

Les Voleurs d'or. 1 act. Th. de Belleville, 28 May 1864.

L'Amour de l'art. 1 act. Th. des Folies-Marigny, 4 June 1865. Paris: Alcan-Lévy, 1865.

Chambre à louer. 1 act. Th. des Folies-Marigny, 20 Oct. 1865.

Un homme compromis. 1 act. Th. des Folies-Marigny, 4 Sept. 1865. Paris: Alcan-Lévy, 1868.

Les Crimes de la mer. 5 acts. Th. de Belleville, 8 May 1869. Paris: Morris père et fils, 1869.

Les Revers de l'amour. 5 acts. Th. des Nouveautees, 28 Jan. 1870. Paris: the author, 1870.

L'Américaine. 5 acts. Th. des Nouveautés, 3 April 1870. Paris: Estienne, 1870.

La Plaideuse. 1 act. Ambigu-Comique, 20 Dec. 1874.

L'Ambition fatale. 5 acts. Th. Beaumarchais, 15 April 1875.

Le Bonnet d'âne. 1 act. 1876.

Entre deux balcons. Fantaisies-Parisiennes, 7 March 1880.

Ma'am Nicole. 3 acts. Folies-Dramatiques, 4 July 1880. Paris: Barbré, 1880.

L'Amour et la rose. 3 acts. Th. des Arts, 10 July 1880.

Pierre Pascal. 5 acts. Music by M. Senée. Ambigu-Comique, 4 Aug. 1885. Paris: Chaix, 1885.

Cordon, s.v.p. Revue. Th. Pépinière, 26 Dec. 1886.

Bastienne.

Le Dernier rendez-vous. 3 acts.

Le Drame de Louvier. 5 acts.

Forgeron d'Ardentes. 1 act.

Marie Margotte. 1 act. Th. des Nouveautés.

Les Petits de Beaufort. 4 acts.

Regain d'amour.

Le 31 de victoire. 1 act.

OPERETTAS

Nédel. 1 act. Music by Marius Boullard. Th. des Champs-Elysées, 23 May 1863.

Militairement. 1 act. Music by Marius Boullard. Th. des Champs-Elysées, 28 Oct. 1863. Paris: Librairie des Deux-Mondes, 1864.

En garde. 1 act. Th. des Champs-Elysées, 14 Jan. 1864. Paris: Librarie des Deux-Mondes, 1864.

Les Pierrots en cage. 1 act. Music by Kriezel. Th. des Folies-Marigny, 9 Sept. 1865.

A la bretonne. 1 act. Th. des Folies-Marigny, 10 Sept. 1868. Paris: Morris père et fils, 1868.

La Tirelire d'Yvonne. 1 act. Music by Georges Rose.

POEMS

"Un chien trouvé"

"Echange d'âmes"

"Les Eglises"

"La Légende du Soldat Pierre"

"Le Marseillais"

Works by Céleste de Chabrillan

"La Mère du Mobile"
"Mes Soeurs de France"
"Mon Petit-fils le Potache"
"Les Orphelins de la guerre"
"Paris captif"
"L'Union"
"Les Volontaires de 1870"

SONGS

"L'absolution" (music by E. Gambillard)
"Adieu romance" (music by Avray)
"L'amour, c'est des bêtises" (music by G. Rose)
"Attends un peu" (music by E. Gambillard)
"Battez tambours" (music by Avray)
"Le chapeau rond" (music by G. Rose)
"Le dimanche" (music by Comte Lionel de Chabrillan)
"Encore moi" (music by G. Rose)
"La fête de Jean-Pierre" (music by G. Rose)
"La Gauloise" (music by G. Rose)
"Le grand cousin" (music by G. Rose)
"L'heure" (music by G. Rose)
"J'ai battu mon homme" (music by G. Rose)
"Je l'ai lâché" (music by E. Gambillard)
"Laissez-moi pleurer" (music by G. Rose)
"Ne boudez pas" (music by G. Rose)
"T'as du chagrin" (music by G. Rose)

In the EUROPEAN WOMEN WRITERS series

Artemisia
By Anna Banti
Translated by Shirley D'Ardia Caracciolo

Bitter Healing
German Women Writers, 1700–1830
An Anthology
Edited by Jeannine Blackwell and Susanne Zantop

The Edge of Europe
By Angela Bianchini
Translated by Angela M. Jeannet and David Castronuovo

The Maravillas District
By Rosa Chacel
Translated by d. a. démers

Memoirs of Leticia Valle
By Rosa Chacel
Translated by Carol Maier

There Are No Letters Like Yours: The Correspondence of
Isabelle de Charrière and Constant d'Hermenches
By Isabelle de Charrière
Translated and with an introduction and annotations
by Janet Whatley and Malcolm Whatley

The Book of Promethea
By Hélène Cixous
Translated by Betsy Wing

The Terrible but Unfinished Story of Norodom Sihanouk,
King of Cambodia
By Hélène Cixous
Translated by Juliet Flower MacCannell, Judith Pike,
and Lollie Groth

The Governor's Daughter
By Paule Constant
Translated by Betsy Wing

Trading Secrets
By Paule Constant
Translated by Betsy Wing
With an introduction by Margot Miller

Maria Zef
By Paola Drigo
Translated by Blossom Steinberg Kirschenbaum

Woman to Woman
By Marguerite Duras and Xavière Gauthier
Translated by Katharine A. Jensen

Hitchhiking
Twelve German Tales
By Gabriele Eckart
Translated by Wayne Kvam

The South and Bene
By Adelaida García Morales
Translated and with a preface by Thomas G. Deveny

The Tongue Snatchers
By Claudine Herrmann
Translated by Nancy Kline

The Queen's Mirror
Fairy Tales by German Women, 1780–1900
Edited and translated by Shawn C. Jarvis and Jeannine Blackwell

The Panther Woman
Five Tales from the Cassette Recorder
By Sarah Kirsch
Translated by Marion Faber

Concert
By Else Lasker-Schüler
Translated by Jean M. Snook

Slander
By Linda Lê
Translated by Esther Allen

Daughters of Eve
Women's Writing from the German Democratic Republic
Translated and edited by Nancy Lukens and Dorothy Rosenberg

Animal Triste
By Monika Maron
Translated by Brigitte Goldstein

Celebration in the Northwest
By Ana María Matute
Translated by Phoebe Ann Porter

On Our Own Behalf
Women's Tales from Catalonia
Edited by Kathleen McNerney